CW00455965

Hɪ-Dɪddʟe-Dee-Dee

Written by

Eddie Webber

Vulpine Press
www.vulpine-press.com

HI-DIDDLE -DEE-DEE

FROM THE STREETS OF BERMONDSEY TO LIGHTS, CAMERA, ACTION!

VULPINE

P R E S S

Published by Vulpine Press in the United Kingdom in 2019

ISBN 978-1-912701-98-8

Cover by Claire Wood
Cover photo Ian Jackio Jackson

www.vulpine-press.com

To my beautiful eternal inspirations Ali, Alfie and Barney.

Let me not to the marriage of true minds
Admit impediments. Love is not love
Which alters when it alteration finds,
Or bends with the remover to remove.
O no! it is an ever-fixed mark
That looks on tempests and is never shaken;
It is the star to every wand'ring bark,
Whose worth's unknown, although his height be taken.
Love's not Time's fool, though rosy lips and cheeks
Within his bending sickle's compass come;
Love alters not with his brief hours and weeks,
But bears it out even to the edge of doom.
If this be error and upon me prov'd,
I never writ, nor no man ever lov'd.

- William Shakespeare

The poet sat upon a hill gazing at the fields, the colours flashing in his mind had caused his thoughts to still – he closed his eyes and raised his hands, they rested on his face – and then his thoughts went drifting on to another time and place.

He flicked his eyes wide open and all the world had changed – the sky had turned a funny green that made it look quite strange – the birds were flying upside down and upwards dropped the rain – a wolf was dancing with a sheep, the sight was quite insane.

The poet changed position so his back was now his front – then took a new perspective and ate it with his lunch – a busy bee went smiling by whilst chewing on a cud – the poet thought he heard a buzz but as he listened it was zzub.

So happy in this element, the poet took a walk and as he reached the forest, the trees began to talk – Hum hum hum the oak declared to the acorn that agreed – a tree that talks, the poet thought, what a clever tree indeed.

The poet took his pen out, started writing in a book and every time he turned a page he took another look – a wolf, a sheep, a zzuby bee he jotted down in ink – what a place to come to, all you have to do is think.

But then a mighty thunderstorm came raging from the ground and everything went quiet except for thunder sounds – the poet didn't like it, all his world had now turned black then scattered yellow eyes appeared that caused him to step back.

A mighty roar within the trees echoed in his ears – his eyes were dancing to and fro and swimming in their fears – he turned to run but vines and weeds were tangled round his

feet – and then the sight he witnessed caused the poet's eyes
to weep.

A big black beast with a thousand yellow eyes and teeth as big
as tusks – there was fire dribbling from its mouth, burning
everything it touched – the beast looked at the poet, the poet
dropped his head – he wished he hadn't found this place as
he registered its dread.

Just as the flames flew round him, everything was gone – the
poet rubbed his sleepy eyes and wondered what went on –
he looked up at the clear blue sky the birds and bright sun
beams – then took out pen and paper and he wrote down
what he'd seen.

– Eddie Webber

PART 1: THE JOURNEY

CHAPTER ONE

Our own self-realisation is the greatest service we can render the world.

- Ramana Maharshi

'Here's a knocking indeed! If a man were porter of hell-gate, he should have old turning the key.' (Shakespeare's *Macbeth*.)

Knock, knock, knock. I flicked my eyes open. It took a bit of time to register the pounding on my front door. I looked to the bedside table, Elvis the clock was singing 5:30 a.m. I snapped into gear. Only two kinds of people jump into people's sleep at this insane hour: drunken girlfriends and the police. My girlfriend had a set of keys. *Shit!*

With my heart pounding and like a thief in the night, I crept out of my duck-feathered womb and headed for Dante's Gate.

'Knock, knock, who's there, i' the name of Beelzebub,' I whispered to myself. I edged to the spy hole in the door.

'Open the door now! Armed police.' There was my answer.

As I peered through the portal to the outside world, the sight left me frozen. High-powered rifles pointed their way into my kingdom. I looked away and like a cartoon character from the TV, shook my head.

Again came the shout, 'Armed police! Open the fucking door

NOW!' This time the demand sunk in. I reached for the lock and turned the key. BANG! The door flew open. I was grabbed by unknown hands and thrown to the floor.

'Who are you?' (Silly question.) 'What do you want?' (Not such a silly question.)

Metal barrels painfully gravitated to the side of my head. 'Edward James Webber, my name is DI Wellend.' *Did he say Bellend?* I thought to myself. I gave out a nervous laugh at the thought. 'We have a warrant to search this house for firearms.'

Sweet, I thought, *last time I checked there were no arms on fire here, side of my head don't feel too good though.* My arms flew to the back of me and a click of a strap bound them together. I was lifted and shoved face first against the wall. 'You are being arrested for suspected armed robbery and murder.' Another officer excitedly entered the fray. In his hand was a sixteenth of prime Charris. Wellend told him to bag it up. I laughed; he pulled the cuffs tighter and leaned into my face.

'Do you think this is funny, Webber?'

I laughed again.

DI bellend (I don't really want to afford this person a capital letter… so this is not a typo, it's out of sheer contempt) and his cronies dragged me, in my boxer shorts, into the street. It was 6 a.m. and with the words 'attempted murder and murder' ringing in my ears, I was pushed against the council flat's wall. I remember the nameless faces whose eyes burnt into me from buses carrying them to their daily grind. It must have been like watching an episode of *The Sweeney* in their eyes. In mine, it was the first level of the fucking divine comedy. I was thrown into the back of a police van and, feeling like Winston Smith from George Orwell's *1984*, I was whisked away to the local metropolitan scuffer's shop. I was in a daze, sitting practically naked, in the back of the van.

A couple of coppers were commenting on my lack of clothing which, in any other circumstance, I might have taken offence at but the only thing that was resonating with me were the charges. When we arrived at the police station, I was put into a cell, my hands released and the cell door banged shut, leaving me still shocked with the unholy 'murder' mantra resonating in my ears like a rusty bell. *What the fuck?* Not a good start to the week by anyone's standards.

A while later DI bellend entered. 'I need some clothes,' I demanded. I now had a dirty, stinking cell blanket around my waist and a dirty, stinking human in front of me. I took comfort in the blanket.

'We have your house keys. If you give us permission to enter your house, we will get you some clothes.' Silly and desperate, I agreed. The cell door closed again. I put my hands on my head and thought, *This is not going to end well*. But, hey, what could happen? I knew for sure that I hadn't killed anybody lately.

A couple of hours later the cell door came to life once again and a bundle of my clothes was thrust at me: grey pinstripe trousers, a white shirt, odd socks and a pair of Gucci shoes that had never been worn. In my defence, the only reason I had them was because someone gave them to me. I dressed and waited for what seemed like an eternity and I must have drifted off. I was rudely awoken by the key turning in the lock. A uniformed lackey escorted me to an interview room where DI bellend and his partner in grime sat around a table with a tape recorder.

'Sit down,' bellend ordered. I waited a few seconds for them to register my contempt then I then sat.

After the spiel of, 'My name is DI bellend and this is the recorded interview of Edward James Webber…blah, blah, blah,' he got down to the nitty gritty.

'On so-and-so day, did you, in Chiswell Street, in the process of an armed robbery, shoot one of the security guards two times in the leg?'

'No.'

'Would you be prepared to stand on an identification parade for this crime?'

'Of course.'

'At so-and-so time, on so and so date, did you pull up outside the Willows Pub on a motorbike, then shoot the doorman twice in the chest?'

'No.'

'Would you be prepared to stand on an identification parade for this crime?'

'Of course.'

'At so-and-so time, on so and so date, did you, whilst in the Pheasantry Club on Kings Road, Chelsea, shoot a man three times?'

'No.'

'Would you be prepared to stand on an identification parade for this crime?'

'Of course.'

'Have you anything to say about the crimes I have mentioned?'

'Yes, I want a lawyer.'

'Is that all you have to say?'

'No, I want a lawyer, please.'

bellend spoke into the machine. 'Interview ended at so and so time.' He looked to his lackey. 'Get him his brief.'

I skipped out of the interview room knowing that I had said nothing and that I was perfectly innocent of all offences mentioned. As I entered my cell it hit me: murder, two attempted murders and armed robbery. I was in trouble.

Paul Robinson, my solicitor, arrived. He informed me of what the day's proceedings would bring, one of which involved an ID parade for all said crimes. Paul said, 'You'll be in and out.'

Famous last words.

Later on that day, I was led into a big room in the station, with Paul by my side. As I entered, I saw a group of men in a line. I was to stand in an identification parade for the murder outside the pub and the attempted murder at the armed robbery. The third charge of attempted murder in the club was scheduled for a later date as none of the witnesses could attend.

An identification parade is where the witness sees the suspect in a line of other people who resemble the suspect. The investigating officer in the case is not entitled to be present at the identification parade. The identification parade should consist of at least 8 people who resemble the suspect in age, height, general appearance and position in life.

When the suspect is brought to the place where the identification parade is held they are asked if they have any objections to the arrangements or the participants in the parade. The suspect is also able to choose their own position in the line.

I was asked to pick a spot in the line and stand there.

The first three witnesses were for the Willows bouncer murder charge. The first witness to enter was the manager of the pub. He was asked to walk up and down the line of men and if he recognised anyone, to stop and let the officer in charge know. He never stopped. This happened another three times and each time the witness kept walking. When the last witness left the room I breathed a sigh of relief.

The next witnesses were for the armed robbery and attempted murder in Chiswell Street. The door opened and one of the security guards who was robbed outside the bank entered. Without any hesitation he moved to me, looked at the officer to his side and said, 'This is the man.' *What the fuck?* I thought. I looked over to my solicitor with what can only be described as swimming pools of fear in my eyes. Paul silently indicated to me with his hands and eyes to stay calm. The witness was escorted out of the room. I elected to change position in the line-up. I moved two spaces to the right and swapped shirts with another man in the line. The door opened and the second witness hobbled in. His left leg had a big cast on it after taking two bullets from a .38-calibre gun.

Again, the witness hobbled straight up to me and vociferously stated that, 'This is the bastard that shot me.' I was shocked, again I looked over to Paul who was shaking his head…not a good look from a brief, I thought. The witness was helped out of the room.

'What's going on here?' I nervously protested. 'I never shot anyone.' I was asked to calm down as there was one more witness for the crime in hand. This time I swapped my shirt with one of the other men in the line-up and changed position again. The last witness entered and, like the previous wretches, unambiguously picked me out. I was fucked; three positive identifications for armed robbery and attempted murder. I looked at Paul. I was led away and formally charged. I was then put back into my cell which, all of a sudden, felt like a safe womb. I remember being shell-shocked and confused as to how these people could have picked me out so positively. Paul entered the cell. I think he was as shocked as me but he believed my innocence. He shook his head.

'Look, we'll sort it out. You will appear at Tower Bridge Magistrates' Court tomorrow morning and will be remanded in custody. It's not worth wasting a bail application.'

I was given a phone call. I phoned my mother to give her an update and to let her know that Paul would be in touch. My poor mum got the burden again. She was not unused to these situations at this point in time; my dad and my brother Jackio were having their own problems with the law and Her Majesty's hospitality.

I'm not trying to say that we were always innocent but sometimes we were.

In 1984 I had a feud with a local beat copper's son called Mark. One night I was in a pub called the Lilliput Arms in Old Jamaica Road, owned by a British boxer called Billy Aird. I was drowning my sorrows with some friends as earlier in the day one of my pals had been given a long borstal sentence for stealing cars. The arresting copper was a man called Arthur (dad of Mark) who, with some of his police comrades, made our lives a misery with their constant harassment which sometimes involved violence. I must say that we were not angels... well, maybe angels with mucky faces. We were just kids growing up on the streets, at a time when boredom led to bad choices, but to have grown men in uniforms hitting us and fabricating evidence against us certainly didn't help.

This particular Saturday night in the Lilliput Arms, Mark walked into the pub. I made it quite clear that he was not welcome but he stayed anyway. After a while, I entered the toilet. As I was standing at the urinal, I felt a blunt thud to my back. I turned to see Mark shaping up for a fight, having just punched me in the back. I saw red, and being young and void of any wisdom I smelt the essence of instant revenge for the incarceration of my mate. I thrust my head into his nose and he went down like the proverbial sack of potatoes. Just as I rammed my foot into his face, the door opened and a friend of mine entered. As soon as he saw the foot rise for the second plunge, he grabbed me. Mark took the opportunity to leave the toilet and the pub promptly.

In retrospect, I'm not proud of acting like that; I was just caught up in a moment and was defending myself. After I calmed down a bit, I rejoined my friends, telling no one what had happened. At closing time, the doors of the pub sprang open and a group of uniformed police officers rushed in. Like a pack of wolves, they jumped on me and dragged me out kicking and punching through the doors to an awaiting police van where one of the boys in blue whacked me over the back with a truncheon, knocking the wind out of my sails. Back at the police station I was charged with assault. When they released me in the morning, I went to the hospital as my back was giving me pain. I told the doctor that I'd been hit with a police truncheon. A few months later I received the letter to appear at Tower Bridge Magistrates' Court for assaulting Messr Mark. I elected to go to trial by jury. I was given bail. After about ten months the letter came to inform me that the case was scheduled to be heard at Southwark Crown Court the next week.

The day arrived and I turned up in my Sunday best and was directed into court. After all the charges were read out the case began. Mark took to the stand and totally turned the story around. He said that I was the one who first attacked him. I took to the box and told the truth of what had happened and my treatment when being dragged out from the pub. I also had a letter from the doctor at the hospital that confirmed that I'd been hit from behind. It was basically down to the jury to work out which version of the story was true. Let me add that my luck was in that day because Mark had the natural look of a thug: bald head and pug-like features.

I, in turn, was blonde and quite angel-faced. The jury, after a few hours of deliberating, believed my side of the story and I was acquitted. Outside the courtroom, Mark was standing with his buddies in blue. I looked at him, smiled and, in retrospect stupidly, informed him that if he ever fancied round two I was available at all times, after indicating, with a limp wrist, what I thought of him and his corrupt cronies in blue.

A year later, I entered the block of flats where I was living called Casby House. I summoned the lift to take me up to my flat on the nineteenth floor. As I exited, a man was sitting on the floor opposite my front door. For the last few years I had been selling little bits of cannabis to friends just to keep the wolf from the door and I thought he was there to buy a bit of puff as his face was very familiar. I greeted him then turned to open my door but realised, after a confused moment, that it was off its hinges. By this time, the sitting man was at my shoulder mumbling something about being in the Peckham drug squad. Then, who should appear from within my house holding a lump of the finest Indian Temple ball in one hand and £2,000 cash in the other (it was 1985 and £2,000 was a fair sum in those days) none other than my old foe Mark. He had followed his father's footsteps and joined the metropolitan scuffers, and in due course had been promoted to the drug squad. As he put the cuffs on me, he whispered in my ear, 'I thought it was time for round two.'

That's a fair cop, I thought. I, again, pleaded not guilty and elected for crown court charged with supplying cannabis. This time I was sent to the Old Bailey.

My defence was that the puff he found was my personal stash. The money was the proceeds of love. I invented a story about having an affair with a rich villain's wife and she gave me money and that's why I couldn't tell the police where I got it from as I feared for my life. I could sense as my nose grew bigger the jury never bought a word of it. When I was giving my evidence the police prosecution sarcastically asked me if I considered myself a bit of a stud. I bowed my head, feeling a bit embarrassed by the jibe. It was the easiest decision any jury has ever had to deliberate. I was found guilty and sentenced to eighteen months in prison. The moral of this story: don't bash up the sons of policemen in the toilets of pubs, it will come back and bite you square on the arse.

Now, back to the charges I was facing: armed robbery and attempted murder. These I was truly innocent of and I had just been positively picked out of an identity parade three times. It didn't make any sense how and why these people wanted to identify me so positively.

Next morning I was shuttled to Tower Bridge Magistrates' Court. I remember a kind old gaoler called Bert who had known me from a young age. Bert would give me cigarettes every time I appeared there over the next three months while I was applying for bail. Kindness transcends all barriers. No one can think bad of anyone who is truly kind.

So thanks, Bert. Even though you were part of the corrupt system, the sentiment meant a lot.

I was led into court and into the prisoner's box. I sat in front of a posh magistrate who was deemed the worst of the lot in local circles. Some say she had been left broken-hearted by a local docker, but thinking about that now, it was probably one of those dangerous urban myths that was started by an oppressed criminal as he was dragged, kicking and screaming, from the box after bail was refused. Nothing like an oppressed criminal-type scorned.

I stood up to answer the charges, guilty or not guilty. It doesn't take the brains of Lloyd George to guess my answer. I was then remanded in custody until the following week where I would appear again for a bail application. I was taken back to my cell to wait for transport to whatever prison they deemed right to hold me in.

I must tell you, never before or after had I felt so down and helpless. These people had come through my flat door at 5:30 a.m., picked me up, thrown me into a police van, taken me to a cell and made me stand in an identification parade where I got picked out for committing the incomprehensible crimes that I was accused of. To say my equilibrium was askew is the understatement of the century.

Paul came to see me and updated me with future plans regarding my case but, to tell you the truth, I was incapable of taking in any information at that time. My head was spinning.

I was in the cells wrestling with God for about five hours before the meat wagon, as it was called, had finished its rounds, emptying other court cells around London. Tower Bridge was the last on its round.

It had separate compartments down each side that held the good and the bad. I was led into one of them. I looked through the small slit of a window as we drove down the road and sadly watched as people travelled to and fro in a completely different time and place to where I was at that present time. The only thing missing was the theme tune to *The Twilight Zone* da, da, da, da. Da, da, da, da!

After a timeless drive, the van entered the underground cells of a holding station in Kennington where the good and the bad were taken into a pit of misery that was the main holding cell. I was in my own world, still reflecting and, by this time, frustrated and angry at the demons responsible for my predicament.

'What you in for?' someone asked.

'I'm innocent,' came my reply.

'Ain't we all,' he added with a hearty giggle. I saw his point.

After a few hours, a prison guard entered and called out some names, mine included. We were informed of the different prisons allocated to each of us; mine was the legend that is Wormwood Scrubs. Never has a name befitted a place better than this. Wormwood Scrubs. God knows how that breaks down. An overriding thought pierced my mind, it went beyond a question. *How, in the name of Odin's teeth, did I get here?*

CHAPTER TWO

The year 1961 was a good one, or so I am told. Mum went into labour on 17 April as Elizabeth Taylor was picking up her academy award for *BUtterfield 8*. B52s were dropping napalm on poor ol' Castro over in Cuba.

Number one in the British hit parade was 'Stay' by Maurice Williams & The Zodiacs. It was also the Chinese year of the metal ox. It is said that if you're born in the year of the ox, you will be stable and preserving, and a tolerant person with a strong character. Two out of three's not bad.

Mum fell pregnant unexpectedly and in those days the man of the outfit had to do the honourable thing. So nine months, a shot gun and a wedding certificate later, there was Mum lying on a table in Guy's Hospital trying to squeeze me out. And out I came, a bouncing 10 lb baby metal ox. The name that was chosen for me was Edward James Webber. *Ta-da!*

Jacqueline Shilling, aka Mum, was a bohemian, catholic eighteen-year-old, growing up in Mill Pond Estate, Bermondsey. I think her mum and dad had middle-class aspirations for their little girl but then my typical fifties Teddy, bad boy dad entered into the mix and, as is inevitable with good catholic girls of that time, she fell pregnant. What I've heard is that my grandparents on my mum's side weren't too chuffed with the match, and for the rest of their lives my dad and his in-laws were at loggerheads, or maybe war would be the better word to use.

My nan, my mum's mum, got pregnant soon after – not by my dad of course, and, by sheer coincidence, they were both in the same hospital ward. I was born in April 1961 and my Aunt Romain was born in June 1961.

My mum's love in 1958, apart from the ol' man, was for dancing and having a good time. There seemed to be a new kind of rebellion spreading all around post-war Britain.

American artists like Elvis, Buddy Holly, Fats Domino, Frankie Laine, Gene Vincent, along with the British contingent, Lonnie Donegan, Tommy Steele (a Bermondsey boy), Cliff Richard and The Shadows filled the airwaves demanding that the youth party and rebel against the stuffy, old-school rule-makers and anything else that fitted that description. Creativity was exploding and breaking down class barriers, and for the first time in history, working-class roots were commanding quite a kudos in society.

Edward John Webber, aka Dad or the ol' man, was twenty-one. As much as Mum was a good catholic girl, Dad was a bad atheist and a natural charmer. They were a classic meeting of angel and demon.

In his formative years, Dad was not always on the right side of the law, sometimes out of necessity. He was a good-looking man and women, so I'm told, used to flock around him. A natural rebel without a pause. What chance did my naive, catholic mum have? But love is blind, as they say. When I think back, my dad never really had too much self-control. Women were most definitely part of his subsequent downfall but there is no doubt in my mind that my mum and dad loved each other very much in the early days.

Later on in life my dad would try to impart what he deemed positive information to me. 'Love is a trick of nature to preserve the species,' he'd say, 'and women are all part of the conspiracy. Once they've had the kids, that's ya lot, they're gone.' No wonder his and mum's relationship went pear-shaped.

When Dad's father, a navy man (navy as in ships, not colour), was eight years old, he fell into a canal. He was so scared of the beating that his strict Victorian father would give him for coming home wet that he let the filthy rat-ridden piss water dry into his bones, which apparently took a bit of a toll on his heart. He died of rheumatic fever when he was a young father. He was also an Eddie Webber but known as Ted and was, by all accounts, a beautiful, kind and humorous man. I can see why he fell in love with my nan, Nanny Lou. She was an amazing woman, straight as a die. I never, in all the time I had with her, heard her swear or say a bad word about anyone. I still miss her when I think of her smiling face. You were a fine nan and without you and Auntie Jean something would be missing from my being. I still hold onto your memory in my heart, Nan.

My ol' man was eight years old, the second oldest of four kids when his dad died, the oldest being my aunt Jean. My favourite uncle in all the world was his youngest brother, Kenny, who went on to have a bit of a shitty life due to multiple sclerosis. Uncle David and Auntie Jean were also amazing human beings. At the time of my grandad's death, my father had to become the man of the house. My nan worked three jobs at the time just to tread water, so my dad started nicking food and whatever else he could get his hands on that might help my nan feed the family.

One of my favourite stories is when he stole a salmon from a boat in the Surrey Docks and brought it home. When Nan saw it, being so straight, she ordered him and his catch to exit the house as she was having nothing to do with stolen goods. As he and the fish were leaving, Nan shouted for him to come back in case he got caught with it. Needless to say fish was on the menu that night.

My Auntie Jean also tells a story: Her best friend's mother and father owned a local baker's shop in their road. One fine day as Jean and the baker's daughter walked down the street, Auntie Jean looked up and coming towards her, smiling, with a tray of cakes freshly pilfered from the baker's shop perched precariously upon his head, was my old man. 'Hiya, girls,' he brazenly spurted, whilst stuffing a jam donut in his mouth. 'Wanna cake?' After acknowledging an embarrassed shake of the head from my Auntie Jean, he happily munched off.

'That's your brother isn't it, Jean?' the baker's daughter asked to a blushing Auntie Jean.

'No, I've never seen him before in my life.'

I tell ya, they broke the mould when they made my father, the proverbial rascal. Having to get married and being cut off in his prime when the metal ox came along didn't sit with him well and has caused us to be at each other's throats throughout our lives.

We all moved into my nanny Lou's three-bedroom council flat in Thompson House, Abbey Street while we waited for the council to house us. My two uncles and Auntie Jean also lived there.

I don't remember too much of that time at my nan's as I was new to the big ol' world, although I would be a regular up there, mostly on a Sunday, for the next thirty years. I loved it – it was the first protective home that I synchronised with. I was the first baby of the next generation and as you would expect, I was spoilt rotten. My nan, aunt and uncles showered unconditional love on me always. I can only remember a few times with my other grandparents, like sitting in their flat on a Sunday eating prawns, cockles, winkles and bread and dripping sandwiches. They have both died now and I regret we weren't close at the time of their deaths but I hope their journey to wherever one goes was a good one. It was a shame that family politics got in the way of the relationship between my mum's family, all caused by my dad, who took their dislike of him very personally.

My earliest memory was when I was eighteen months old at All Hallows caravan site in Kent. The caravan belonged to my great Aunt Kate and great Uncle Albert. Aunt Kate, who I always remember as a force of nature, was my great grandmother's sister and, as they say, a money earner by hook or by fiddle.

Aunt Kate was born in Holloway prison and took her first breath on the bleak Victorian spurs. Her mother was a money lender and a bookmaker, an all-round old-school fiddler. Some silly fellow made the mistake of borrowing a few quid from her and tried to knock her. One night she waited outside the Cock and Monkey public house in Rotherhithe until the tanked-up knocker showed his person at closing time. Armed with a fork, she stabbed him up the arse.

Even though she was pregnant, she received a year in HMP Holloway and out popped Aunt Kate, born amongst brasses, thieves and murderesses. What a start!

Aunt Kate was married twice, first to a naval sea officer. They had one child, named Albert, who she spoilt beyond belief and who, later on in life, was a musical inspiration to me, introducing me to jazz and blues in my teens. Kate sang and danced in the Vaudeville scene in the 1930s, which accounted for her hitching her skirt up and flashing her knickers at any given time to the sound of a piano and leading a good old drunken sing song. Albert and Aunt Kate featured heavily throughout my life. Sadly they have both passed now but she was a character never to be equalled, as was Uncle Albert. I remember your advice Aunt Kate: 'Never a lender or a borrower be.' Regretfully I chose to ignore it to my own detriment.

When my mum was pregnant with me, all the clan were convinced that she was having a girl. I think some gypsy told them in a tent in Margate or somewhere. So, with the gospel of the gypsy ringing in their heads and a few pieces of silver lighter, they all set off down the shops to buy my wardrobe: pink cot, pink blanket, pink clobber, pink, pink, pink, a colour that sickens me even now.

Anyway, there I was pottering around the front of the caravan on the grass in my pink baby clobber minding my own business, probably eating worms and dirt, when the pain came. I had stepped barefoot onto a wasp. I remember it like it was yesterday, my first ever bit of real conscious pain. Funny ol' thing, the power of the canister (head).

Wasp stings were to feature many more times in my life as, when I was kid, I had white hair and for some reason wasps were attracted to it. Many a time I'd put my hand on my head and feel the nasty yellow beasts staking their claim in my barnet.

In 1962, we moved out of my nan's to a block of council flats by the River Thames by the name of Park Buildings, situated in Paradise Street, opposite a huge Catholic church and close to my nan and granddad on mum's side in Cherry Garden Street.

Our flat was almost on the sand of the River Thames. I think 'boat' was the first word I blurted out. I think 'dad' was the seventh after 'hedgehog'.

Park Buildings had its own claim to fame, a certain Max Bygraves grew up there. Something that he would never admit in the years to come. I think I can remember, many years later, Max being called a 'ponce' by an old, jealous resident.

Show business must have run in the brick work as Princess Margaret and her fancy man also had a bolthole in a house a hundred yards away. I can't for the life of me think why, with all those palaces and stately homes lying about, they chose Bermondsey as a venue. I suppose a bit of rough doesn't do anybody's relationship any harm. Thank God she didn't run into my ol' man, that's all I can say. Who knows where the monarchy would be now!

I was, apparently, a restless baby with a lot of excess energy, causing mayhem at any opportunity I could. Not a lot has changed to this day. I've been told that I'd never go to sleep without the radio on. When I think about it, all the music that I was exposed to whilst looking out over the Thames with baby eyes still features high in my life, as does the feeling I get when I look at the river vista now.

The sixties had arrived and with it, the future. I believe it was a turning point in history never to be repeated with regards to creativity and the breaking down of the class divide. Me and my sponge-brained generation were, subliminally I'm sure, absorbing all that was thrown at us through the transistor airwaves.

The Beatles, The Stones, the rebirth of Muddy Waters, who I am listening to as I write this, The Who, Michael Caine, Harold Pinter, Terence Stamp and the rest of the working-class thespians and writers took urban culture to a new level. What more could a growing seedling's ears and slow-forming mind ask for?

Mum and the ol' man got busy and two more tots arrived in as many years. As far as I know they came into the world without any fuss, well, Jackio did anyway. Jackio and I have been at loggerheads all our lives. Never a day went by when we were holed up at home without us being at each other's throats. But saying that, we couldn't be any closer these days; he has turned out a fine, principled man, a hard worker and a devoted father of four kids, but in the early days I have got to put our strained relationship down to him stealing a bit of my thunder as the first born. I had it cushy until he came along but, more importantly, an incident happened when we were nippers, four and five years of age. This is how I remember it:

We were playing at the bottom of our flats when, out of nowhere, a strange man came up to us and asked me and my brother to go with him and get some sweets. Somehow, inherently, I knew we shouldn't go but Jackio's perception was different. What can a five-year-old boy do when his brother walks away with a strange man but to run and tell his dad. With my bat powers in mind (I'll explain that later), I flew up the twenty or so flights of stairs as fast as my five-year-old legs would take me. 'Dad! Dad! Jackio has just gone off with a strange man,' I blurted out manically. For the next, I don't know how long, my dad systematically bashed me up and down a street whilst frantically looking for my abducted brother. I remember being very confused as to why my dad was being so violent towards me. Surely I'd done the right thing by telling him, hadn't I? As we rounded a corner, there was Jackio and the man. Jackio was filling his face with ice cream – it was one of my dad's mates who had wanted to treat us both. I can't remember the outcome between abductor and Dad but hope the ol' man gave him a clump as well.

I was battered and bruised. When we came back home, I remember climbing into bed with my mum, who was having a bad time with the pregnancy of my sister. That was my first recorded experience of comfort but also the first account of loss of trust in a human being. How could my dad, who was my hero, hit me like that? From then on, I was always paranoid that a clump could come at any time. So started the contemptuous rot.

Years later, I had a chat with my dad about all this and we concluded that he wasn't really that happy about getting married at twenty-one and having three kids by twenty-four. I think that is one of the reasons that mine and the ol' man's relationship was forever strained. It led the way to his now-mediocre existence.

When I look back on my life from time to time, I realise that I have always found it hard to maintain any kind of human relationship. I think that when one gets so royally let down by their superhero, there is no going back. Ultimately, trust certainly doesn't loom large in my legend.

CHAPTER THREE

In 1963 we moved from Park Buildings, new destination: No. 54 St. Vincent House in Abbey Street. This is where my youngest brother was born on 7 August 1963, the day before Messrs Reynolds, Wilson and Edwards relieved Her Majesty of a few million quid in the Great Train Robbery.

Apparently, he nearly died whilst my mum was giving birth to him at home, so the relatives, all being mad Catholics, called in the local bag of yeast (priest) to christen him. He was blessed by the holy water and made a complete recovery, earning him a middle name after a saint.

God knows why they did that but that's miracle-witnessing Catholics for you. After his recovery, it was confirmed to the crazy mumblers of prayers that there was a god and a miracle had indeed taken place in our little old flat in Bermondsey, and for many years I believed it too.

Ma and Pa made us learn our flat number and the name of the road we lived in off by heart as we were all prone to wandering off, especially me. I really came into my own when I was about four or five. I would climb up and down trees, jump over roofs and almost killed myself one day with a daring feat which caused many residents on the landing a near heart attack.

I was obsessed with *Batman* in the 1960s, the one with all the POWS!!! and HOLY COWS!!! and, of course, the camp superhero and arch baddy disguises that any existentialist worth their salt would kill for now.

I used to be transfixed with the regular scene of Batman and Robin walking up a building effortlessly whilst having a strategic conversation about what was going to happen to the arch villain in the next couple of minutes and pulling all sorts of craziness from the faithful 'Bat Utility Belt'.

I think I might have taken it all a bit too literally.

Dressed in my loose-fitting camp *Batman* outfit, equipped with a hashed together Bat utility belt, made from one of my dad's docker belts that hung around my arse, I tied some Bat string onto our second-floor landing railings. With a swift Bat look to the right and left to create the right mood, I began my climb over the safety rail with the full intention of abseiling down the front of the building. Mum and the neighbours were terrified as they tried to softly coax me back over to safety with anything that came to hand, sweets and all sorts of sticky offerings. I think the toffee apple was the thing that clinched it. Even Batman has his addictions.

I loved watching TV and films in the cinema. The first movie I went to see was Walt Disney's *The Jungle Book*. It was as if I had entered into another world. Animals singing songs and, of course, Baloo the bear. Now that is a couple of hours I will never forget: me and dad sitting down watching this giant screen come to life, with lit-up faces, one smeared with red sauce from a sacred hot dog.

A few days later Dad came home with *The Jungle Book* soundtrack on vinyl and I played it constantly on the old radiogram we had. I must have listened to it hundreds of times over the years. It lived in the cupboard with Buddy Holly, Fats Domino, Frankie Laine, Elvis and the Rolling Stones, some of the records from my dad's selective LP collection. *The Jungle Book* stayed my number one right up until my teens. I still know the songs word for word.

Baloo was my favourite, he didn't give a monkey's about anything except that is…The Bare Necessities…BOOM!

Another passion of mine, at that time, was swimming. Dad taught me to swim at a young age by throwing me in the deep end of a swimming pool then informing me to sink or swim. I obviously chose the latter. I took to swimming like a drumstick to a drum.

I used to spend my hours sitting on the roof of a bicycle shed that was situated at the side of the road in front of the flats, waiting for my dad to come home from his work at the docks. When he stepped onto the landing from the lift, he used to get my attention with a hearty tongue in lips whistle and off we would go swimming. He and I were always at the swimming baths on Grange Road and, if I can remember rightly, so was a lot of fine-looking 1960s swimwear, filled with fine 1960s female, hippy, free love bodies. As much as I was there for the swimming, Dad, I'm sure, was secretly there for the women, no doubt spinning the old chestnut of how hard it was to bring up a child on his own.

A man used to be in the pool quite frequently. In retrospect something was definitely not right with the geezer. He would let the young kids clamber all over him and he'd throw them back into the water, arms and bodies would be everywhere about his person. He also used to give us submarines. We would lie prostrate on the water while he placed one of his hands under our tummies. His other hand would be on the soles of our feet, then he would push us and we'd glide through the water like a submarine.

He used to make fart noises with one hand wedged into his armpit whilst chicken flapping his other winged arm, resulting in a perfect wet fart noise. In retrospect, he was definitely a suspect in the bacon bonce (nonce) department in my book.

The swimming baths in Grange Road also doubled as washing baths as many people didn't have washing machines in those days. I know we had one, because I drank a quarter of a bottle of bleach, which my mum had left on top of the machine. It was another Batman moment for poor Mum - I remember being violently sick and my mother making me drink gallons of water. She had to have eyes in the back of her head with us lot. When I hear the lyrics of Ella Fitzgerald's version of the song 'Black Coffee' it always reminds me of my mum and the tough time she had bringing up our family and putting up with the ol' man.

I used to love it when we finished at the swimming pool, we would have a cup of hot Bovril and a bag of crisps. If it was Saturday we would take the short walk to Tower Bridge Road and then to Manzies Pie 'n' Mash shop. We'd have double pie 'n' mash soaked in liquor then swamped with vinegar and pepper. I drool with the memory as I write.

My young prowess in the pool got me noticed by the coach of the local Bermondsey swimming club. I ended up joining and excelling in the club, winning a few big races.

St. Vincent House was a beautiful place to live and every once in a while I still happen upon someone that lived in the flats. They all have stories about the Webbers to reminisce about.

One morning Mum woke up and, in a sleepy daze, headed for the kitchen to break her brood's fast and have her first cup of tea and fag of the day. It took her a while to register the silence. With fear in her eyes she ran upstairs and like Goldilocks found all three beds empty. As she rushed downstairs again, she noticed piles of pots and pans stacked up against the front door and the door ajar (when is a door not a door?).

She ran up and down the flat's landing, frantically scanning and calling for us but alas, there was no sign of her nappy-filled fledglings. Whilst panicking and having her fifth fag in the flat there was a knock on the door. 'Do you have three children, two blonde, one dark?'

Mum got worried. 'Yes, where are they?'

'Follow me.'

'How did you know where to come?' Mum enquired.

'The bigger of the three knew your address.'

So well done Ma and Pa, job done on the learning the address front.

The kind stranger and Mum walked down Abbey Street until they came to a crowd of chatting black women, fresh over from the Caribbean sun. They all worked in the metal box factory up the road. The sight was reminiscent of Custer's Last Stand as they circled us. As Mum and the kind stranger stepped towards the gathering, she noticed three pairs of little legs in the middle of the crowd, two I might add, supporting heavily shit and piss-laden nappies.

Like the parting of a bad 1960s haircut, the protective crowd stepped aside and Mum walked through, revealing me and my two brothers. I informed Mum, in a happy four-year-old kind of way, that, 'We were going swimming.' We always kept our mum on her well-worked toes.

I was in my usual solitary place on the bicycle-shed roof one day, waiting for my dad to get home from work for our weekly fix of the swimming pool. I heard the familiar whistle as he walked along our landing. When I saw him, I jumped off the roof. I was so excited that I didn't see the car. I landed bang in front of the iron horse and my face smashed into the headlight as the car ran over me. I can't imagine what my dad was feeling as he had a bird's eye, step-by-step view of the accident. He told me in later years it was like watching a film in slow motion.

I was wearing strong boots. The kind that had a compass in the heal and animal footprints on the soles. My mum swears it was those boots that saved my foot as the wheel of the car had ended up resting on my ankle. I can vaguely remember Dad cradling me in his safe arms, the taste of blood and loose skin in my mouth still resonates, then arriving at the hospital and being pulled from pillar to post. It was all mighty confusing for a while, then bang, no more.

I had to have forty stitches to hold my face together. Apparently one of the finest surgeons about at that time was on duty that night and did a first-class job of stitching me up.

I can remember one or two things about being in hospital. Uncle Albert, son of Aunt Kate, bringing me up some ice cream, but mostly I remember my face being stuck to the pillow by goo every morning. I was in hospital for what seemed like months while my head got better, as now it had become the size of a scabby green melon. I had so much time off school.

My primary school was St Joseph's at Dockhead, a Catholic institution in Bermondsey run by dastardly nuns – a gross generalisation I suppose, as there were some nice ones too. The headmistress of this holy institution was called Sister Baptist, a powerful name in itself, I'm sure you'd agree. She was a stern-faced woman that would take no shit off anyone.

If you had to be chastised, Sister Baptist would chastise you. She was fierce and fair, reminiscent of her biblical namesake.

Sister Baptist had half an index finger on her left hand. Us kids were always intrigued as to what had happened to the unfortunate carpal, that is, until my ol' man came up with the answer, much to my mother's disgust.

'She lost it sticking it up a priest's arsehole.'

Mum, a dedicated catholic to the core, didn't appreciate the revelation at all.

'You'll go to Hell saying things like that about the sister,' Mum scorned.

'Well, if the sister ain't there before me,' my dad said, 'I'll say hello to the priest who's keeping her half finger safe up his bottle and glass [arse].'

Mum shook her head in resignation knowing that if she carried on conversing about the subject it would gradually get more derogatory.

But could it be true? Us kids debated it in the playground the next day. Could it be up a priest's arse? We all came to the conclusion that losing a finger up the arsehole of a priest must have been an act of God, so indeed, she must have been a messenger of the Messiah, or, at the very least, a very naughty girl.

Before the car accident I can always remember enjoying school. In those days they used to give you a pint of milk in the morning and some toast with glucose on it for energy. We used to race to see who could neck the pint of milk in one go. My two best mates back then were Ted Power and Stephen Greasly. I think of them fondly, especially Stephen as he lived in the next block to St. Vincent House and we used to walk to school together in the morning. I was pretty content to have them and my two brothers as friends on this part of my little life journey.

When I was released from hospital I had to get back to school as soon as possible as I had missed so many important educative lessons, especially concerning English grammar and the mechanical workings of vowels and consonants.

I remember my first day back, my face had healed a bit but not much. It was still a mass of scared skin, scabs and faded red bruises.

I was excited to enter the school gates and see all my friends again after being away so long. I remember getting strange looks from the rest of the kids but took no notice, I was just happy to be back in the collective company of small people again. I walked down the corridor to my classroom.

When I entered, all hell broke loose. Girls started screaming when they saw my face. Mary Shelly would have been proud. Although the doctors had said it was fine for me to go back to school, the kids in class made it clear that they did not agree. I was very confused. I was taken out of the classroom and put in the deformed messenger of the Messiah's office to wait for my mum to take me back home. That was the time when me, the world and its occupants fell out. It took months to heal properly in order for me to return back to school but by then I had missed so much that, although they put me back in my year, I never really caught up. I found it hard to concentrate which led me down a shaky road of thinking I was stupid. I started to hate the place and the overzealous nuns with a vengeance and, with my wingmen Ted Power and Stephen Greasly beside me, we started to cause a little bit of havoc, especially in the playground.

Let slip the dogs of war; that this foul deed shall smell above the earth with carrion men, groaning for burial.

- William Shakespeare's *Julius Caesar*

I started to become a bit of a bully to younger kids (to my shame now). There was a little girl in my class called Delores and we used to sneak off with each other and experiment with our pants down – I laugh out loud at the thought. Hope you're well, Delores.

The only time school became worthwhile, in my eyes, was when swimming and galas were on the agenda. I won a few trophies for the school in local inter-school swimming competitions. I won one certain trophy three years on the trot which meant the school got to keep it. I used to look at my name inscribed on the cup and felt validated every time I walked past the trophy cabinet.

When the nuns felt the need to punish kids they brought you out in front of the class and smacked the back of your legs with their bare hands. I remember being quite confused about these women in black who gave their body and mind to their holy written legend but, at the same time, could dish out abusive punishment to children willy nilly. My dad used to say, 'It's because they all needed a good fuck.' Damning himself to hellfire again.

The scars of the accident were not only on my face but inside my head as well. I thought, sod school and its unholy authority, a philosophy that has followed me through life.

In retrospect, having kids of my own now, school was and is a precious thing. A place to meet other young travellers on the start of their life journeys and, most importantly, to learn life skills. I'm being a bit harsh on the nuns as, deep down, they did really care but it seemed the tunnel vision of their call to arms did, every now and then, turn them into beastly penguins.

Education, education, education, a fine thing to have and as the Child Catcher from *Chitty, Chitty Bang Bang* declared, 'All free'.

I adored reading books. We used to get a menu of books sent to the school by publishers. They had lists of recommended books by people in the know which you could buy. They were subsidised, so were affordable and I fell in love with the Swedish *Moomintroll* series written by Tove Jansson.

I avariciously read every book of the *Moomintroll* series. The bizarreness of the Moomin family, with their big hippo-like noses and quirky friends, was right up my street. There was even an asteroid named after the series.

It was the last knockings before I finished primary school. I must have been about ten or eleven and every day seemed to be a little bit more of a struggle. The nuns seemed to have developed a penchant for the back of my legs as their handprints were permanently embossed on them.

We had to wear grey above the knee shorts for school uniform. I hated it. I have a great big red birthmark on the back of my right leg from ankle to arse. That was the butt (no pun intended) of many a sarcastic schoolboy's jibe. I used to put a pair of original Levi 501 jeans over the shorts to cover my infirmity when I left the house, then take them off at the last possible moment before I entered the school gates.

I fell even more behind in my lessons in the last year of primary school, I just couldn't be bothered anymore. So began a losing battle between me and the people responsible for teaching me that was to last all the way through my adolescent school years.

I used to try and feign sickness every day when Mum woke us up in the morning in the hope of getting a day off.

Then along came another couple of additions to the family. My little sister, Sian, and a car. A green Mini Cooper. I don't remember much about the occasion of Sian's entrance except being fascinated by my mum breastfeeding her. So now we had a little girl as well, our lives were becoming like SimCity™. One morning, as the brood and I were eating breakfast, my dad stormed in shouting, 'Some bastard has nicked the car.'

His pride and joy had been stolen in the night and so began the search of the century. We found the car a couple of miles away, parked in a block of flats. That night the ol' man slept in the car, cuddling an axe, waiting for the offenders to come back. He was ready to dish out some eastern punishment and chop their arms off to make sure the villains never stole a car again, but alas, the fortunate offenders never returned. In my experience, lightning very rarely strikes twice in spontaneous crime. I was glad because I have no doubt there would be a couple of one-armed bandits running about today.

By then, things at home weren't so good. Mum and Dad's relationship was becoming more strained day by day. Mum had three children in nappies at twenty-one years old at a time when modern-day conveniences like microwaves, online shopping and disposable nappies were not yet available so everything had to be done by hand. My dad was twenty-five, with four kids, a Mini Cooper and an eye for the birds. It must have also taken a lot of money to keep us clothed, watered and fed.

Dad worked as a docker in Surrey Docks and many nights after he finished work I'd witness my mum administering ointment to the blisters that sat like hill mounds under his armpits. I have two children of my own now and know how hard it must have been for my dad to keep above water and I doff my cap to him. We always had food, clothes, an occasional trip to Canvey Island and an abundance of Christmas presents every year. He was a good provider, even if there was a lack of physical love, but you can't always have everything, can ya?

Lots of strange boxes, filled with all sorts of everyday commodities, used to appear in our flat every now and then, as if by magic. My inquisitive questions were answered with, 'They fell off the back of a lorry.'

Dad was stealing goods from work to subsidise his wages. Lots of like-minded dockers did the same at that time as there was not a lot of money about. Add to that four growing kids, a flat and a wife, and one had to be on top of all the finances. My dad was, and always has been, a hard worker. When the sleeves needed to be rolled up, up they went. Bravo, Dad.

Now with six of us St. Vincent House was getting too small and, because of the Batman and car incident, a bit dangerous, so Mum and Dad put in for a new council flat.

Chapter Four

No.2 Traps House in Southwark Park Road was a little bit bigger than St. Vincent House, but the winning factor was that it was a ground-floor flat and was situated around the corner from a colourful street market called The Blue.

The six of us moved in. Myself and my two younger brothers shared one bedroom, my sister had another and Mum and Dad the third. At least if the Batman urge came again it was not such an issue on the ground floor. There was a park behind the flats with swings, a seesaw and a set of monkey bars. I remember Traps House being a happy place, except for the rows between Mum and Dad every Saturday, which was racing day. My old man was a gambler and a compulsive one to boot. Horse racing was on the TV every weekend. I have a hatred for the sport and the silly voiced, fast-speaking commentators even to this day. One Saturday afternoon my mum had left for her weekly bingo fix, a rigid ritual, faithfully kept. I believe it was her only saving grace and gave her the precious time she needed for herself to stop her going insane with family life. The old man was left in charge of us kids, the blind leading the blind so to speak.

'I know,' he would say excitedly, 'let's play a game of Cowboys and Indians.'

'Yeah,' was our happy response.

With that, the old man dashed to a cupboard in the passage and brought out a rope.

'I know what we will do. I'll be the Cowboy and you be the Indians.'

Myself and my brothers debated the concept for a bit. Being loyal Saturday morning picture-goers, the American Westerns that we viewed in the picture house at New Cross, with a couple hundred other tykes from the surrounding manners, led us to believe that the Indians were always the bad guys and the Cowboys always victorious…but, hey, fuck the politics, Dad wanted to play with us so we'd swallow our pride and get on with it and stick a couple of feathers on our heads. He then proceeded to tie us up with a rope, tightly binding our arms and legs. He'd do a super fine job with the knots. When he finished, he made safe the rope by tying it to the big old homemade wooden drinks bar that sat in the corner of the living room.

'Right,' he said, 'I'm the Cowboy and you have to escape and find me.'

With that, he left the house. It must have looked a pretty picture, us three wriggling about laughing trying to get free from the bonds that bound us. After a couple of hours and not making any sort of dent in the fabric of the rope, we all agreed that this Cowboys and Indians lark was hard work. Another hour later, exhausted with the job of trying to untie our hempy nemesis, we gave up. The front door opened and my mum walked in and, seeing her brood in a broken mess on the floor, enquired passionately, 'Where's your father?'

'We're playing Cowboys and Indians, don't know,' we replied together, but not as enthusiastically now. With that she stormed back out of the front door, still leaving us shackled. Maybe she wanted to play a Cowgirl? A while later she returned with my dad who she'd dragged out of the local betting office. This scene has turned up in a film called *Freebird* after I told the story to the film's director.

Traps House was situated in a part of Bermondsey called The Blue. The market was in The Blue; I'm not too clear why it's called The Blue, possibly because of Bermondsey's nautical ties or its location to Blue Anchor Road.

In the olden days, the area, including Southwark, was under the corrupt, watchful eye of the Bishop of Winchester. I think it was not looked upon by the holy head as anything but a pox-ridden place to throw undesirables, thieves, brothels and anything else the earthy voice of God wanted rid of from the centre of the city but, when I was growing up there, it was a vibrant place with market stalls lining both sides of Southwark Park Road and a great community spirit, everyone helping each other when they could. In those times you could just open anyone's door on the landing and ask to borrow milk, sugar and many of the other elixirs of life.

My dad ended up with a market stall that was situated outside a branch of Woolworths. He sold all sorts of fabrics which catered for homemade shirts, trousers and curtains. My mum made three sets of purple velvet trousers for us when my Uncle David got married, all made from material from the stall coupled with black lace, see-through long collared shirts. We looked the nuts.

The market was full of wooden, old-school stalls lined up next to each other with all their 1960s colourful wares proudly displayed. Record stalls, shops, a café. At the start of the market, a beautiful lady called Anna, who owned a fruit and veg shop, would give us young people the occasional apple…*por gratis*. She was a real, old-school native of the place and was greatly missed by the community when she fled this mortal coil, but the real bonus for us was that the market was ripe for picking.

I once stole an Elvis double LP from one of the stalls as I could never have afforded to buy a majestic treasure like that with my measly pocket money. I was thrilled when I got home to play it. Later that evening, when the ol' man had finished his day, he marched into the living room. There was I, hugging our old radiogram in the throes of listening to the hip-shaking King of Rock 'n' Roll's version of an old gospel classic called 'Peace in the Valley'.

'Where did you get that record?' Straight to the point as always.

'I found it…honest.'

'Yeah. Where'd ya find it then?'

'By a wall. I can't remember exactly where.' I wasn't doing myself any favours. The old man clumped me round the head. 'Don't lie to me, I hate liars.' That was fucking rich coming from him, I thought.

'You fucking nicked it off my mate Jimmy's record stall.'

'I never.'

Whoop, another clump hit its mark.

'Now, I will ask again. Did you nick it from my mate's record stall?' I was, somehow, busted. I thought I was being so careful at the time. How in heaven's name could he have known? I pondered for a second on the edge of telling another porky pie (lie). Then thought better of it.

'Yeah alright, I nicked it but you've always told us to nick things.'

'Yeah, but not off my mates. He saw you take it and marked my card. Now take the record back to him and say sorry.'

Another clump.

'What's that one for?'

'Getting caught.'

I took the record back to Jimmy and apologised. Jimmy smiled and plainly said, 'Don't get caught, that's the secret, kid.' Great minds think alike.

I soon found a new partner in grime that was as dedicated as me to the art of skulduggery. His name was Mark Gudgeon. We were next-door neighbours and became best friends with a lasting bond. Both of us were up for any kind of mischief that was put our way, always daring each other to jump the gaps between garage roofs or somersaulting off the swings in the play area. We also devised a money-making scam. One of us would stand outside a public toilet entrance. In them days you had to pay a penny to use them, if I remember rightly, or it might have been a threepence coin. Anyway, one of us would stand outside the unholy smelling entrance, holding our stomach and feigning a belly ache. If one could muster up a wet fart as well that was almost certainly a deal clincher.

A kind, concerned adult would come up and ask if you were okay. After spinning a yarn about having diarrhoea and there being no one in my flat to let me in, they'd nearly always give you the entrance money for the toilet. A few of the people who we had nipped for money previously would walk by and give us a smile as they witnessed another kind soul affording us the entrance to the karzie. It was a good day's money for a couple of sweet addicts like Mark and me.

Another money-making scheme was to stick tissue paper up the refund hole of a red phone box.

It was like a fish trap, you'd come back at the end of the day and, if another little firm hadn't got there first, you'd pull the tissue out and walk away with a handful of sixpenny pieces.

Not everything was a walk in the park for us though. One Saturday we were up to our old tricks in the play area, doing outrageous death-defying stunts on the monkey bars, when one went a bit pear-shaped. I fell off from a great height and to my horror, when I looked at my arm, the bone inside my left wrist had popped out to say hello, a sight not to be recommended, especially to a pain coward like me. I ran to the flat, my wrist as limp as limp can be with the bone still exposed. My ol' man was just off to the betting office. After cursing my stupidity, he reluctantly shoved me in the car and had to spend the next couple of hours whilst they sorted me out at Guy's Hospital. He'd keep looking at his watch and asking the poor A&E nurses how much longer I would be. The call of the betting office is a strong one; it transcends all things.

I ended up with a plaster cast for two or three weeks which put me and Mark right out of the game but, in saying that, the plaster cast made people sympathise a lot more in the diarrhoea scam. Wished I'd broken my right wrist though – school couldn't have argued with that fact.

By this time I had started my secondary school education (for want of a better word), at St. Michael's in George Row situated opposite my old hell St.Joseph's. With it came a new uniform, which I'm pleased to add had long trousers. I was, for some bizarre reason, put into the school's A stream.

There were four streams: Alpha which was the top; A a close second; B a far-away third; and C sub-zero. I hated being in the A stream, most of my friends from St. Joseph's were put in B and C. The only advantage of being in the A stream was music lessons. That's when I first heard the piano at close quarters. I fell in love with it. Mrs Gregory was the music teacher, I'll never forget her for a number of reasons. I used to sit with her during the lunch break and she would show me chords and finger exercises on the piano. I loved music and found myself quite attentive in the lessons. Apart from music, nothing had changed with my war with academia and its dealers of education.

If I disliked my first school, I despised my second school. With all my mates being in the B stream, I immediately set about getting demoted.

I still couldn't understand anything that the teachers were trying to teach, especially now in the A stream where expectations were a lot higher. So after a while, and a lot of swipes from our sadistic headmaster's cane, I planned to completely give up on school. The plan worked. I was demoted to the B stream at the end of the year. What I now know is that I am dyslexic, but this ailment wasn't flagged in the seventies. The next blow was a hard one to ride. Music lessons were exclusive to the A stream – getting demoted to the B level meant no more Mrs Gregory and her magic piano. I was gutted, the one and only consolation was being united with my fellow B-stream reprobates once again.

Our form teacher was a hippy by the name of Mr Washington; he was an English teacher.

I remember him being a good, kind and gentle hippy soul who was tormented by us all daily. He used to bring his guitar into lessons and play Donovan and Bob Dylan songs. My mates would take the piss but I loved it. Mr Washington was a teacher that encouraged colourful creativity and I'm sure that my love of words is down, in part, to him.

I once wrote a story in his English class, inspired by the seventies psychedelic vibration hanging in the air and the TV series *H.R. Pufnstuf.* My story was about a boy who fell down a drain hole and entered into a psychedelic world where animals spoke. The animals in this world were governed by a tyrant monster so the young boy, together with the animals, set about dethroning the beast and restoring peace and love to the land. I was called to the office of the Head of English, a crusty old lady called Miss Jackson. She told me that the story was fantastic and well done. I skipped out of her office as if walking on air. It was the first time any teacher had praised me for my school work and it meant the world to me. So thank you Mr Washington and Miss Jackson, your presence has been fixed forever in my fried, creative, dyslexic brain.

Inevitably, I started to hop the wag (bunk off school). I would hang out in the Montana Café. Around this time, I had started putting on weight, zooming up to about twelve stone at the age of twelve; not a good look for a five-foot-seven schoolboy with bright blonde hair and a travelling fan base of wasps.

I started to become very self-conscious, especially when my dad used to call me 'Jumbo' and 'Big tits'.

That, I must admit, after a while, caused an inferiority complex as big as the universe and its inner workings. It was years before I could take my shirt off in front of people. Even now I look in the mirror and see the tits. The times when I have had to take my shirt off in front of the camera when doing a scene have filled me with dread. So thanks for that one, Dad!

There is so much more that I want to say about my early home life but I shall refrain from doing so as the objective of this epistle is about going from A to B in life. Some things in life should be held in the chest, so that's what I will do.

Another dreaded lesson was Physical Education, aka PE. Going to the gym for PE lessons at school was painful, having to squeeze my fat, insecure, adolescent body into tight shorts and a tight T-shirt. The school would hire a coach and take us off to a wooded area called Malden in South West London. I always had a couple of cheeky bags of smoky bacon crisps tucked away. It was an open sports area, surrounded by woods, with muddy football and rugby pitches, all needing a bit of TLC. The PE teacher, Mr Murphy, was a fair teacher, who also, like Miss Jackson, wouldn't stand any old bollocks off anyone. He would send us all on cross-country runs. I hated it. It was cold, muddy and too much like exercise for me and my fat body. I still feel dread when I think about taking my kit off at the end of the lesson and standing naked in the shower with everyone else. I felt like the elephant man.

I used to love sailing with the school. Our cane-happy headmaster would take us to Surrey Docks in the days when it had water in it. We used to sail Wayfarer boats. After doing the necessary bits and pieces, like putting the sail, jib and tiller in place, we would glide off, capturing the wind around the dock. I became quite good at it. When we arrived back at school we had to head off to the changing rooms and the dreaded communal showers. Our headmaster must have liked keeping an eye on us as he always joined us, naked in the shower, minus his cane I might add.

The school, in its wisdom, issued all the students with journals, little light blue rectangular books for writing our timetable inside. There was also a little box at the bottom of each page to write notes or to get parent's signatures if we were to miss lessons. I became an expert in the craft of forging my mother's signature and getting out of as many PE lessons as I possibly could. Until, that is, the day my mother received a letter from the school asking if she would like me to be seen by the school doctor on account of my frequent physical ailments every PE day. The fraudulent forgery came to light. I had to confess my crime to her. When the ol' man came home and Mum told him what had happened, he said, 'Fuck school,' damning himself to Catholic hell once more.

CHAPTER FIVE

It was 1971. The Montana Café had three pinball tables and a kicking jukebox.

I used to love the sounds that emanated from the colourful glass box standing proud in the corner of the café. For the price of a tanner (sixpence) you could hear the great tunes of the time: 'Lola' (The Kinks), 'Maggie May' (Rod Stewart), 'Soldier Blue' (Buffy Sainte-Marie) and 'Ruby, Don't Take Your Love to Town' (Kenny Rogers). Every time I hear that song, the wonderful memory of red-and-brown ketchup-filled sausage sandwiches subliminally assault my senses – I can almost taste them.

The café also had a one-armed bandit, not the car thief sort but the fruit machine type. I remember, if you got three cherries, a pile of silver tanner bits would crash into the money plate. To a starving teen-ager with a penchant for ketchup-soaked sausage sandwiches that was all the wonders of the world in one place. I bleeding loved that café. I used to love hearing the banter from the big boys, talking about their sexual conquests in dark corners of garages and toilets, tarnishing the reputations of the fair Bermo maidens that fell foul to their charms.

John Lennon was putting songs out as a solo artist. I listened to his 'Imagine' album and I was smitten. I loved the jaunty nature of a song called 'When You're Crippled Inside'. I had always loved The Beatles and after their acrimonious split, 'Imagine' was Lennon's first commercial solo album. I wanted a guitar. I went on and on at my parents to buy me one, then, one Christmas morning, there it was, an electric guitar without an amp. I tried and tried to get to grips with it but couldn't seem to achieve anything. I wanted to be able to play it immediately and didn't realise how hard it was.

I took it to school but, alas, no help there. The curse of the B stream took care of that. So I put it down and eventually gave it away.

I started to swap school for the Montana every chance I could. The fine old institution that was Woolworths was situated about two hundred yards from the Montana. I used to go in there and nick pencils, rubbers and even Airfix model aeroplanes. I would go back to school and sell them to the kids. If my mum had known this, she would have been pretty pissed off, nay pissed off, she would have bloody killed me and waved the way to Hell but I had to fund my pinball and excessive sausage and ketchup intake somehow.

Mark, my next-door neighbour, and I would love the weekends. We'd jump on our chopper bikes and, like two urban cowboys on our steads, would head for the area's wastelands – nothing happier than two pals in their early teens on bikes looking for adventure.

Greenwich Park took about two hours by bike from our flats. When we arrived, we'd make straight for the highest point of Greenwich hill and, with a yell and an insincere prayer, ride our bikes down at full speed. God knows how we survived doing that so many times. There were quite a few serious accidents that happened on that hill. A friend from the flats, David Streek, a fearless lad, known for his temper and his fist, rode his bike down the hill one day and the front wheel hit a hole. He came off it and, as the bike landed on him, one of the handle bars got stuck in his leg.

If only Santa knew the havoc he sometimes caused with his two-wheeled presents.

Santa was the cause of a Christmas Eve clump that I received from my dad the year I got my chopper bike. My brothers and I would stay awake on Christmas Eve, listening out for the bells that were supposedly attached to Santa's sleigh. We'd be asking each other unanswerable questions, questions like, 'How does he get in places that don't have chimneys?' and 'What landing does he park his sleigh on?' or 'Does he start at the bottom and then take the lift?' All normal questions for young enquiring brains. This one Eve, I was elected by the other two to catch the fat man on the job and get the answers once and for all.

I sat at the top of the stairs and waited for the jolly white-bearded enigma to make his entrance.

As Catholics we have to go through a Christian ceremony called confirmation where we take the name of a saint. I took the name of Thomas, as in the doubtful one. I think my mum chose that moniker for me.

So there I was, sitting at the top of the stairs, waiting to pounce, when the street door opened. I was about to make my presence known, when my dad entered, carrying a brand-new chopper bike, oops. Needless to say, he saw me and wide-eyed and swearing, put the bike down. I flew back into my bedroom. My brothers were both feigning snoring noises knowing the outcome. I was on my own with this one, brothers or not it was an 'every boy for himself' moment. The old man flew in and made it quite clear how angry he was. I think that he was more angry at himself for getting caught than dispelling the myth of Santa.

I now realise how important Christmas really was to my father. When he was a kid, growing up without a dad, he never really got any Christmas presents because of the lack of family funds, so he really did go overboard for us. Me catching him probably killed a bit of that magic…sorry Dad, you and Mum always did us proud at every Christmas that I can remember.

Playing in the streets of Bermondsey in the early seventies was amazing. I remember the vivid colours and the hippies in outlandish psychedelic clobber. There was something freeing, gentle and sunny about it all, probably down to the strange, earthy, pungent aroma that was forever lingering in the air.

I was sitting on the balcony of my flat one sunny day. My prized portable 45s record player was on my lap, blasting 'Can't Buy Me Love' by The Beatles. *H.R. Pufnstuf* was still my favourite TV programme; a world of weird-looking creatures with pumpkin heads and all sorts. There was also a wicked green witch in the mix, who chased the stars of the show all over the gaff.

The programme stared Jack Wild of *Oliver Twist* and Artful Dodger fame. I was a Jack Wild fan, in fact, his was the first 45 RPM record I ever bought with my own money. It was a cover version of Joe Brown's classic 'A Picture of You'. It cost fifty pence from the wise man that was Jimmy on the record stall…at least I paid for it. You'd often see me skipping down the road singing the *H.R. Pufnstuf* theme tune, trying to imitate a few of Jack's shapes.

Muhammad Ali was another great hero to us all down south. I remember his fights being spectacles, viewed on our black-and-white TV. The TV cameras monitored all the celebs that had paid extortionate amounts of money for their prime ringside seats. One fight in particular, Ali was fighting the Argentine heavyweight Oscar Bonavena, and knocked him down on the canvas three times in the fifteenth round. After the fight he shouted to all the cameras, 'Ain't I pretty' and 'I am the greatest'. I'm sure that some people watching hoped that someone would knock him out but that never happened. Muhammad Ali, in retrospect, transcended all race, creed and colour. He was like a god to us kids.

Bermondsey was traditionally an all-white area. I can't remember seeing too many black faces about the place back in the day. I think there was only three or four black kids in our school. They always seemed to be fighting due to destructive culturally based name-calling.

In those days it was very rare to see mixed-race relationships. They usually consisted of a white girl and a black man. The girls that favoured the exotic West Indians went through hell with some pretty nasty derogatory labels attached to them as well.

Saturdays, in those days, were always fun. The day would start with Saturday morning pictures. Gangs of youths from all over the manor would converge onto the Old Kent Road, making their pilgrimage to the Regale cinema. The other choice of cinema was the Elephant and Castle Odeon and ABC but that was a longer walk or you had to get the bus. We were excited and ready for our weekly fix of old black-and-white movies.

My favourites were Cowboy and Indian movies. Flash Gordon (who was played by Buster Crabbe and whose image is still embossed in my mind), and the Three Stooges who were a comedy trio. When we were all nestled into our fag-burnt seats, you'd hear the 'dadadadaaa' organ music intro and the whole cinema would raise their voices to sing the Saturday morning pictures song in not-so-perfect harmony. Then an MC would come out onto the stage clutching a handful of birthday requests. He would try and read them out over the vociferous abuse he was getting from the impatient baying youth. 'Fuck off and start the film' or 'Sit down, you cunt'. Somebody always ended up chucking a well-aimed chocolate brazil at him, hitting him square on the nut.

There were also a few little raggedy, bully gangs there. They would sometimes make kids' lives a misery, prowling round and trying to pick fights with them. But our gang was never bothered. It is another fond and nostalgic memory.

CHAPTER SIX

The summer of 1972 crept in and our car pulled up outside a block of flats that had just been built. Corrugated iron still circled the base of the unfinished block. We headed up an almost-finished stairwell. The sweet smell of the big Peek Frean biscuit factory on Drummond Road hit us like candy floss at a fun fair. As we synchronised with the air and the buildings about us, we all marched down the landing to No.79 Lockwood Square.

Built in the early 1970s, the Four Squares Estate was made up of 691 homes across four, nearly identical, seven-storey blocks: New Place Square, Lockwood Square, Marden Square and Layard Square. We entered number 79. It was like heaven. A four-bedroom maisonette with a massive kitchen and a big living room with three big windows that looked out over the estate. Stairs led up to four bedrooms and, get this, there was even a toilet upstairs and down. It was like we'd won the lottery. We watched as the flats started to fill up with other families from Bermondsey. Some that had come from the same blocks where we had previously lived. David Streek of Greenwich Park Hill and handlebar fame from Traps House, the Arnells from St. Vincent House. Even my nan and grandad on my mum's side, who had to battle the hate-ridden, icy stares of the ol' man many times as they passed each other on the street.

Families would bring their fledgling teenagers and kids, some of whom would become life comrades.

Soon we had our little gang and we would troll the estate playing run outs (a game of hide and seek), and truth, kiss or dare, a game which was played sitting in a circle, usually on the grass at the back of the flats. When all seated, you then had the choice of a dare, tell a truth or kiss a girl – each one resulted, in one way or another, in some kind of embarrassing predicament, usually ending up with a kiss with one of the fairer sex or a broken arm as a result of one of the dares going pear-shaped. All innocent fun. I started to become besotted with one of the girls.

She lived on the other side of the building but I could see her front door from my back balcony. I was obsessed with watching her door. If I saw her leave her house, I'd dash down to the porch of my block and sit there, trying to look cool. When she emerged from the block I'd be there, my heart banging like a drum. I don't think her mum and dad liked my family or our gang, as we were starting to shape up as undesirables, so nothing really came of it. Donny Osmond's 'Puppy Love' was floating about the charts at the time. And puppy love it was. One of our gang, Terry, had a bit more luck with her sister, so, indirectly, all was not lost on the knee-trembling front.

I saw my first grown-up female naked body in a pub called the Southwark Park Tavern. Billy Tarent, who owned the pub, was an old friend of my dad's and a legend to boot. He was, at one time, the road manager of the band Manfred Mann and, by all accounts, was a promising boxer which was hard to imagine due to the rugged, unblemished good looks he possessed. Billy was a good-looking man in a Charles Bronson kind of way – the actor not the prisoner. He also had a wife, Sheila, and two daughters called Nicola and Natasha who were also stunners but totally a no-go for us estate oiks. Billy gave me a job bottling up in the pub, which meant every morning I would have to replenish the empty bar shelves with bottles of beer and mixers. One fine day I was late arriving. It was an hour away from opening time and the salivating, Sunday rush.

In those unpolitically correct days, most pubs traditionally had strippers performing on a Sunday afternoon. Working ladies who would take their clothes off whilst seductively dancing to the music of the time. This particular Sunday Billy opened the pub whilst I was still on the last knockings of bottling up. As people started to file in I finished my work, left the bar and went to get my coat. I opened the door to a room at the back of the pub and nearly died as my eyes met with the sight of a naked woman bending down putting some high heels on getting ready for her show. I must have regressed at least ten years at the sight as I started mumbling like a baby with a raspberry-coloured face. She just laughed and said, 'Don't worry, I bet you've seen it all before.' I had seen it, many times, inside my head but never in reality. I ran past her grabbing my coat with a face now the colour of a beetroot, and I fled the room like the wind, but the image has been branded on my brain forever. Thank the universe and traditional Sunday pub afternoons.

My mate Terry had an unusual hobby: he used to collect birds' eggs. Every Sunday we'd catch the 47 bus and ride it for miles to the end of the line which was a place called Farnborough in Kent, just on the outskirts of London. We'd exit the bus and head for the local café. As there were four kids in our family, Mum couldn't always afford to give us much money. I'd watch as the other members of the gang munched into their ketchup-soaked bacon and sausage rolls, then we would pound the country lanes for our objective. Terry had eyes like a hawk, he'd spot a nest from yards away.

He'd put his disposable gloves on, climb the tree and gently feel inside the nest for the treasure. He'd gently take out the eggs and put them into a little cotton wool-lined box. It was a magical time, especially for a group of urban city boys swishing away at bushes with sticks making pathways through Farnborough's green and pastured forests. When we arrived back home to the flats we would go through the ritual of blowing the eggs. You would make a pin hole at the top and bottom of the egg and gently blow the yolk and egg white out then place the empty egg in one's customised egg collection box. I had a pretty impressive collection I can tell you. My favourite was the egg from a small bird called the Spotted Flycatcher. The eggs were tiny, brown and speckled and also very rare, like all special birds are.

Every now and then our school would put together a disco for the students. The nights were chaperoned by the teachers. The disco was held in a place called the Feltham Club Hall just off Jamaica Road, in a building almost connected to my old primary school St Joseph's. Obviously booze wasn't allowed but someone always managed to smuggle in a bottle of vodka and keep it hidden from the teachers. It was one of those typical seventies discos where the DJ would sit behind a home-made box with flashing lights and, in a silly Tony Blackburn voice, big up each song before he played it. At the end of the night you would have a slow dance with someone you fancied. That night my dance was with Sandra, she was in the year below me at school and another girl I obsessed over.

You couldn't get too close as you danced as you'd be a bit worried that the lump in your pants would give your devilish intentions away. Many a horny teenager would go back to his gang after the dance almost bent in two trying to hide their excited embarrassment.

After the disco we would head to a local youth club called the Cambridge University Mission or CUM. The Mission, first founded in 1907 and then refurbished in the 1940s, became a second home to us.

That club loomed large in many Bermondsey legends. It was maned by a group of posh, middle-class Christian university students and some indigenous Bermondsey folk who were born-again Christians. The club was overseen by a fine man called Snowy Davoll. Snowy was probably the straightest man that I have ever met and the only person who could really control us.

He and his wife, Sybil, were a holy couple with two kids called David and Andrew. They hailed from up north. Snowy and Sybil had a calling to work with inner-city kids and thank their God they chose Bermondsey. We had great fun with him and the Christians - the club was subsidised by a charity so we didn't have to pay too much money for the trips that Snowy would take us on. We used to go on wild adventures up mountains in Wales, camping far and wide and battling the elements, all to keep us off the streets. He also knew what the local police were like and how they treated us. What was most important was that our parents trusted him unequivocally. He was a true man of his word and of his God.

There were private living quarters in the club for Christian volunteers that usually came from either Oxford or Cambridge University. Some stayed and were abused for months. Luckily, they had a private space to return to at the end of the sessions to lick their wounds after the nightly battles with the unholy Bermondsey lion cubs. My lord, did they go through it. There was nothing Christian about the kids that used to attend. Every night the volunteers were mercilessly taunted, sometimes violently by the drug-infused older boys; the violence was sometimes borderline biblical. But, I must say in their favour, it was very rare for any of those good people to lose their tempers or their faith, even when faced with the angst of feral, teenage, pugilistic adversity. They never got angry and, like their messiah, always turned the other cheek. A good training ground for any young, middle-class missionary preaching the word of their God.

CUM was a little nugget in a land of oppression, especially when it came to a part of the evening that was called 'Epilogue'.

Epilogue was a compulsory section of the night where the young Christian soldiers would act out or voice a lesson from the bible. There was always a slight smell of fear coming from the chosen speaker of the night as the ruthless city lads of the club were gathered and herded into a space in the recreation area to listen. A few of the members were armed with gummy bears to launch at the speaker while reluctantly listening to his interpretation of the holy written word.

In retrospect I can honestly say that these young soldiers of Christ get top prize for the sincerity in their belief as they battled through the twenty minutes of abuse and jelly missile throwing, never missing a beat.

Another older Bermondsey friend of mine, who also went to the club, was a guy called Dookie Ash. Dookie was an exceptionally gifted guitarist. He had formed a band made up of Bermondsey lads and volunteers from the club and used to rehearse in the basement. They were a brilliant and competent band to boot. Dookie and his fellow minstrels would be banging out tunes like 'Rock Bottom' by UFO and 'Free Bird' by Lynyrd Skynyrd. This music was like finding the holy grail for me. I bought my first acoustic guitar from the Kay's catalogue, paying in instalments of two quid a week for twenty-five weeks. What an investment.

I synchronised with my universe there and then and decided to lock myself in my bedroom, never to come out until I had mastered the sacred instrument and the words and music to The Animals' cover of the famous folk song 'The House of the Rising Sun'. Many blisters and much blood later, my crusade was over. I had learnt to play the guitar. I saved up and bought an electric guitar and amp, much to the annoyance of the ol' man, who couldn't concentrate on the runners and riders showing on Saturday afternoon's *Grandstand*, as I'd now progressed to playing the Johnny B Goode opening riff at full blast. 'Shut that fucking noise up before I chuck that cunt guitar out the window,' he'd shout up the stairs. He'd look to my mum as she was getting ready for her weekly bingo fix. 'Tell your son I'm trying to have a bet.' I'd lock the bedroom door, just in case the threat carried weight. 'Mother, tell your children. Not to do as I have done. Spend your life in sin and misery. In the house of the rising sun.' The chords of Am, C, D, F and G surely must equal Om as sacred letters of the universe because they paved the way for many other chords and songs to break through. I had got myself a repertoire of magic sounds.

My other passion was the ancient marshal art of kung fu. Kung Fu was fast becoming the new fad. I, like every other teenager at that time, was besotted with the coolness of kung fu maestro Bruce Lee. I would kick at anything, coupled with a silly noise, every chance I got.

There were no videos or Internet around in the seventies so we had to depend on TV to show Bruce's masterful executions of the deadly graceful art.

A scene from one of his films *Way of the Dragon* was shown on the Saturday sports programme *Grandstand*, before the horse racing, obviously. If the horse racing was on there'd be no chance. The conversation with the ol' man would have probably gone like this:

'Dad, Bruce Lee is fighting Chuck Norris on *Grandstand*, can we watch it?'

'No, I'm watching the racing.'

'But it's Bruce Lee.'

'I don't give a fuck who it is, it's my telly, I bought it.' That one would kill the debate stone dead.

We'd never seen anything like it before. Bruce Lee, kicking ten shades out of Chuck Norris, who was then the world karate champion.

One day I was ambling about the house when I heard the magic words, 'Come on, I'll take you to the pictures and see *Enter the Dragon*.'

'Eh? *Enter the Dragon* is an eighteen certificate.'

'Don't worry about that, you are eighteen.'

'I'm not, Dad, I'm thirteen.'

'Well, they don't know that do they.'

'What about lying?'

'It's okay to lie sometimes.'

So off we went to the Elephant and Castle picture house. As we entered my dad bought two tickets. The lady behind the kiosk looked at me, then at the ol' man.

'You do know that this film is an eighteen certificate, don't you, sir?' Only thing missing from the scene was a fag hanging out the corner of her mouth.

'Yeah,' the ol' man replied and gave me the proverbial wink.

'I don't believe that boy is eighteen.'

The old man, feigning outrage, demanded to see the manager pronto! The smiling, eel-like manager slithered over. The ol' man took him aside and had a word in his shell-like ear whilst I was standing there feeling like a blob of brown sauce on a bowl of jellied eels (very out of place). Moments later the manager sycophantically ushered us into the house. I looked at my dad in wonder.

'How did you manage to do that?'

'I told him you were a midget and asked him to not make any kinda scene as you were self-conscious about your height.' Touché, I thought. I sat through the first film red-faced and a tad embarrassed. It was a weird science-fiction movie called *Zardoz* starring Sean Connery and Charlotte Rampling. I'd only ever seen Mr Connery play the suave James Bond, innocently messing and flirting with the heavily made up Bond girls, but now here he was fifteen foot on a screen kissing Miss Charlotte OBE's bare breasts. I didn't know where to put my face. The manager would pop in and out throughout the show and every time he'd make dodgy eye contact with me.

'Dad, I think he knows.'

'Fuck him, we're in now…wanna hotdog?' Does a bear shit in the woods?

For the next two hours I sat there mesmerised, filling my face with hot dogs and popcorn as Bruce Lee systematically took down everyone who dared challenge him. Kung fu, I was hooked.

A local sports centre had opened opposite my flats in Scott Lidgett school. In Bermondsey there were only two schools worth their sort. The Catholic one, of which my brothers and I attended, and Scott Lidgett which was Protestant. These was another school on the periphery called Bacon, but that was always just an option in case one never got into the other two. Most of the people that mattered went to St. Michael's or Scott Lidgett. The sports centre had a sort of youth club attached to it where we would hang out in the evening. I started meeting new mates like Ian Burns and Peter Shearer. The activities at the sports club included badminton and trampolining. It also had its own swimming pool in which canoeing was taught. Karate and judo classes were also on the menu. I opted for karate but you had to be over sixteen to do the class, so I ended up signing on for judo. I got pretty good at it as well. I progressed to an orange belt. The guy teaching the judo class was called Alan, and by night he was an old-school Teddy Boy. Every now and then the youth club would hold a disco. Alan would come dressed in all his prized Teddy Boy clobber, looking great with his massive sideburns and blue suede shoes. He also taught my new mate Peter Shearer to play the drums.

It was at this time that I had my first encounter with the law, a relationship that was to last for the next fifteen years or so, on and off.

I was in a supermarket in Lewisham and stole a packet of Wrigley's spearmint gum. The shop detective caught me, called the police who then took me to the local scuffer station. I had to go to court. I think I received a conditional discharge. I was thirteen years of age. Maybe if I'd just got a slap on the wrist it could have led me onto a different pathway but, as we say in my part of the world, if me aunt had bollocks she'd be me uncle.

By this time school had become intolerable. There was a maths teacher called Mr Shields, who, for some reason, had it in for me. One day during the maths lesson I was being my usual disruptive self and he hit me so hard on the side of my face my ears didn't stop ringing for the rest of the day. I was so embarrassed that the rest of the class had witnessed the unholy event. I hated this man with a vengeance. He made my already hated school life even more of a misery, but it was the seventies and teachers' abusive behaviour was totally par for the course. We also had a headmaster called Mr Blake who loved to whack us across the arse with a cane but no one really worried about that as it was a time-honoured headmaster's tradition. But Mr Shields was something else, a grown man clouting a young boy, would no doubt, in these politically correct days, be looked upon as a form of abuse. That night I told the ol' man what Mr Shields had done to me in front of the class.

'Fucking liberty, how dare he. I'm the only one who's allowed to do that.' All irony lost.

'When is your next lesson with him?'

'Tomorrow.'

'What time?'

I referred to my trusty journal. 'Three o'clock.'

The ol' man nodded and got back to the horse racing page of the paper.

Next day, there we all were in the maths class. Half an hour into the lesson, the classroom door opened and the ol' man casually strolled in and sat at an empty desk. The rest of the class downed pencils, all eyes on my dad. He put up his hand.

'Sir?' he questioned.

Mr Shields, in a confused state, enquired who he was and with that, the ol' man got up, walked to the front of the class, grabbed the now freaked out Mr Shields by the scruff of his neck and dragged him to where I was sitting.

'This is my son, if you ever lay a finger on him or any of my children again'—the ol' man opened a window—'I'll throw you out of this window.' With that, he left. Mr Shields was shaking like a leaf. Doubtless to say that cowardly man never laid a finger on me again, nay a finger, he never even let his eyes fall on me. The ol' man instantly went down in St Michael's folk law and became a hero to the boys and girls of Class 3 B. The incident was talked about in the school playground for months to come. Even the headmaster I'm sure thought twice before leaving imprints with his trusty bamboo on my young gluteus maximus but it still didn't stop him.

In 1975 Pete Townsend and The Who released 'Pinball Wizard'. Music and pinball were my only saviours, with The Who's rock opera *Tommy* ringing in my ears.

I used to try and play pinball in the Montana Café with my eyes shut, frantically pressing the flipper buttons but, alas, the deaf, dumb and blind kid was an impossible act to follow and the big silver ball was swallowed up effortlessly by the machine. The pinball machine had its own unique sound. There was music and constant clicks of replays as the proficient fingers of older boys nimbly worked the flipper buttons. Single and double clicks. Now the double click was a lucky number. When the game was finished the machine decided whether or not the last score number was a lucky one, and if so, it gave out an extra game. I still sit with the memories of the Montana Café.

CHAPTER SEVEN

Then another life-altering event occured: my dad came home one day with the news that he had bought a caravan in Dymchurch, Kent, a sleepy little place a few miles from Folkestone. So come the weekend we all jumped in the car excitedly and headed for what was to be another great coming-of-age adventure. We'd never had a holiday before, so although it was just Kent, also known as God's garden, to us, it might as well have been on the other side of the world.

The drive down there was like travelling through another planet. Fields of corn, rape and apple trees, it was magical. Only downside was that I suffered from hay fever and the pollen played havoc with my sinuses. I'd arrive at the caravan a sneezing red-eyed wreck.

Dymchurch ended up familiar territory, half of Bermondsey had caravans down there. The Saunders, the Morfords, the Stupples, to name but a few. All respected Bermondsey families, but even these people were not prepared for the havoc the Webbers and the gang from the Four Squares were to bring. Roll on the six-week summer holidays.

The caravan site that we were on was connected to another bigger site called New Beach Holiday Centre. It had a club house full of fruit machines and pinballs and would hold singing competitions, discos and live bands in its bar room every weekend.

New Beach Holiday Centre also housed two site shops, a swimming pool and, most importantly, lots of girls. Outside the club house above the road was a big wall that separated the land from the good old English Channel.

In World War Two when Hitler was determined on world domination, Dymchurch was one of the coastal batteries that kept him at bay. There were hardy stone-built pillboxes scattered all around the coastline. Their other important use was for the act of teenage deflowering. Usually built in a hidden spot they were perfect for a sexual fumble or knee trembler in the dark. They also seemed to double up as a recycling point for used condoms that unceremoniously lined the cold concrete floors.

Around the back of our caravan were big fields full of lambs and sheep that would lazily graze on the pasture. Every Sunday Mum would dish up a traditional Sunday roast dinner and lamb covered in mint sauce was always our meat of choice, but I tell you, looking at the cute animals skipping about in the fields whilst digging into a lump of their brother's or sister's carcass with our forks was somewhat off-putting. So needless to say the Sunday menu was changed to beef.

The club house became the nucleus of our fun, only trouble was that if you were not a resident of the site you weren't allowed into the club. Unless, that is, you had a visitor's pass. This was never a problem for us as a few of our Bermondsey pals that were signed up members would sort it out for us and bring us in as guests. We had a lot of fun and games in that place and, needless to say, robbed it blind.

It was the Chinese year of the dragon and that bode well with the now fifteen-year-old ox. It was also the British year of the heatwave. Jesus, it was hot but what did we care, we had Dymchurch and New Beach's swimming pool.

The real bonus of that year was my first proper, full on sexual encounter with an Irish girl from Cork. She was on holiday with her family and we met at one of the club's discos. I must have impressed her with my moves as I was head banging to Status Quo's 'Down down'.

Tina was fourteen with red hair and a fiery seductive temperament well beyond her years. Was that an Irish thing? I think not, just teenage rampant hormones I would say. 'Save All Your Kisses For Me' by Brotherhood of Man was number one in the charts. Who would have thought that a year later, Steve Jones of the Sex Pistols would be swearing on prime-time TV, propelling the ol' favourite BBC drunk,

Bill Grundy, onto the well-attended dole queue. But this Irish lass was definitely saving her kisses and everything else for me. All we did, at every opportunity, was attend to our teenage hormonal calling. It was very fumbly at first but I soon got to grips with the inherent wisdom as to what goes where.

After this there was no stopping me. I had found sex, but unfortunately, the gang had other pastimes on their mind. Soon every shop within the vicinity was unmercifully robbed and the safe house, or flop as we would call it, was our caravan. By this time, our parents allowed us to go down to Dymchurch and use the caravan on our own. We used to get a train from London Bridge station to Folkestone. When out at Folkestone station we would steal a car and drive to Dymchurch. We could all drive as most of us had perfected the art of 'TDA' as the police called it (taking and driving away).

On the mean streets of Bermondsey often there were stolen cars doing handbrake turns and mad racing down roads. We were always armed with a set of FT, FS and blacktop car keys that we would jiggle in the car's ignition until it started. I remember we nicked a Mini Clubman at Folkestone and parked it outside the caravan – God knows what the other residents of the caravan site thought. We'd use it like it was our own car. It was a wonder we didn't all got nicked.

After the holidays or sporadic weekends when we decided to go down, the car got dumped. I must add that I'm not proud of stealing people's cars, as I have since been on the other end of it once or twice and it causes absolute mayhem – especially if one has a family they need to ferry to and fro. I sincerely, with hand on heart, apologise to all our faceless victims and their families.

We met new gangs that lived in and around London, Kent and in the far-off worlds of Croydon and Maidstone. One of these new comrades was a skinhead with the unfortunate nick name of Skid (I'll leave you to do the maths on that one). Skid was a big mouth and prone to being a bit of a bully to younger kids. One weekend the gang had all gathered in our caravan to smoke a bit of hash. The trouble was we didn't have that much stock so while we would roll and smoke joints housed with the finest Red Leb money could buy, we'd grab a few beef oxo cubes from the cupboard and sprinkle them into a Rizla paper then pass them to Skid. Skid would smoke the beef gravy-laced doobies then pretend he was stoned. We'd be in fits of laughter as the beef-flavoured smoke would fill up the caravan and Skid's announcement that 'this shit is good, man'.

One night, after a night out with my little Irish banshee, I walked into the caravan to be faced with a mountain of frozen perishables: boxes of Bird's Eye fishfingers and burgers, bars of chocolates, sweets and, of all things, digital watches all freshly pilfered from the village shop in the night. The contraband had been piled up in the middle of the floor. I left to take a shower. The showers were situated on the other side of the camp. On my merry way and whilst eating some of the stolen sweet proceeds, I ran into Little Jock, the waif-like owner of our campsite shop, freshly robbed the night before. He was furious and who could blame him.

'The young buggers!' he whined, in his incomprehensible high-pitched Glaswegian accent. Knowingly, I asked what the problem was.

'The young buggers. They've had all me burgers, sweets and frozen food.' I stifled a giggle as I thrust my stolen sweet-riddled rubber band (hand) behind my back and cast my thoughts back to the vision on the floor of my caravan.

'Who?' I innocently asked.

'I don't know but they'll all go to hell!' A foregone conclusion I thought. I did feel sorry for the poor little fellow though I must say. None of us in those days had too much regard for anything or anyone – we were young and from an area where kindness was always taken for a weakness. Looking back, I can't believe we thought it okay to do these sorts of things.

When I think about it, I really feel that it was due to the area we came from. Everyone who we were close to had someone in the family who was hooky. Hookiness saturated our hood.

I sometimes feel a little sadness when I think back to those days. We were all intelligent boys that should have all gone on to do great things legally. Mums and dads, in those days, had their hands full just keeping the family afloat let alone time to educate us about life and our futures. Kids of my generation usually had to go out and just get on with it. So it was odds-on that sooner or later you would have run-ins with the law. I quote Pete Townsend: 'A hero or villain is what you become or take the road in between'. I, after many painful life lessons, chose to try and be a hero. I have two amazing, conscientious, creative kids called Alfie and Barney and would never expose them to any kind of world that is connected to the sort of unempowering one that I grew up in.

When summer was over in Kent, it was back to the flats and Bermondsey life resumed its never-ending cycle of police and parent harassment – the boys in blue must have missed us as they went at it tooth and nail to arrest us all again. It was also coming to the end of my time in the institution that was school; it was my last year and I couldn't wait to walk out of those fucking gates.

In 1977 Dub reggae started hitting our scene. The finest red seal cannabis with the dub base and powerful working-class lyrics of oppression seemed to somewhat marry up perfectly.

Back in school we had to choose what last-year exams we wanted to take. I, in a moment of head-filled dumb madness, chose to do about six CSEs. God knows why, I couldn't even fill a in Marvel Comics subscription.

The school brought in a careers officer to talk to us about what kind of futures we saw for ourselves. I remember sitting uncomfortably in a room with him as he was telling me my options. I could be a plumber, bricklayer or a forklift driver. I told him I didn't know what I wanted. He laughed. I told him that I didn't want to be any of the things that he was offering. I left the room and jumped over the back fence, never to return to St. Michael's school again, and good riddance to it as well. Months later they sent my family a bill for exams not taken. I think the ol' man chucked it straight in the bin.

I had left school, now to get a job. I started to ask about whilst underwriting my gap year with the occasional petty crime. There was a statutory police law in force at that time called 'Suss'.

The full charge was 'Loitering with intent to commit an arrestable offence' which translated to, you were susceptible for the charge at any given time. If you stopped in the street near cars one had to be on the lookout for the scuffers or they'd have you. That was all the bully boys in blue needed to carry on their persecution of us.

We had names for these offending protectors of society like Spotty, a tall, lanky loud wanker with a face full of acne. He seemed like the type who, when growing up, possibly at one time took the brunt of much bullying himself. I think the uniform gave him the power over kids that he probably always craved. Another horrible copper was Fat Alex, a complete, all-round (no pun intended) son of a bitch who loved to beat up on young teenage boys. Then you had a couple in the nasty upper echelons, Paul Bard, Barry Plod and a snake, we nicknamed Blondie. Blondie used to drive a police dog van and always had a fierce Alsatian that drooled at the sight of our oike buttocks accompanying him. He was very slippery and sly. All these second-rate troopers would think nothing of sitting for hours somewhere, waiting for us to amble by, then ramming us against the wall to search us, only to produce a magic eighth or sixteenth of cannabis from our pocket that we had no idea about – in those days cannabis was a big deal. Many of our gang ended up in Borstal or detention centres down to these outrageous, fabricated crimes. No wonder we formed a dislike for police officers and any sort of authority at an early age. In our eyes, none of them could be trusted.

My ol' man's opinion was that no one, not even himself, could be trusted. And that's the philosophy we adopted. Trust no one.

Once in the young offender's prison system, your life would change. Aside from the internal violence with other meat-headed inmates, whose sole mission was to become the daddy of the gaffs, you'd meet other kids that went on to bigger crimes when released. Borstal was the breeding ground for the future Brink's-Mat and train robbers – our gang weren't any different. Many of my friends are still with Her Majesty serving many years for audacious crimes committed. A few of them, at some point in their lives, targeted by the named officers above. It was shameful how this handful of police acted in those days but to us it tarred the whole authority system with the same brush.

A few years later a friend of mine got his first job as an apprentice carpenter, which was always an early morning start. The few bent coppers would wait for him almost every morning. When he would leave for work on his bicycle they would stop him, question and over-the-top search him. They did this so many times at the start of the day that he was often late for work so, after a while, he was fired from his job.

Others who had this sort of stuff happen to them took the stance of, 'Fuck it, we'll be what the police want us to be.'

I hope that some kind of karma caught up with each and every one of those disgraceful demons in uniform, as they made everyone's lives, including our parents', not to mention our future paths, a misery.

In my opinion, teenage years are the most informative era of our being, deciding on what roads to travel in life, leading to our futures. Having to leave the so-called safety of our flats, always looking over our shoulders in case grown men in uniforms jumped out from nowhere to grab us, plant incriminating evidence then send us to the justice courts where we'd nearly always be found guilty of the charge, didn't make for a good nurturing environment. Sometimes it seemed that we were living in an alternative universe, a world where angels and demons took on another meaning. What chance did we have?

From the age of thirteen until my early twenties myself and a lot of my friends accumulated high, double-figured police convictions that would hang around for years on paper because of these bad cops. Guilty or not guilty, the perverted games of Messrs Spotty, Barry Plod, Paul Bard and Blondie and his dog infected us for the rest of our lives.

CHAPTER EIGHT

My first job after leaving school was in a bonded warehouse in Tooley Street. It was filled with booze. St. Olive's Bonding was controlled by HMRC as no duty was paid on the alcohol stored there. I got the job through my next-door neighbour in Lockwood Square, a guy named Danny. He and his family had moved in about the same time as us. They were a nice family. The youngest was a girl called Jane who had something about her. She became a good friend.

I remember their mum, who was a lovely straight down the line lady, tragically died at a young age, leaving her husband to bring up the kids as a single parent. A fine job he did too as they all grew up to be successful. My mate Danny was a lovely man with a very dry sense of humour but unfortunately had his own demons to contend with. He passed recently, but another deserving doff of the cap to that beautiful family.

Next door to them lived a family called the Walkers. Terry Walker, the son, was part of our gang. His claim to fame was that he could run like the wind and would show it every night as he took a sprint around the circumference of our block. Also now passed but remembered fondly.

Terry's parents were much older, I think in their sixties. His father, who we named Winkle, was a little man but a big boozer. We would all be sitting down to dinner in our flat when, without a knock, the front door would open and Winkle would stumble in drunk, his flat cap tilted to one side of his head caused I'm sure by a drunken mishap, mistaking our flat for his. There were times when Winkle returned home really drunk after closing time and his family would lock him in the dust cupboard outside on the landing. Many a time you would walk by stoned and hear the muffled protests of the incarcerated drunken Winkle pleading for release. You'd put the muffles down to the puff you'd been smoking and sometimes walk straight past. I smile at the memory.

At the bonded warehouse it was hard manual work lifting boxes full of bottles of alcohol but I enjoyed it.

The world and I were finally connecting: I was getting a small but regular wage every week which allowed us the luxury of going over to Brick Lane to buy our treasured Oxford bag trousers and spoon-like shoes. Another good thing that happened was my puppy fat started to drop off me like wet tissue paper on a rain-soaked window pane. For once in my life my body started to become defined and stronger, no more 'Jumbo' or 'Tit' ascorbic jibes from the hardened mouth of my old man.

I started to steal bottles of booze from the warehouse as a fiddle to subsidise my pittance of a wage. I think, if I remember rightly, I was earning about twenty-four quid a week. I used to sell the ill-gotten gains around the flats but getting the booze out of the place was a bit of a mission in itself. That's where the Oxford bags came into play. Trousers that had no shape other than a thirty-inch flare from groin to feet and an extra-wide waistband. They were handy though, as you could hide four bottles of twelve-year-old single malt whisky in them, at one time worth twenty quid on the Lockwood Square Estate black market. Two bottles under each flare. We'd tape the bottles to our legs and let the flare do the rest. When our shift ended at 5 p.m., you had to walk the gauntlet of custom officers that were lined up on each side of the exit, who in turn could search you at any time. I got away with fortunes, certainly got the tax back that I paid in.

One of my jobs inside the warehouse was looking after the vats of sherry and wine. Me and my pal, Alan Shearer, brother of my Scott Lidget youth club mucker Peter, worked in the vat department.

The wine was stored in huge fibreglass vats before being bottled up on the conveyer belt, packed in boxes and taken away by forklift.

One of the drivers was my next-door neighbour Danny, who was often pissed as a fart at the wheel swerving everywhere.

Alan and myself were allowed to open the side door of the warehouse onto the road. Our reason was to meet the wine tankers that delivered to us and empty the containers into the vats. I'd take orders from the drivers and bring them a box or two of the finest tipple, cash on delivery of course, which came in handy as Farah trousers were coming onto the market then and were a bit more expensive and stylish than the Oxford bags. Alan was oblivious to my dodgy dealings as he was not that way inclined. Although Alan was a Bermondsey boy through and through, he was as straight as a die, and a lovely fella and good friend, so I had to keep it all low profile. As the ol' man would probably say, 'Ignorance is bliss'.

There was an older woman who worked on the warehouse floor and liked a drink. I used to bring her a bottle of vintage whisky every now and then and she'd let me have a feel of her tits behind the box room. I laugh at the thought! I worked at the warehouse for about a year before they started suspecting me and my extracurricular activities. I was diplomatically tin tacked (sacked).

I went straight into another job as a hospital porter which took me to another level in my life.

St. Olave's Hospital was smack in the heart of Rotherhithe, Bermondsey and built in the early 1870s. Sir Michael Caine was born there and there is a blue plaque nailed to a wall to prove it.

It was our local life saver and everyone in the community, at some point in their life, passed through the hospital either to give birth, to prolong life or to die. Working there was one of the best periods in my life. The fun I had with the other porters like Danny Draper and George Caten, was unequalled at that time. Danny and George were old-school Bermondsey to the core. George spent his life working at the Courage Brewery then was made redundant and got a job at the hospital. Danny and George were two incessant practical jokers. Their merciless acerbic antics used to make me belly laugh to the point of pain.

I fitted in at the hospital like a hand in a glove. It wasn't like a job, it was a life experience. The porters would do three different shifts: 8 a.m. – 5 p.m., 3 p.m. – 11 p.m., and 11 p.m. – 8 a.m. The day shift was great. The afternoon shift was a bit of a pisser as it took the middle of the day away and we also had to work weekends. The night shift was a nightmare as, for some reason, old people usually chose the early hours of the morning to shed their mortal coil. Our job as porters was to take the dead bodies to the mortuary. I was famed for not wanting to go near dead bodies or the mortuary.

I was eighteen and I was happy at that point in life. Someone once said to me, if you didn't get up every morning whistling whilst you went to work, you were in the wrong job. I was in the right job; my whistle was getting brighter day by day. I had started to get close to a local girl named Sue who was a year or so younger than me. She was a cleaner in the hospital and, after a while, it started to turn a bit more serious. Another friend who frequently showed her boat at St. Olave's was Mo Bass, better known now as Laila Morse of *Eastenders*, *Love Honour and Obey*, and *Nil by Mouth* fame. Mo's ex-husband, Gerald, was a rascal and a friend of my father – birds of a feather and all that. Mo has a book out about her life, a must-read but I never got a mention in it though (*wink, wink*). Mo was a hospital driver and used to deliver to the X-ray department. We'd always have a bit of time for a chat in the corridor. Mo is and always will be a beautiful friend. She is a genuine and lovely loyal human being...old-school.

When St. Olave's Hospital closed down in the late seventies, they moved a few of us porters down to New Cross Hospital. Myself, Danny and George were chosen for the move.

My relationship with Sue continued when I left for New Cross Hospital. I was falling deeply in love with her – only trouble was, I didn't know if she felt the same so I kept it under wraps, a life pattern of mine when something comes along holding a bit of longevity. I would melt every time I saw her. She was, in my eyes, quite beautiful. One day we kissed in the outpatient department at the hospital, and that was it. Sue and I were inseparable and bird twittering for the next two years. I loved being in love. I loved the comforting cushion of it; I'm sure there is some cognitive reason for the condition. I was quite a shy person but with Sue I could be myself.

I stayed away from trouble with the law in those few years as well. Sue also became part of the gang but we only saw them now and then as we were happy and content with each other's company. The gang were now getting involved in much more serious crime but nothing concerned me and Sue as we cuddled up on her parents' sofa in her family flat, listening to Diana Ross. Sue's parents, Alice and Tom, were such lovely, old-school Bermondsey folk. Sue had two brothers as well. One of them, David, who died too early in life, was such a nice generous man who most certainly loomed large in all our legends.

Sue had a very close family and they accepted me hook, line and sinker.

New Cross Hospital was a psychogeriatric set up. It was sad to see these old people that had lived life leave this planet from a pissy hospital ward. Some of them, I felt, just gave up and I don't blame them, sitting in one's own excrement for hours on end must have been miserable. Myself, Danny and George used to try and cheer them up a bit by leading sing-songs, much to the protest of the nursing staff as it would be them that had to calm the patients down after we left the ward. We tended to try and get our shifts together as the New Cross porters were different to our Bermondsey comrades. This one particular time, I was working with Danny and George on the night shift. We had a little system: one porter would man the phones, one would do the work and one would go back to the porter's lodge and get his head down until it was time to take the breakfast trolleys to the wards. On this particular night, I was the one tasked with doing the work. At about 1 a.m. we got a call from the ward to tell us someone had been absorbed. The procedure for picking up a dead body was to go to the mortuary first and get a metal aluminium box that was disguised as a hospital stretcher. I offered Danny, who was on the phones, twenty quid to go and collect the body instead of me. He said no. After cursing him for a bit, I took a deep breath and headed off to the mortuary which was, for some reason, situated in the darkest part of the hospital. Mortuaries are strange places, they have an aura of their own and always seem to have a layer of orange mist around them due to the building's outside lights. So I arrived at the mortuary door to the sound of hidden owl hoots, took a few deep breaths and unlocked the door.

Gawd knows why they locked it up, can't imagine why anybody in their right mind would want to break into the place. After another breath, I quickly entered. I grabbed the aluminium trolley and exited as quickly as I could. I then had to wheel the contraption through the eerie hospital grounds to the ward, still accompanied by the haunting owl hoots. With the help of a nurse, we respectfully lifted the blue shrouded empty body from the bed and placed it inside the aluminium box. I could feel the dead bones in its legs as we put it in the box. I then had to make the journey back to the mist-ridden, hammer house of horror building and I don't mind admitting I would be shitting myself. I made wobbly tracks through the hospital corridors to the lift. Standing alone in the lift with a dead body was another thing altogether and sent my imagination running all over the place. After what seemed like an eternity the lift door opened and I resumed my frightful journey. Fuck me, I thought, it's one in the morning and I'm trudging through dark, Victorian hospital grounds with a dead body in a box. And the hard work hadn't even started yet. I ploughed through the orange mist, my mind expecting the horned Lord of Darkness to make an appearance at any given moment. Terrified about the next stage of the process, I stood outside the door to try and gain some sort of composure. My heart would be beating at the prospect of what I had to do in the next five minutes. The owls were hooting louder now and were joined by the sound of crows cawing. I toyed with the idea of running off and leaving the box and its lifeless contents until it got a bit lighter but thought a little better of that one.

I made my plan of action. I would rush in, open the fridge, whose compartments were already holding more of the reaper's catch of the day, place the body on the fridge tray, bolt the door and get out of dodge ASAP. All went to plan; I opened the fridge, ignored its lifeless contents, lifted the body out of the box and put it onto the tray then promptly closed the door and was ready to hightail it out as fast as my little SE16 legs would carry me. On my way to the exit I noticed, out of the corner of my eye, that the light was on in the chapel of rest, a room where they laid out the deceased for relatives and close friends to have some time and say their goodbyes to their loved ones. For some irrational reason I decided to be conscientious and turn the light off, saving the hospital's electricity. As I entered the room, I noticed that a dead body was under a sheet on the table. The moment I set eyes on it, the body started to move then rise making cliché 'dead body rising' noises. A moment later I was staring at a groaning, shrouded figure heading towards me with its hands stereotypically held out in front of it. A 'zombie alert' sign flashed in my mind and then all rationale left my being. Without thinking, I made for the exit door. I was so scared that my brain couldn't coordinate my hands enough to turn the handle in order to escape the vision from hell. I was bouncing, back and forth, on the door like a cartoon character. In the corner of my eye, I could still see the undead creature advancing. I turned to face my fate and resigned myself to becoming his undead comrade. Then the zombie, to my surprise, crumpled onto the floor in fits of laughter.

Was this creature so cruel as to taunt me with its undead humour as well? The sheet came off. I focused on the face, still in zombie mode, then slowly all rationale returned and smiling up at me was my ol' mucka George Caten. Danny had phoned him in the porter's lodge and told him of my dead body mission. George, ever the joker, just couldn't resist the opportunity to frighten the living daylights out of me. It was such old-school humour. To say I was pissed off at the time though is an understatement. If George hadn't been an old man, he would have certainly joined the ranks of the fridge's residents that night. After a while though I did see the funny side of it. Danny and George have long since left this planet and I'm glad for the memory, you pair of old, beautiful rascals.

The pub back in Bermondsey in favour at that time was the prized Southwark Park Tavern that I mentioned earlier. It was a pub used by all sorts of different characters, the likes of the Brink's-Mat bullion robbers. Buster Edwards and Bruce Reynolds of the infamous Great Train Robbery also used to water down there, basking in the romanticism of their unique crimes. This congregation of the criminal elite always seemed to rub off on to ordinary working people who also drank there and, when in their presence, they would pretended to be gangsters. It was quite laughable watching these people who went to work every day in ordinary jobs talking out the corners of their mouths like they were one of the chaps. Pubs were an intricate networking place in our area. They were where certain people based themselves for work. Local gangsters were our heroes when we were younger.

We would watch them pull up outside the pub in their expensive cars, all paid for by their daring raids on London's security and post-office vans. They would reverse cranes into the back of security vans in the middle of the road then rip the back doors off and make tracks with their big paydays. It's fascinating talking to these people, some of whom are one hundred per cent, genuine geniuses at their craft. There was always an aura around these robbers of the country's roads and trains. If I had to give a job description about what they did, it would definitely fall under the umbrella of highway robbery. Outside of it all, though, they were nice, polite people…until crossed.

A new live band venue had recently opened in a warehouse by the Thames called The Crunchy Frog.

Its other claim to fame was that The Sex Pistols used the basement as a rehearsal room. The name Crunchy Frog was taken from an old *Monty Python* sketch.

The Crunchy Frog would open its doors at 10 p.m. and stay open until about 2 a.m., which was later than other pubs in the area which closed at 11 p.m. in those days. The club was full of stoners, many left behind from the now-fading hippy era but still armed with the leftover stashes of the dreaded Black Bombers.

Black Bombers were a combination of amphetamine (speed) and Dextroamphetamine (active salt in Adderall). The pills were typically 20 milligrams. Effects included a mild to moderate euphoria, increased hyperactivity, increased awareness of surroundings, increased interest in repetitive or normally boring activities, decreased appetite and decreased ability to sleep.

What more could teenagers, who were looking for kicks, want? It was an amazing place, with some nights there hilariously etched into my memory. One night, when the club had finished and we had all consumed much of Africa's finest seed and stalk-ridden weed, we decided to run the gauntlet in our cars to get to a hamburger stand on Blackheath Common. Blackheath was about three quarters of an hour drive from The Crunchy venue. The downside was, you had to drive through Bermondsey, Deptford and Greenwich. No mean feat for two carloads of stoned and speeding oikes from the flats of Bermondsey who were known to all the police in the area as nuisances, but the powerful, proverbial munchies would ruthlessly take over.

So this night we all piled into our cars and headed for the greasy oasis on the heath, there to meet with Mcbeef.

The hamburger van had been around for years and was known as a watering hole for passing bearded Hells Angels on their god-given Dantesque missions of destruction and chaos – most of them leftovers from the mods and rockers era.

We pulled up in a lay-by next to the food wagon then joined the hairy queue of bikers. One of our crowd, who was fearless and a wind-up extraordinaire, started tapping one of the Angels on the shoulder, then when the offended Angel turned, he would nonchalantly whistle and feign ignorance to the act. This happened about five times before the Angel had finally had enough. He raised his voice in anger at my pal, who, in turn, put one on his chin and he dropped to the floor. Two more Angels got involved. My good friend Charlie Nunn sent them both the same unholy way. We headed to our cars for a quick getaway. Then it came, the dogs of war were let slipped. We looked around and saw a sea of studded leather jackets heading towards us, all wanting to avenge the fallen Angels. We jumped frantically into our cars. Luckily, Sue had jumped into Charlie's car that promptly took off. I had an old Hillman Minx. Myself and two of my other pals, Rob and Lee, jumped in just as the screaming herd of Angels entered the lay-by. I thrust the keys into the ignition. Lee and Rob, by this time, were out the windows giving wanker signs and spewing out derogatory names to the oncoming angelic chaos, confident in the fact that we'd be zooming away at any second. I turned the key to start the car and there was nothing.

I quickly found religion again, said a quick prayer then turned the key again getting the same result. Nothing. Not even a teasing flicker. The holy concept must have been thinking, 'Is he having a laugh? The only time he wants to talk to me is when he wants something or he's in trouble, give him another kick up the bollocks and liven human Eddie up.' Lee and Rob, needless to say, looked at me now with a tinge of fear in their mince pies (eyes). Lee gave his assessment of the situation and blurted out, 'Fuck it, we're dead.' We braced ourselves for the pain that was to come in the next few moments as, by this time, the Judus Hillman Minx was surrounded by the angered Angel choir. The windows of the car started to cave in and shatter as the studded Angels from hell started to systematically take the car apart with whatever came to hand. I'm sure I saw one of them biting into the metal frame of the car with his teeth. A hand grabbed me and proceeded to drag me out through the shattered glass side window. Lee was truly a prophet and we were all a little closer to finding out the esoteric answer.

I took a couple of clumps to the head before, somehow, breaking free. I hightailed it across the grassy heath. What about Lee and Rob, still in the car, I hear you think. Well, the same thought went through my mind at the time but some situations in life require a selfish attitude and this was one of them, another 'every man for himself' moment.

I must have run about three miles at a sprint with a lot of help from the Black Bombers that were coming into play again, because the next thing I knew I was running into Greenwich police station – of my own accord which was a first – screaming like a mad man possessed that my friends were being butchered by Angels on the heath. The police calmed me down enough to make some sense of what I was saying. After taking note of my saucepan-like eyes, which I think they put down to shock, they put me into a police car with one other officer and off we went to the heath, there to meet with McCarnage.

As we approached the lay-by, the scene was empty, no Angels, no Lee and Rob, only the sad sight of my unfaithful, wounded Hillman Minx and the dejected face of the food wagon owner. The doors to the mechanical traitor were hanging off their hinges and not a window remained intact. I stepped out of the police car and walked over to the wounded beast to say my last goodbye when I spotted the keys, still in the ignition. I turned the key and lo and behold, God must have finished his bacon sandwich as the engine fired up first time. I managed to get the unhinged doors shut and asked the cop if I could drive it home rather than leave it there and wait for it to be towed away. I had all the relevant road documents. He looked around shiftily, thought about the proposition for a while, then succumbed to a resounding yes. I kangarooed down the road. It was about 4 a.m., my mission was to get back to Bermo as soon as I could, hoping the Minx had one last fight in it to transport me back to SE16. As I was driving through Deptford, I heard a shout and looked around only to see Lee running towards the car.

I dared not stop for fear of the car not starting again, so I slowed up and Lee, with a death-defying leap that equalled any circus performer, coupled with a lit joint in his mouth, bundled through the window. We looked at each other and burst out laughing all the way back to the plot. Lee relayed his story of escape. He had pleaded with one of the female Angel's maternal side. Lee had told her he was only thirteen years old, his baby face regressing younger and younger and his nose getting bigger and bigger with each plea. Mumma Angel took pity and waved the way to his and Rob's freedom. When we got back to Lockwood, the rest of the gang, including Rob now nursing a black eye, and Sue were all at the block entrance. When they saw the battle-scared Hillman chugging down the road, there was a well-earned standing ovation and doffing of caps. Another interesting night was had by all.

CHAPTER NINE

Sue and I broke up a year or so later. I was devastated, I thought we were going to get married and be together for life. I gave my notice in at the hospital and for weeks I didn't eat or leave the house, even Winkle Walker's mishaps ending in the dust cupboard couldn't lift me. The selective trick of nature to preserve its species thought jumped in again.

I threw myself back into my guitar to take my mind off my first real relationship breakup. My next mission was to have a go at writing my own songs. For some reason writing songs came easily to me, especially love songs with the fair Sue in mind. The first song that I wrote was called 'Nobody Loves Ya', still a good little tune. I had an epiphany: I was now going to become a pop star and one day meet John Lennon. I was crazy for his music, his philosophy on life and his song lyrics which spoke to me in a deep way. 'Working Class Hero' by John Lennon was the next song I mastered. For once the ol' man liked this one. 'They hit you at home and they hurt you at school, hate you if you're clever and they despise a fool, till you're so fucking crazy you can't follow their rules'. That will do.

Four months later, on 8 December, I received an early morning call from Sue telling me that Lennon had been shot. I was stunned and shocked. I switched on the TV and it was confirmed – he was dead. What kind of mind could do that and take John Lennon so violently when he had so much more to give? I loved George Harrison as well, especially his 'All Things Must Pass' triple album. Two heavy, bang-on artists who were helpful in the making of many great creative and spiritual minds. 'Tomorrow never knows', eh?

The next few years saw me and my guitar rarely apart. I bumped into my old friend Charlie Nunn one day. Charlie had learnt to play the drums and learnt them well. Charlie and my brother Jackio had been partners in mischief since their early teens. They would think nothing of staying in a building connected to a warehouse all weekend in order to knock down a wall to gain entry to the Aladdin's cave. One time they spent the weekend knocking a wall down, only to emerge onto the road outside. The weed they were smoking led them to do a left instead of a right, as sometimes happens in life.

Charlie and I decided to start a band. We incorporated a bass player called Jimmy Maynard and hired out a studio next to Peek Frean's biscuit factory. The studio was called Mr. Clean but there was nothing clean about it at all. In fact, to call it Mr. Dirty would have been a Starsky and Hutch (touch). We started to arrange the songs that I had written. It took a while before my dyslexically penned compositions started to shape up musically.

I personally felt that we were ready to do a gig in a local pub but nerves got the better of the rest of the band so it never materialised, which was a shame really as it could have become a bit of a moment.

It was at this time that I was offered my first council flat. It was a bedsit on the Arnold Estate, not far from where I went to school in Dockhead. I hated the place at first; it was a pokey little dive where the living room doubled as a bedroom, a bathroom you couldn't swing a cat in and no bath just a shower, but as they say 'beggars can't be choosers'. I took the flat for the purpose of getting onto the council-flat ladder. Across from me lived another soon-to-be partner in debauchery, Tony. He was from another old-school Bermondsey family and it wasn't long before Tony and I would pal up.

Our common denominator was women and Dionysian fun. There was a constant stream of females toing and froing from our two flats. There was a group of married women with kids that lived on the landings above us who used to monitor our exploits and would label us, in jest I might add, as slags due to the volume of smudged make-up and tousled-haired women they'd see exiting our boudoirs every Sunday morning after a bit of Saturday night fever.

These lovely mumsy residents would also bring us down an occasional Sunday roast to keep our energy up but really I think the dinners were payment for the entertainment myself and Tony brought to them, and of course not forgetting the bit of flirting banter in the mix as well.

I was always a bit embarrassed about my flat being so small, so I set about doing something about it. A friend of mine's girlfriend was pregnant so I got her to give me a urine sample and got my girlfriend at the time to go to the doctors to say she thought she was pregnant.

They asked for a urine sample and she duly gave the one that was with child – you couldn't go to the chemist and just buy a test back then. Of course, the test came back with the desired result. I went up to the council office and told them that the Arnold Estate flat wasn't big enough for two people and a baby. A month later I was picking up the keys to a two bedroom flat on the nineteenth floor of a high-rise block called Casby House, situated parallel to Jamaica Road. I remember walking in for the first time and stepping onto the balcony and seeing the skyline of London. My bedroom window had a view of the River Thames that people would pay a fortune for nowadays. My new next-door neighbour was a lovely woman called Lil who was a bit of a boozer. Her husband, Freddy, used to work in the flower market at Covent Garden. He'd leave for work at 1 or 2 a.m. every morning and return about 6 p.m. pissed as a fart. I never really got to know him but he seemed a nice man. Lil has long since passed now but she was a good friend and got me out of copious amounts of trouble. She was always on the end of a phone whenever the police decided to kick my front door in and drag me out. She did me untold favours unconditionally. Thanks Lil, gone but not forgotten...*hic.*

At this time, the gang had become good at being on the wrong side of the law and had progressed to relieving Her Majesty and security firms of their excess wonga. The thought of running into places and demanding money was not for me but people were making some serious money and, to tell you the truth, I felt a bit left out because of my principles. Until one day, that is, when someone approached me with a proposition. He had a stolen access credit card which, he informed me, if we handed across a bank counter and signed the same signature as was on the back of the card, they would give you money. As long as you stuck to a sensible limit, of course. Could it be that easy? I took the card and practised the signature for a bit and then trotted off to a bank. My heart was beating as I approached the counter and spoke to the bank cashier. I asked for ten pounds. She took the card and ran it through a contraption, as computers and cyber space was something you only read about in sci-fi comics in those days. She came back with a slip of paper that I had to sign. I signed it, she checked my signature, went to the till and gave me a tenner.

I stepped outside the bank feeling elated. To my shame now, we entered ten banks that day. I found out later that you could go up to twenty-five pounds without them phoning the request through to head office. We'd got two hundred and forty pounds for a day's work and in those days that was nothing to grumble about. We were also informed that the person who lost the card was guaranteed by the bank for up to fifty pounds, so, as long as we stayed under the fifty pounds limit, the person whose card it was wouldn't lose the money.

The only losers were the banks. Power to the people, we justifiably thought. We also found an ingenious way to clean the original signature off the cards by running a bit of car brake fluid across the strip then dipping it into a glass of Steradent teeth whitener. The break fluid chemicals would erase the ink signature but would sometimes leave a dark stain on the strip so the Steradent took care of that and we could then sign it in our own hand. We never, ever thought that there was anything wrong in it as we were saturated with the ruthless hooky vibe.

We would work the card for a day then throw it away, so you can imagine the need for cards was constant. We had a couple of friends that worked as postmen and they used to deliver fresh cards to us straight from the post office, the benefit being that the cards were not reported stolen so instead of twenty-five pounds we used to take the card's limit which could be up to £300 and the postmen would take a fifty per cent split. I'm not proud now of what we did but sometimes needs must when living in those ignorant, creatively unproductive days on the mean streets of the eighties.

Fridays became a sacred day. We'd work all week with the credit cards and Friday afternoon, we'd all meet in Southwark Park. If it was a hot day, we'd meet in the open-air baths.

Acid trips were in fashion at the time, little bits of blotting paper and tiny blue pills that took you to Lucy for a while. I loved tripping, it seemed to take one's mind to places in one's future. The dreaded lysergic acid diethylamide could transport you to utopia or a dystopia at any given time.

Our gang had got bigger by that time, with added mischief makers from an estate called Silwood, another breeding ground for misguided youth. Skinner, aka Michael Flynn, and Baldy, aka Johnny Wright, became part of our group. Johnny was a promising boxer but unfortunately also a natural rebel without a pause. Johnny died at a very young age. He was an amazing spirit. Skinner was later shot in the back and killed by the police whilst committing an armed robbery, which, in our opinion, must have been grassed from within our ranks. Both are still greatly missed. The suspected grass was a mole planted by the police and after the incident he disappeared off the face of the planet.

There was a local geographical eclectic mix of people in the gang but no matter what corner of the plot you came from, the thing that bonded us all was partying and, fuck me, did we party. I salute you all.

People were getting their own council flats all over the place so there was always some sort of hedonistic party going on somewhere.

Another crazy scene that came along was people chopping off the padlocks to railway arches and setting up what was known as Spiels – illegal drinking dens with bags of cocaine and well-stacked shelves of booze. There were some crazy nights in these darkened dens of iniquity as there were no windows and only one way in or out so you didn't know what time or day it was. You walked in on a Friday night and next thing you knew it was Sunday and off you would go to Mum's for a roast dinner, much the worse for wear, with loud eighties music ringing in your ears.

One Friday night, all in a stupor, the gang decided to go night fishing. We all met at a designated place at 6 p.m., about fifteen of us, one armed with a pocketful of dreaded acid microdot pills called Blue Lagoon. Some of the gang even thought they would do a bit of fishing and brought a couple of fishing rods – fat chance. We all dropped our pills, except for our pal Russell, who was designated to be the straight one on the firm. It's always good to have somebody who is not tripping because it can be a risky business if it turns bad. Our pal was a good man to be in charge. Although he gave up the dreaded lysergic in his later years, in his younger days he had dropped enough for all of us so there was nothing he didn't know about the mind-bending pitfalls. He also knew the area we were heading to as he had spent some time in a naughty school there in the seventies.

So off we rolled in three cars, destination a place called Frensham Ponds, deep in the Surrey green belt. Frensham Ponds was about a two-hour drive from Bermondsey. After an hour or so, the mischievous lysergic started to kick in. It was a bumpy journey as lights from other cars created amazing mesmerising images, like dragons wafting through the air. To say my pal who was driving the car was a crazy driver is an understatement, but here we were, all out of our box in a car, tripping on acid.

Trying to follow two other cars on the A3 carriageway was a nightmare in itself. We all thought that we were gunning at great speed but in reality we were stopping and starting and driving at 30 mph, trying to avoid the impressive, translucent dragons that were gliding all around us. We took the slip road off the A3 at Thursley and were immediately plunged into the darkness of leafy Surrey country lanes. At one point Jackio opened the passenger door and jumped out while the car was moving. We stopped the car and looked at each other as Jack lay flat out in a bush, somewhat mind-bended. Then it came, the obligatory giggles. We laughed until it hurt.

Jackio got back into the car telling us he'd thought that he'd seen a strange form heading towards us, full on. That was all we needed, we all exploded into irrational, belly-hurting laughter again. We carried on laughing for the rest of the journey. After a while the lead car stopped; we had reached our destination.

We parked the cars wonkily and stood in file behind the rational Russell and, like a platoon of soldiers, followed the leader into the unknown, none of us saying a word. We were out in the open now and were subjected to the sounds of strange animals and the rustling of leaves, heightened by the acid trip – no place for city boys, mangled up, with augmented realities. We scrambled silently behind Russell through the bushes and undergrowth until we reached a clearing, still marching, giggling and heavy-eyed. Moments in the world of acid seem like an eternity. Out of nowhere, lights appeared. We all looked at each other cautiously. We heard Russell start to panic at the realisation that we were in someone's back garden. 'RUN!' went the shout. Our guide and leader ran past us at full speed. Confused, we were all bumping into each other as equilibrium and perception merged precariously into panic. Then began the exodus, bodies falling over each other and scrambling through bushes for dear life.

'I've left my fishing rod,' Paul exclaimed.

'Fuck the fishing rod. I've left all reason,' came the reply from someone with one leg over the garden fence already. Paul dashed back, apprehensively, to retrieve his rod. We managed to find calm with the help of Russell, the Wise One, whose sole job that night was to manage us and let all know that things were cool.

We all stumbled back to the cars and carried on our navigation to the pond which was about a mile wide. We couldn't miss it, could we? It was becoming a mission, which was the whole point in the first place.

After another bout of gut-wrenching laughter, we reached water at last and parked the cars on the bank.

By now we were deep into the acid trip. Nothing made sense at all as we left the cars, our insides tingling, and headed for the pond. I heard the tuneful sound of a blues harmonica emanating from a wooded area and stumbled over to investigate. As I peeled away the bushes, I saw a group of young, posh dandies, sitting pagan-like amongst the trees. A fire was flickering and, I kid you not, one of the guys was sitting in a red velvet, smoking jacket playing the harmonica while another played a guitar. The group looked up at me and smiled. Without saying a word, I headed back to the gang and got Russell's attention. 'Russ, come with me a minute please.' I led him to where I had seen the action. I peeled away the bush and the group of guys looked up and once again smiled. 'Are these people really here, Russ?' I nervously asked.

'Yes,' Russell said.

'And does one of them have a red velvet, smoking jacket on?'

'Yes.'

We said hello and called some of the others over. We sat with them for a while, basking in the calming effect of the music.

By this time, the rest of the gang were trying to get a fire going, unsuccessfully. A shout went up from Paul, he'd managed to set up his fishing rod and catch a fish. We all rushed to see the spectacle. Paul turned to Jackio. 'Take it off the hook, will you?'

Jack looked at the wriggling silver fish from lysergic-effected eyes. 'Bollocks, I ain't going near the thing.' No one would unhook the wriggling, two-inch beast. Paul put it back in the water and let the bail arm off his reel. The fish swam away.

He then spent the next part of an hour letting the fish swim up the pond, then reeling him back again. I swear the last time Paul pulled it out of the water the fish's tired out face was like, 'For fuck sake lads, give me a break.' Someone had managed to get a little flame to the fire, when, all of a sudden, three aggressive local lads entered the mix. They were trying to intimidate us. Russell the Wise informed them that we were tripping and for their own sake, go in peace, but being country folk and faced with silly, wired Londoners on their turf, the bumpkins weren't having it. One of them took his cock out, which looked a bit like the fish Paul had caught, and pissed on the fire. We all looked at each other trying to work out what was going on, when Paul, now fed up with playing the 'fuck the fish' game, ran at one of the aggressors and started bashing him over the head with a fishing rod rest. That was our cue. Fourteen monsters from Bermondsey, tripping on acid and fighting for what seemed like life itself, systematically and, in retrospect, regretfully kicked the shit out of the three amigos.

Somehow they managed to crawl away over the sand dunes and to safety. Russell the Wise imparted new information to us about how he knew these country folk and that they all had shotguns hanging on their walls. Gulp, could it get any worse? We all dashed to the cars and, taking the historical lead from old George Armstrong Custer, positioned them into a triangle. We then took our socks off and filled them with rocks and crouching down with the cars as cover, we waited nervously for the locals to come back with their army and double-barrel fire power.

God knows what we thought rocks in socks would do against shotguns but that's acid for you. We were in the triangle for ages waiting for the bad guys to return. Someone declared that we were lacking skins (Rizla papers) to roll a joint.

Our mate Wriggly, who is one of life's soldiers and was a few years older than us, stood up and declared, nonchalantly, that the only thing that we were all lacking was common sense. He then took off, on foot, into the mist-ridden woods, not to be seen again that night. God knows how he got back to Bermondsey. I live in the same area today and I know the distance from Frensham to Haslemere or Farnham train station's, not to say he was tripping as well. Again, my hat is well and truly doffed to Wriggly's great effort. When we finally caught up with him, back on the mean streets, he told us that he'd thought we had pulled the numbers on him and had set the whole thing up to put him on a downer. Oh my, that was a good night and another one that is forever etched in my memory.

CHAPTER TEN

Another local pub to spring up in Bermondsey at that time was Coopers. This became our regular haunt. The movie *Scarface* was doing the rounds and with it came the cocaine era. Tony Montana had started a movement and the poison of choice became oats and barley (Charlie). I loved it. I'd have a line of coke and would become totally free, but with it came the downside where all principles and integrity were wiped aside. At this time, another member of the powder family wanted in.

Heroin started to infiltrate the streets of Bermondsey and good people, that unfortunately had weak minds, started falling foul of the horrid, sickly brown Niki Lauda (powder). In its own inimitable way, heroin started to cause quite a bit of chaos within our ranks. Friends that succumbed to the chemical demon didn't remain friends for long. People with any sort of class A chemical habit, in my experience, cannot be trusted as far as the old proverbial spit. The police were of the same assumption and so began another level of corruption. The police would arrest a known heroin user and leave them in a cell until they started to cluck (withdraw). They would time their entrance strategically and walk in holding a ten-pound bag of heroin, then wave it in front of the unfortunate addict. By then, the addict would sell his own mother for a shot and would freely give information about certain teams on the manor and what they were up to. Although we were a closed shop, the police would work on the best-friend syndrome, that is, everyone has one person who they trust implicitly and confide in but that trusted friend also has that one person he trusts and confides in and so on and so forth until, sooner or later, it would reach the ear of an addict who ends up in a police cell with a local scuffer waving a ten-pound bag in his face.

So we took it upon ourselves to try and clean the area of the scum that peddled the poison. We would find out where the dealers lived and, in military style, smashed through their doors, took what powder they had and flushed it down the toilet. The dealer would be told, in no uncertain terms, that his peddling of filth would not be tolerated.

There was a dealer, who as far as I know is clean now, who was sitting round some flats in an estate called the Avondale, a known place in Old Kent Road where junkies would buy and sell their smack and anything else to hand. A car pulled up and three geezers stepped out, marched over to where the dealer sat, banged a carrier bag over his head and lifted him into the car. They took him to a flat on the top floor of a high-rise block, where he was hung over the balcony by his ankles, still with the bag over his head. Someone took the bag off. The dealer screamed like a wounded hyena when he saw the drop, and who could blame him.

He was held there for a while, then pulled back up and told that if he didn't stop dealing, next time he would be dropped. He was returned back to his flats, a shivering wreck, and left to review the last hour and half of his life. The moral of the story is that after a week he was dealing again, despite going through all that. The power of heroin made it a pointless battle, the drug and its addiction was too powerful – if people would value it more than their life, how can you beat that dependency?

I personally have never ever had any interest in it. I've seen what it does. A few friends of ours managed to kick the habit and I, again, doff my cap.

The heroin was coming down from up north and the people supplying it were none too chuffed about what we were doing. They thought that we were trying to muscle in on their business so they sent an armed team down to take us out of the game, but a few of the big local villains, who were our friends, interceded.

They had words with the northerners and explained that we were not trying to take their business but were trying to clean the place up. They were told that the heroin was causing addicts to give the police information about people's activities.

The northern contingent conceded. As long as we were not jumping on their business, they understood the reasoning. The whole affair could have turned out sticky because we were not going to stop.

Coopers became the in-place for us. One night the door of the pub flew open and a friend of ours Terry, a lad from Deptford, who has also recently passed away rest his soul, barged in waving a sawn-off shotgun. The pub stood still as the crazed Terry started shouting about how he was going to shoot one of our other friends called Reg. It was a bit touch and go for a while but somehow someone managed to calm him down and take the gun off him. Unfortunately, someone outside saw him enter waving the beast, and phoned the police. They arrived and Terry got nicked, minus the gun that someone had got rid of.

I started seeing another local girl, let's call her Lorna, who I met at a fancy-dress bash in Coopers. I was dressed, bizarrely, as a school girl and she as the grim reaper. She kept putting her hand up my skirt. She was thirty-two and I was twenty-two. I suppose it was a bit of fun at first. It suited me as I didn't really want to get tied to anyone. Lorna ended up a loyal friend and was instrumental in my release from prison on the armed robbery and attempted murder charges. Thanks, Lorn.

It was at this time that I received a letter telling me that I was to appear at the Old Bailey for the cannabis charge that I mentioned earlier with Messr Mark. I received eighteen months for suppling. I started my sentence on the A wing of Wormwood Scrubs. I would serve nine months of the sentence as a B-category prisoner, if I was a good boy that is.

The prison category system was AA, A, B, C, D, depending on the crime committed.

When entering the prison for the first time you were escorted to the reception where you were issued a prison number, clothes, a plastic bowl, cup, knife and fork, shaving soap, bed sheets and a pillow case. You were then marched onto the wing and allocated a cell. My cell was on landing two. My cell mate was a guy called Gary who had been to prison many times before. His crime, this time, was for fraud.

I always believed that the reason people went back to prison time and again was because they forget that first morning when the cell door opened for slop out!

The smell of ammonia from the piss and shit was like a whack in the face with a sledge hammer, as cons marched to the landing recess with full buckets that were then poured into the communal slooshes.

The recess was the meeting place for a good old natter. Every evening there was 'Association' where your landing was allowed to go downstairs to the ground floor and play table tennis or watch a bit of TV. I was always quite lucky that every time I went to jail, I knew quite a few faces there from Bermondsey, so I never really had too much aggravation from the prison bullies. I'm told cells nowadays have toilets installed and cons are allowed TVs. That must be a bit of heaven in hell.

The black and white cultural divide in jail was huge and never the twain met. Any white men that hung out with black men, and vice versa, were always contemptuously ostracised by each of their cultures. It always amazed me how working-class white and black kids had reason to dislike each other when they came from the same areas.

After slop out, we would then be locked up again for half an hour then unlocked for breakfast where we would all file down to the hot plate, which was situated on the ground floor. The hot plate was one of the most dangerous jobs in the prison. I have seen a man get his face cut with a spatula for giving a man a few fried chips more than the person lined up next to him. Breakfast was a cup of tea, powdered scrambled egg, a manky old bit of streaky bacon, some beans and as much bread as you wanted. Food that was supposed to be cold was usually always warm and food that was supposed to be warm was usually cold.

You could get about four single bread sandwiches out of each breakfast which would sustain a growing lad until lunchtime where you would repeat the procedure all over again.

Currency was tobacco and cannabis and it was a big thing as wages from prison jobs were miniscule. Prisoners who were not employed in the prison received a weekly basic wage of £1.75. Prisoners who were fortunate enough to obtain work could receive up to £5.80 per week depending on what job you did. Half an ounce of tobacco, at £1 a shot, took the bulk of wages if you were unemployed. I was okay as I had a pal from Bermondsey, Leon. He worked in the prison canteen and used to bung me a bit of tobacco, no strings attached. He was a few cells away from me and every night we would sing 'Life Is Just a Bowl of Cherries' out of our cell windows.

Loved ones on the outside could send in money for your private spends but you could only buy cornflakes, powdered milk, chocolate and shampoo. No tobacco. A lot of cell mates that were doubled up for the long game would combine their wages and share the shopping list. The dedicated smokers would go through the half-ounce of snout in no time resulting in them having to borrow another half-ounce from a tobacco baron, who, in return, required the half-ounce plus a quarter back for the service. Some people would get into so much debt that it led to violence. I was walking past a cell one day and a person that I knew to be a tobacco baron's lackey was walking towards me with a steaming bowl of boiling water. He stopped at a cell and entered it. I heard an ear-splitting scream as the lackey quickly left the cell with the bowl now empty. He was followed by a man holding his scorched face.

He'd had boiling water, mixed with sugar, thrown onto it. I found out later that he owed the baron an ounce of tobacco, which was probably worth two quid in those days, and now he was scarred for life.

Another no-no in prison was sex offenders. A friend of mine, who was doing eighteen years for robbery with violence, made a point of sniffing out these bacon bonces (nonces) and viciously hurting them. When a prisoner comes onto the wing, he can be whoever he wants to be as the convicted uniform was the same grey jumper with a bit of blue in it, a white blue striped shirt and jeans, so everyone looked the same. The only way that the sex offender could be found out is if one of the staff marked a card.

I was walking back to my cell one day after getting my dinner, when this friend of mine, armed with an empty metal dinner tray approached me. 'Webber,' he said, 'come with me. I need your help.' I followed him, blindly, to a cell. He looked about, then, with metal tray raised, told me to make sure no one comes near the cell and to let him know if a screw is about.

'Fuck me, mate, what's happening?' Without answering, he darted into the cell. I heard a smashing sound and screams. I looked in to see my friend was manically, mercilessly smashing a geezer to bits with the metal tray. I turned and reluctantly kept watch. After a while, my friend, now blooded, appeared from inside the cell, mumbling something like, 'Nonce cunt.' We both walked away sharpish.

'What the fuck was that all about, mate?' I enquired.

'He's a nonce.'

'How the fuck did you know that?'

'One of the screws told me.' This fella was, most definitely, the prison's modern-day *Van Helsing*.

When a sex offender gets found out there is a Rule 43. It's a protection rule. The prisoner is moved to another wing, occupied with like-minded monsters. Paedophiles, rapists, child murderers and any other cases that inflict harm for their own perversions. These people are vilified by all cons. The screws hate them as much as the prisoners but my pal *Van Helsing* took it to another level. Prison was a tough place to survive in, whatever the crime.

Gary and I were both allocated the job of wing cleaners which meant we had to get up early in the morning and clean the inside landings and outside yard of the wing, which I didn't mind as it got you out of the cell. The downside was that we had to clean up the shit parcels that were thrown out of the cell windows every night. There was a code of conduct with certain people in the 'boob' that you never shit in the bucket in your cell. So people would do their stuff on a newspaper, in socks or ripped-up sheets and pillow cases then throw the offending waste out of the window for muggins here and Gary to sweep up off the yard in the morning. Despite this, one great plus for being on the cleaning party was that we had to clean out the visiting room after visits. Ashtrays were filled with half-smoked cigarettes which we would crumble into a tobacco pouch. We would always end up with a good couple of ounces of dry, stinking, second-hand smoked tobacco. Back at the wing, we would find the dedicated smokers and trade our booty for half an ounce of the good stuff.

In the Steve McQueen film *Papillon* (1973) he has a line that prisoners are the only animals that have to stick things up their arses to survive. I've seen things go up people's arses that would make a billy goat puke, me included.

Visitors needed a V/O (Visiting Order) and were allowed to visit every two weeks. Lorna would visit me without fail and bring an ounce of weed, and sometimes Mogadon (a tranquilliser), all wrapped up in cling film. Before I left my cell to go on the visit, I would spread Nivea cream around my arse then at the visit, when the screw wasn't looking, I would surreptitiously take the parcel of weed from Lorna and slip it up. Fuck me, it used to bring tears to my eyes sometimes, I can tell you.

Gary had finished his sentence so off he went back to the outside, no doubt to return at a later date. My next cell mate was a guy called Mark and we got on like a house on fire. He was from North London and connected to some of the top villain fraternity over there. Mark and I would take a few of the tranquilisers, roll up a couple of joints, tune the trusty Roberts Rambler radio to Radio London and listen to David Rodigan. Radio London unified the prison and David Rodigan's reggae show played in every cell. All tucked up and feeling good, Mark and I would play a game of monopoly until one of us crashed out from the effects of the drug. The rule was, the first to crash was open to anything the other person wanted to do. I woke up once with no eyebrows, thick black specs and a moustache drawn on me.

Time in the scrubs moved slowly. Mark moved on after his B cat was dropped to a C cat.

After a few months I was made a C-cat prisoner and was moved to a C-cat prison on the Isle of Sheppey called Standford Hill.

HMP Standford Hill is on the site of an ex-Royal Air Force station and was first used in 1950. It consisted of army billets which were used as dormitories. There was also another couple of prisons on the island, one B cat and another A cat. I moved into a dorm with five other people. The C-category prison was far more relaxed than the one I'd just left. The prisoners were more or less left to their own devices and, as luck would have it, Mark had also been moved there. I bumped into him the first day as I was walking to my dorm. He was sharing a room with three other good lads from North London who eyed me with suspicion when I first met them, but one of the lads, Johnny, knew my brother Jack from prison. Later on we realised we had a lot of mutual friends on the outside and I was accepted into the new gang. Also, I had half an ounce of weed stuck up my arse which helped the bonding situation somewhat. The new gang was Jimmy, a pickpocket out of South

East London, Johnny, a robber from North London, Footsie, also out of North London, Steve from South London, myself and Mark. We kept ourselves to ourselves and had so much fun. John would talk to the screws in a backward language and do it so straight that the screw would think that his hearing was going mad. Mark had also mastered the technique of lighting his farts. That was the centre of many a stoned night of laughing.

Standford Hill was surrounded by a tall wire fence. It was quite easy to escape but the trouble was, the prison was situated on an island with only one way to get off: a bridge. It was either that or you had to brave the choppy North Sea. If you were to escape and get caught they'd send you to a B-category prison for bad boys called Camp Hill on the Isle of Wight. No one wanted that as it was a mission for visitors to travel to from South London. If you were thinking of escaping, you had to run your plan by the escape committee (I kid you not), which consisted of a group of bored cons with nothing else better to do. As it was a tall wire fence, the escape committee put together some makeshift tools consisting of two blocks of wood with spikes and would embed them into the toes of your shoes so you could scale the fence. They would also give you a couple of pieces of wood with hooks in them for your hands (God knows where they got them from). It was quite a funny sight and we had many a night of entertainment watching the cons, lizard-like, scaling up the fence for dear life with a screw not far behind them. Why anyone would want to escape is beyond me, we had it cushy. Most of the cons that flew the coup were captured. One even dressed up as an old lady – purple wig and baggy knickers included. He was scuffed trying to hobble over the bridge. That cheered us all up, not him getting caught but the sight. The police were well-tuned in to all the disguises as they had been the guardians of the bridge for many years. None may pass.

Time in Standford Hill passed with nothing too eventful happening, apart from Mark lighting his farts and John forever at the wind up with the screws.

I swear Mark got so good at igniting his trumps, he could have toasted bread if he so chose. Then an event happened that kicked my universe into play again. The billets that we all lived in were made of wood and one day some bright spark set the prison alight. I had two and a half months of my sentence left. Lorna had kept the puff supply coming faithfully at every visit and life was good. Because the wooden huts were now a fire hazard, the powers that be decided to rebuild the prison, so we were all relocated. I was moved to Northeye prison in Bexhill-on-Sea, another C-category establishment. The only trouble was that Lorna's ex-husband was there doing four years for possession of a class A drug. All was going so well in Standford Hill but that would be too easy, wouldn't it. Lorna's ex-husband had been in Northeye for a year or so and was established with friends and comrades. For some head-fuck reason, myself and a mixed-raced lad called Peter were the only ones shipped there from Standford Hill. I explained my predicament to Peter and, hats off to him, he said he would make one with me if there was any trouble, which, in the circumstances, was very likely as Lorna was still going to be visiting me. I felt so down as we approached the entrance to Northeye. Peter and I were inducted and allocated separate billets. We marched off with an armful of sheets and pillow cases to our new abodes, which was up a big hill. I was looking over my shoulder at all times. I hated the place already. The only saving grace was that I had some puff stored. I entered the room, and there were three cons already there.

I'd never met these people in my life but they all seemed to know about me. One mentioned that Lorna's ex was expecting me. I put my stuff away and made my way to the toilet to relieve myself of the puff I was carrying, then rolled a joint. I laid on my bed trying to block out the trouble that was most certainly afoot.

Next morning, as I headed down to breakfast, I passed one of the billets and saw him standing at a window peering out from inside. Our eyes met. Fuck it, I thought, might as well get this over with, I'll show face and take the mountain to Muhammad. I indicated for him to come outside. He complied. The cold and swift conversation went something like this.

'How are you, mate?' I asked, looking into his eyes.

'I'm okay,' he lied.

'Look, mate, I've got to tell you, Lorna is still going to visit me in here. I don't really want any trouble.'

'I'm sweet,' he lied again. 'I've nearly finished my bird, so I don't want any trouble either.' His nose was growing by the second.

'Let's just stay out of each other's way,' I answered. I had two more months of this, there was no way that he couldn't show face sooner or later as every con in the nick seemed to know about our situation. The pressure would have gotten to him to do something sooner or later whether he wanted to or not. I'd like to add, he was no fool. I was with his ex-wife, who he still loved, and who I was falling in love with. Everywhere I walked for the next few days, I was expecting the fight to come from anywhere.

It was so oppressive I could feel myself slipping into a bit of madness. I could see him and his pals everywhere I walked. Lorna came up to visit me and I told her what had happened. I suggested that she write to the governor and tell him that it wasn't really a good idea that me and her ex-husband were incarcerated in the same place. After the visit, I looked for Lorna's ex and found him outside his billet. I explained to him what Lorna and I had discussed and he was in agreement. I also told him that I was going to make an application to see the governor and ask to be moved to a D-category prison. It made sense to do it that way as he was convicted of a much more serious crime than me so I had more chance of getting moved. Again, he agreed. I made my application and was scheduled to see 'el jefe'.

I was lying on my bed and caught a glimpse of an article in *The Sun* newspaper with the headline 'Attic Siege Man' and the mention of Southwark Park Road. As I looked at the picture in the article, I realised it was the road where my brother Jackio and his girlfriend lived. Later that day, Lorna visited with the news that the attic siege man was indeed Jack. I was shocked as I knew nothing about the situation.

The next morning I was invited into the governor's office. I laid it on thick about mine and Lorna's ex's situation, telling him that it would inevitably end up in a fight between us.

I wasn't expecting his answer which was, 'Have a fight and I'll send you to Camp Hill.' I tried to reason with him but, in the time-honoured traditional tone of the majority of prison governors, he told me to fuck off. I went back to my hell and lay on the bed. Things were just getting worse. Maybe we should have just had the fight and got it over with. Even Camp Hill was a better prospect to where my head was now.

A day later, I was reading on my bed when a prison officer entered the dorm and told me to pack up my gear and get down to reception as I was to be moved to another prison. He didn't have to ask twice. I was off to Ford open prison in Arundel. Lorna had written her letter to the governor explaining the problems this situation could bring. It's one thing when a prisoner voices concerns to a governor internally but quite another when someone writes from the outside. The powers that be have to act just in case.

I was at reception, beaming from ear to ear, and was told a taxi was on its way to pick me up. I was elated as every prisoner in England would kill to finish their sentences in Ford.

The prison was initially RAF Ford before it became Royal Naval Air Station Ford, a Fleet Air Arm station. The site was converted to a category D open prison in 1960.

The taxi arrived and I climbed into it and waited for my escort, but it just moved off.

'Mate, where are you going?' I nervously asked the driver.

'Arundel.'

'But we have to wait for a screw.'

'No we don't,' he said and off we went. The cab journey from Hastings to Arundel was amazing. It was the first time in months that I'd been outside walls or fences in anything other than a prison van and handcuffed. We arrived at the prison. I got out of the taxi and walked through the welcoming gates. The prison somehow had an old-time holiday camp feel. I was almost expecting a Red Coat to come and greet me. An officer approached. I told him where I'd just come from and he pointed the way to the governor's office then made his merry way in the opposite direction. I must say, it was a bit of a mind-fuck, I couldn't really understand what was happening. I heard my name being called out and turned around to see my old friend Rob from the Hell's Angel incident up on Blackheath looking like he'd been on the Costa for a month. He was as brown as a berry due to the fine weather England was having at the time. We had a cuddle then he gave me a rundown of the prison.

'Mate, it's like a fucking holiday camp here, you'll love it.' I cracked up laughing.

'Have you been in to see the governor yet?'

'No.'

'Go and see him and I'll see you in the games room later.'

I sat at the desk in the head honcho's office. He told me that this was a good prison but if I wanted to escape I was most welcome to. I wasn't expecting that one, but then came the old Camp Hill, Isle of Wight threat again. Damn that dastardly island. He gave me my dorm number and told me that I was to be employed as a Womble.

'Excuse me? You want me to be a Womble?' He explained that the prison cleaners were nicknamed Wombles as they had to start at 5 a.m. and clean the grounds and empty all the bins. Never in a million years would I have thought, whilst watching the hairy do-gooders of Wimbledon Common on TV as a kid all those years ago, that I'd end up one of them. I left his office and, for some reason, started running about the place like a rabbit caught in headlights. It smelt of freedom.

I was allocated a dorm with six other residents – the thought of having to go through all that getting to know strangers again filled me with dread. There were eight beds, four on each side in a straight line and they were divided with partitions. All the spaces were empty when I entered as everyone was out doing prison things. There was a guy who was busy mincing about mopping the floor.

'Hi,' he gayly squealed, 'my name is Hughie.' He showed me to my bed then gave me a rundown of the residents. There was The Dread, a true Rasta Lion from Zion; John, a con from the same SE London streets as me; another John who was used to the finer things in life; and another fella who I can't remember his name. He was from traveller stock and a nice fella who kept himself to himself. Last but by no means least, Winstone, a black guy from Brixton who, according to Hughie, was a man that couldn't be trusted as far as one could throw him. I thanked him then quickly headed for the toilet to retrieve my puff. I offered Hughie a joint. He told me he didn't partake but knew a man who did.

I gave him enough weed for a couple of joints then bid him adieu and shot off to look for Rob.

I found him walking aimlessly about the grounds. We went back to his dorm. I met his dorm mates, a couple of brothers who were bottle workers (pickpockets) from Walworth Road and a guy named Alex, who was as slippery as an eel and a piss-taker but, all in all, a nice bunch.

Later I returned to my dorm, which was now filled with the hateful six. I said my hellos and made a mental note to applaud Hughie on his appraisal of Winstone, who radiated treason and malice in spades. I gave everyone a joint which was appreciated by The Dread, who responded with a hearty, 'Jah Rastafari.' All was going swimmingly. I was woken up next morning at 5 a.m. by Pat, aka Great Uncle Bulgaria, the head Womble of the cleaning party, and for the next two hours I wandered in and out of the prison emptying bins. I even caught a sunrise. I sighed with relief at being on the outside once again.

One night, something stirred me from my sleep in the early hours. I looked around my bed space hazily and thought I saw someone with the vague essence of Winstone, creeping about my space. Putting it down to the weed and vodka the night before, I turned over and resumed my sleep. When I awoke in the morning to start Wombling, I realised my watch had gone missing from the side table. I turned my space upside down looking for it but, alas, it was gone. I didn't make a big deal about it as I had to go to work. Later that day, when we were all back, I broached the subject of my missing watch.

I don't know what I was expecting but everyone swore it wasn't them. The only one that I didn't believe was the evil red-eyed Winstone, but what could I do without proof? The non-existent relationship between Winstone and me dropped to another level and, for the next week or so, was strained to say the least.

Ford prison was surrounded by low fences. After visits, our people would hang about until evening and chuck goodies over the fence for us to retrieve. The rule was that after 9 p.m. no con was allowed to be outside their dorms, so you would have to creep outside, dodge round all the billets and then make a suicide dash to pick up the offerings, which had hopefully landed in the preordained spot, before the screws found it on their rounds. Our billet's missions were always successful and there was often a lump of hash and litre bottle of vodka to enjoy. I decided that the evil Winstone was never to benefit from my parcels and excluded him from the feasts.

A few days later I was in the kitchen of our dorm when, suddenly, a pair of arms thrust me against the kitchen sink. As I turned, I was faced with the demon Winstone who had a Stanley knife in his hand which he promptly put to my neck. I felt the blade sitting on my jugular vein. The Dread entered the kitchen to see what the fuss was all about and he managed to take the blade off Winstone. As soon as the blade was out of the way, I punched him. We started to scuffle before it was broken up. I felt my neck, there was blood. I still have the scar to this day. I started to plot my revenge there and then. I ate humble pie and walked out of the kitchen, to return at some point in the future.

I spent the next few days inside my mind, tortured about the liberty Winstone had taken. I found a bit of wood in the shape of a mop handle whilst outside wombling. I hid it up the sleeve of my shirt and put it under my mattress on my return to the dorm. I was going to pick the right time, when it was just me and him alone, then I'd smash the wood over his head. A week went by and no opportunity arose. I decided to wait until the next time he went to the toilet alone then I'd rush in and do my thing. I was keyed up the whole day waiting. Then came the time Winstone went to the karzie. I took out the mop handle and headed for the toilet. The Dread blocked my way. 'Don't do it,' he said. 'I've been watching you all week, I know what you're thinking.'

'I got to do him, it's driving me mad.'

'No, your ego is driving you mad.'

'Eh?'

He sat me down, rolled a joint and spoke to me in such a sensible way that he defused the situation in my mind. 'If you want to do it, wait until you are out.' Then he ambled off. At some point over the next two days I went into Winstone's space and got his home address from one of his letters.

Winstone was released and a peaceful vibe returned. I'm glad that The Dread made me see sense as with the way I was feeling at that time I could have got in a lot of trouble. Jar Rastafari.

A few weeks later an Irishman came into our dorm. He had been talking to Rob.

'I hear you play guitar.'

'Yeah.'

'Do you sing as well?'

'Yeah and I write songs.'

'Do you fancy doing a gig next week in here? We had a guitarist who sings but he's been ghosted out.'

The gig in question was for all the prisoners. I'd never done anything like it before but agreed to do it. I was given an electric guitar and told that we would be doing 'Down in the Tube Station at Midnight' by The Jam, plus a few others. I asked if we could do one of mine.

'Is it good?'

'Well it's goodish.'

'Goodish is good enough.'

So, that was that, I was to have my first audience experience playing to a room full of thieves and lost souls. The original song I chose was 'Nobody Loves Ya.'

We rehearsed for a couple of days and, if I may say so myself, it sounded shit. But the deal had been struck at the crossroads. On the day of the gig I was sitting in Rob's dorm shitting myself and having doubts about performing to a room full of the UK's undesirables. Piss-taking Alex was there. He offered me a faded prison jacket and said I would look the bollocks in it. He rolled up the sleeves and asked Rob's opinion. Rob coyly agreed. I fell for the wind-up, hook, line and sinker. I looked like a cunt.

Time came for the gig and it went well. I felt at home playing music and being up front. It was a profound life-changing experience that put me on a future road.

Ford had a TV room where everyone would congregate to watch an afternoon movie or a bit of television in the evening. It was here that I saw the first ever episode of *EastEnders* – it was a JFK moment. I remember my friend Jimmy saying it would never last because the cast couldn't act for toffee. Famous last words.

Lorna had been great throughout all of this. I received a letter from her nearly every day of my sentence. She visited me every two weeks for ten months and I fell for her genuine loyalty and loved her for that but also felt obligated to take the relationship further when I came out. After three months they gave me my release date which was to be on a Thursday. I told everyone on the outside that it was on the Friday to avoid any fuss. Thursday came along and I was given the train fare to Kings Cross. A taxi took me to the station in Arundel. It took a little while for it to sink in that I was free. I sat on the train looking out of the window and for that first few hours everything was from a new perspective: the fields, people walking up and down the train having alien conversations about their everyday life.

I arrived at Kings Cross and got on the tube to London Bridge. There were so many people about, it was a bit intimidating. I felt like *Pinocchio* with a million foxes at my heels.

I had spent the last nine months in a completely controlled, regimented environment with walls and fences. I jumped onto a bus at London Bridge. My belly started tingling as I got closer to familiar Bermondsey territory.

The bus stopped at Jamaica Road. Lorna had a flat in Cherry Garden Street, funnily enough on the same estate my mum grew up on.

I was sniggering to myself about how she was going to react with me just knocking on her door, as she was all set to pick me up from Ford the next day. I knocked on the door with my best, mischievous face on and Lorna opened it. The look on her face was similar to my hospital zombie alert: total confusion. I moved in with her and, for a while, it was nice.

I had been out of prison for six months when an incident happened one Sunday evening in a pub called Willows that undeniably defined my future.

Lorna had a sister who was drinking in the pub when a fight broke out – a real, old-school Western-type brawl. Bottles were smashed behind the bar and chairs were smashed over body parts. The doormen were throwing people all over the place. Her sister somehow got in the face of a crazed doorman enough for him to punch her so hard that some of her back teeth were knocked out.

A couple of weeks later, someone pulled up on a motorbike and shot this doorman dead as he stood outside the pub.

It was six months later when DI bellend and his band of merry SWAT men introduced themselves to me.

Chapter Eleven

M y mind snapped back into real time to the holding cell in Kennington. We were all herded into vans, destination Wormwood
Scrubs again but this time with a fabricated charge of attempted murder
and armed robbery. After the reflection on my past colourful life I truly
wondered what my future held.

The van entered into the eerie Scrubs prison gates. I had been
charged with two nasty crimes with another ID pending for the
attempted murder in the Chelsea club. I went through the reception
process again but this time as a remand prisoner.

We arrived on B wing. My mind was spinning like a top and
dreading the smell of piss and shit in the morning. I was allocated a
cell. I remember writing a heart-breaking letter to my father who was
serving four years himself at that time. He told me at a later date that
the letter didn't do him any favours as he couldn't do anything to help.
A father's nightmare. After a restless, sleepless night the door opened
and, bang, there was the smell and the line of cons making their way to
ablute themselves. I was bang in trouble and saw no immediate way out
of it. I kept reliving the ID parade where I was picked out and could
find no rhyme or reason for it.

I walked to the recess and spotted the towering figure that was an
old friend called Ted, one of the Southwark Park Tavern elite. He was
on remand for a number of robberies that had happened in and around

London, but was also innocent of the charges. The police had managed to convince one of his firm to turn Queen's evidence, the biggest no-no there is in the criminal world and for some reason the Judas stuck Ted's name in the mix. Ted was an old friend of my dad's from the docks. I told him what had happened to me. He was shocked. Everyone knew who had really done the crimes that I was being charged for but the code prevented anyone talking about it. After ablutions we were locked back up again in our cells. I felt a bit better after seeing Ted, at least I had a friendly, trusted face around which, I tell you, helped immensely.

After breakfast a group of us remand prisoners, Ted included, were marched over to C wing, the main remand wing. We had to gather on the bottom floor of the wing to be allocated our cells. An officer started to read our cell numbers out. I didn't like the look of my cell mate and I was in no frame of mind to cater to anyone's authority. I was innocent and I shouldn't have been in there in the first place. I was not going into any cell with anyone other than Ted. I protested. The prison officer again told me to get to the cell. I refused. I told the officer to look at my charges and if he didn't put me with Ted I would hang myself that night. He went upstairs to an office and when he came down, he gave me and Ted our cell number.

We settled in but I was still an innocent man locked up in a stinking jail for no reason other than going to bed the night before. The frustration of not being able to do anything I wanted to do was sometimes a bit too much to bear. I decided then and there, that I would not follow any of the regime rules. Lorna came up to visit; it was the first time that I had seen her since being arrested. She was shocked and promised to do all that was in her power to get me out.

Before I got arrested Lorna and I were about to split up but she was not going to let me roast in jail for a crime she knew I hadn't done. When the visit was over, I went back to the visit holding room and who should appear but my old pal Terry, of sawn-off shotgun in Coopers fame. We said hello and how ironic it was that the last time I saw him he was running into the pub with a gun and now we were both in this stinking hole. I told him what I was charged with and he was shocked because he knew who had really done it. We started hanging out together on the wing and became quite close.

One day, after a visit, myself and Terry were in the back room waiting to return to the wing when Terry, out of nowhere, approached another man in the holding area and smashed him in the nose so hard that the bone popped out. He then started kicking him. The screw in the room just turned his back. A couple of us dragged Terry away as the screw turned around and walked up to the man on the floor. The man started shouting through his tears and blood that he wanted to go on Rule 43. The screw picked him up then looked over at the bloodied Terry and told him to wash his hands.

I looked at Terry confused. 'The screw told me he was a nonce,' Terry said. *Oh fuck,* I thought, another *Van Helsing.*

Terry was from Deptford and from proper old traveller's stock. There was always a little feud dating back eons between Bermondsey and Deptford and usually never the twain met. Terry was dating one of the barmaids of Coopers who he later married and had kids with.

Back in the cell I used to share the puff I received from visitors with Ted as he was not the sort of man that would put anything up his arse, not for love, money or jail. 'My bottle is for one-way traffic,' he'd say to me. Ted helped me a lot with regards to coping with my situation; he was very level-headed. I used to be fascinated with his exotic stories about his dodgy dealings with the kings and queens of Asia. Without him I probably would have gone under from this absolutely diabolical fit-up. Ted taught me to play backgammon and we would spend hours playing it in the cell.

After a few weeks Ted's co-defendant, Johnny, came into the jail. He had also been grassed up by the same supergrass and was innocent of his charges. Ted asked if I'd mind if Johnny moved into the cell as they had a lot to talk about regarding their case. I was fine with this and set about moving in with Terry. A cell change was quite a big administrative deal but I wasn't going to take no for an answer. I was innocent of my charges and I would create a holla any chance I got. I think that I was the only prisoner in Wormwood Scrubs who other prisoners actually believed was innocent. Throughout my detention not one day went by without me protesting my innocence.

On my first day with Terry in the cell we decided to put down some rules. Due to the loyal Lorna, I always had a lump of cannabis on my person so we decided if we had a cell search, whoever was not holding onto contraband would distract the screws whilst the other took care of getting rid of the gear. This one afternoon our girlfriends brought us a Chinese meal – as we were on remand visitors were allowed to bring up a hot meal for us. It was also permitted to have a pint and a half of beer brought in. So, there we were, sitting in our cell, the Chinese sitting on the radiator pipe keeping warm, and as I was rolling up a pre-dinner joint, we heard the key slip into the door lock. It flew open and a screw walked in. Terry immediately jumped up, grabbed a towel and wrapped it around the officer's head whilst I was busy stuffing a parcel of Mogadon (sleeping pills) and a quarter ounce of puff into my mouth. When my mouth was empty, Terry took the towel off the screw's head. He started dancing around telling the screw he was only joking. The screw exited the cell double sharpish. We looked at each other and burst out laughing, that was, until we remembered that I had swallowed all our contraband. Half an hour later I started to feel the effects of the drugs, and an hour later I was lying on my bed, almost comatosed. Terry was eating his exotic food as the door sprang open again and three prison wardens rushed in shouting at us to exit the cell. I informed them, dribbling at the mouth, that we didn't have any drugs as I had eaten them all earlier. They helped me out of the cell and draped me over the landing railings. There were cons milling about on the ground floor on Association, Ted included.

Ted later informed me that I was shouting down telling everyone I was being fitted up again, this time for drugs. The cons just looked at the state I was in and started laughing. I was a dribbling mess. The screws searched the cell and helped me back in realising, by that time, that I really had eaten the shit. The next thing I knew it was morning. Terry told me what had happened but I couldn't remember a thing. The one thing I did get out of it was a new pair of felt tip glasses and a moustache.

Thursday came along and a return to my weekly court bail appearance. I was up at 6 a.m. getting my things together. I looked out of the cell window, the sky was red as the sun was rising. It looked beautiful but was also soul destroying not being free and I felt an element of self-pity creeping in. My emotion then turned to anger. I promised myself that I would never feel self-pity again in this place.

Terry woke up. 'Good luck with the bail app today, Webber.' He was just going through the motions. We both knew that I would be coming back.

Every Thursday an armed escort would take me to court for my bail application. I didn't have to appear but I elected to go for two reasons: it physically took me out of the prison and it caused the authorities a lot of aggravation. Having to cater for a so-called high-security risk prisoner to be scuttled back and forth from the Scrubs to Tower Bridge Magistrates' Court took some logistical planning. I packed up all my stuff. Every time you leave prison you have to go through the processing system again. In and out.

I was getting ready to leave the cell when I turned to Terry and asked him not to let anyone sleep in my bed. Getting processed again meant that one was not guaranteed to get back in the same cell. It becomes open and the administration can move in whoever they like. Terry laughed and shook his head knowing that if anyone else entered the cell he would have to eject them, which, in turn, would cause trouble with the screws. I headed down to reception. It was a real palaver, I was led into a holding cell where I was handcuffed. They brought me the obligatory powdered egg and a cup of stewed tea then I had to wait for the security forces that were to escort me.

It was crazy. Every time I would go to court I was accompanied with armed escorts, a van in front, one behind and a helicopter above. I used to look at the gun-toting policeman that sat opposite me feeling like Alice after going through the looking glass but in reality it was more like Dante on level four of his twisted comedy. I was spiritually and mentally empty. All I could do was just sit there and let it all unravel in front of my eyes like a bad movie. I was so scared at the prospect of spending the next twenty years in prison for a crime I did not commit. It filled me with anxiety and dread I had never experienced before.

I'd arrive at the court and then be herded to its cells. Bert the jailer would always be waiting with a cup of tea and a cigarette. Then I would be led into the court room where the magistrate would look at me with contempt and remand me once again until the next Thursday.

Screaming my innocence, they would drag me from the defendant box and take me back to the cells to wait for the van to transfer me back to the Scrubs again.

'You don't do yourself any favours, young Webber,' Bert said as he handed me a cup of tea.

'Bert, I'm innocent, I'm not having it. I demand justice in life.'

'Justice in life? I'm afraid there is no such thing, kid. Good luck.' He gave me a cigarette and left.

Back in the Scrubs I entered the wing again and made my way up the Victorian spurs, so pleased that I was returning back to mine and Terry's cell. I was met by another prisoner called Cyril from up north, who had been in and out of the prison system all his life. He was there for shooting a security guard. On the robbery in question Cyril and his team flew across the pavement armed to the teeth. Cyril confronted the security guard holding a box of money and told him in no uncertain terms to give him the money or he would shoot. The security guard failed to comply. Cyril shot him.

I'm not saying that Cyril was right to hurt the guard as he did but, as he used to say, he gave the guard fair warning, plain and simple, give me the money or I will shoot you and the guard chose to ignore it. There is a moral to the story somewhere in the fact that if people like Cyril come at you, armed to the teeth demanding money, give it to them.

Cyril stopped me on the landing and told me that there had been murders earlier on in our cell. I dashed to the cell and Terry was lying on his bed listening to the radio. As I entered, he started laughing.

He went on to tell me that a couple of hours after I left for court, they opened the door and an African con stepped in with all his kit. After the screws shut the door the African introduced himself to Terry. Terry told him to ring the bell and ask to be moved as he wasn't going to get near his mate's bed. The African con started to try and reason with Terry, who repeated the order but this time a bit more aggressively. The African con again refused. Terry smashed a table and waved one of the legs in a threatening way in the poor guy's direction. 'Ring the fucking bell now or I will smash you around this cell.' The guy came to his senses and hit the bell. A few minutes passed and nothing. He hit the bell again, this time keeping his finger on it. After a while a screw came to the door.

'What do you want?'

'I have to leave this cell.'

'Fuck off.' The screw walked away. The finger went onto the bell again. This time the screw was a bit peeved.

'Stop ringing the fucking bell.'

'I am afraid for my life, sir.'

'What are you talking about?' The African moved away from the spy hole. The screw saw Terry with the table leg in his hand. 'Don't be silly, put down that weapon.'

'He is not coming into this cell, guv. Webber told me to not let anyone sleep in his bed and until I know for sure that he's not coming back, that's what I'm going to do.' The key went in the lock and the African bolted out of the cell.

'This is not over,' the screw said threateningly as he and the relieved African marched away up the landing.

A week later Terry had to go to court. As he was leaving the cell he turned and said, 'Don't let anyone sleep in my bed, Webber.' I smiled at him as he left. When the doors opened for slop out, I made my way to the office on the landing. The same screw who dealt with Terry and the African was there. I told him not to even attempt to put anyone else in my cell. 'You and Russell are fucking nightmares, Webber.'

'I know, guv.'

'Go back to your cell, I'll see what I can do.'

'Cheers, guv.'

Terry returned to the cell. I had had a visit that afternoon so a plate of Chinese and a can of beer was waiting for him. 'Did they try to put someone in the cell?'

'No, mate.' Terry looked a bit pissed off that I didn't get the same drama. 'But if they did, it would have went the same way,' I reassured him. He smiled as I gave him his platter of chicken chop suey, rolled a joint and we settled down for the night. Times like these helped me to cope with the nightmare that I was living. I had one more identification to attend for the shooting in the nightclub in Chelsea but, as of yet, no fixed date had been reached.

By this time the news of what had happened to me had spread around Bermondsey and people were angry about this miscarriage of justice. There was a local community centre in Bermondsey run by a middle-class woman called Lois Acton and an old school friend of mine, Julie Donovan, who was born and bred in Bermondsey. Two very strong women, both with very left-wing political tendencies who helped people around the area that were unjustly treated by the authorities.

Lois was a bit older than us. She had settled in Bermondsey many years before and started up an organisation that helped young local kids and their families. I went to school with Julie who was also a good friend of Lorna's. So the three of them set about putting an 'Eddie Webber is innocent' campaign together to bring a bit of media awareness to my plight. As there was no Internet around in those days everything had to come via newspapers. They got the local Southwark and Bermondsey News involved.

Terry and I were in the cell one night smoking a joint and playing the card game Kaluki when the door opened and an S.O. (Senior Officer) stepped in.

'Which one of you is innocent?' he asked. Terry and I looked at each other – the cell stank of weed.

'Both of us,' we answered in unison.

'Webber, get your kit packed, you are moving.'

'Moving where, guv?' It was 9 p.m. and no one gets moved at 9 p.m. unless they were being ghosted out to another prison. 'I ain't going nowhere.'

'Just get your kit packed, one way or another you are leaving this cell.' There was a big hint of a threat to his words. I started to pack. I said my goodbyes to Terry and left the cell with the S.O. He took me downstairs to landing two where the A-category prisoners were held. He opened one of the cells, turned and said, 'Welcome to the big league, Webber, the home office has made you an A-category prisoner.'

As I stepped into the single cell my heart sank. I lay on the bed and the self-pity came again. The divine comedy had reached the next level.

In the morning when my cell was opened I stood at the door and looked up. Terry was looking over the landing with a sadness in his face. I feigned a smile. The next few days were spent acclimatising to my new A status. I was taken to another part of the prison where I had some photos taken that would be put into a book that records the movements of prisoners of my category. I wasn't allowed to go anywhere outside the wing without two screws and usually a dog accompanying me. Everything about my day had to be written into the book. Even my visits had to be behind glass. My new neighbours were a fascinating but dangerous bunch. An IRA soldier; a Sikh assassin; John, an armed robber from North London; and George, a big-time cocaine smuggler. The Sikh had spent two days lying in wait under a bush in the front garden of his target. When the target walked up his front path, the Sikh jumped from under the bush and decapitated him with a sword then waited there with the headless corpse to be arrested. I must say, though, he was one of the nicest, politest murderers I had ever met. It was a political assassination and, in his eyes, one that was an honour to perform. The IRA prisoner was called Quin. He was there for shooting a female police officer in Hammersmith. The armed robber, John, was there because he shot at a taxi driver as he and his comrade sped off on a motorbike after committing a robbery. John was riding pillion and started shooting at the taxi that was now chasing them. The bullet travelled up the steering column of the cab and lodged itself in the steering wheel. A lucky escape for the taxi driver. We called him Dirty Den.

He would walk along the landing and someone would nearly always jump out holding a fictional gun and shout 'Taxi!'

It was not all doom and gloom though. One evening I rang the bell in my cell. A screw came to the door and unlocked it. As soon as the door opened I ran out onto the prison landing and headed for the top floor. Whistles started piercing the air as the screws chased me around the landings. I ran past a cell and I swore that I heard 'Webber's out again.' When finally the panic-stricken screws cornered me, I would just start laughing and tell them that this was all but a dream and I'll wake up any moment and be in my bed again. They looked at me as if I was bonkers (they weren't wrong), as I calmly walked through them and back down to my cell. I'm sure it did me no favours with regards to what was written in the book. The next day I was taken down to the prison psychiatrists who would ask me silly questions like, 'Do you hear voices in your head?' To which I would answer, 'Yes.'

Thinking he'd found a worthy patient, he would ask, 'What kind of voices?'

'The voices of justice, or maybe God laughing at me,' I would answer. I wasn't lying. He would write down what I said on some report sheet, no doubt to come out on a rainy day. I was taken back to my cell.

I remember, in retrospect, a defining moment of my time in there. I was lying on my bed and I actually started to converse with what, at that time, I thought was God. As I mumbled towards the sky, I was fucking desperate and demanded that I be given justice and my life back.

The deal that was struck was that if I got out of this situation, I would be finished with crime and would do what I always wanted to do, travel the world and further my musical aspirations.

A few days later I was told that my last identification for the shooting in the club would be held the following week at Chelsea police station. By this time my mind was adjusting to the fact that I was going to spend a long time in this place. I'd had three positive IDs for the crime I was held for. If someone in this next ID picked me out, that would corroborate the evidence they had already. The next week arrived far too fast. I managed to borrow another set of clothing as I wasn't going to make the same mistake again.

The day of the ID I put the spare set of clothing under the top set that I was wearing so nobody saw them before the ID.

When we arrived at Chelsea police station, as the back doors of the van opened, I hid my whole body under the big coat I was wearing then proceeded to bunny hop into the station, making sure that my face and body was not seen by anyone. I'm sure I must have had some funny looks but I didn't give a monkey's what people thought, I was not taking any chances. I had already been picked out originally by, what I now know, was the clothes I was wearing – it most definitely wasn't going to happen again. I was led to a cell where I crouched in the corner with the coat still covering my whole body, not moving a muscle. A while later I heard the door open and looked through the opening of the coat to see three or four police officers standing there, and one of them told me to stand up.

I told them to fuck off and asked where my solicitor, Paul, was. They informed me that they had to go out onto the street to find my identification parade and needed to look at my description so they could find people of a similar appearance. *That old chestnut*, I thought. Again I told them to fuck off and get my solicitor. Shaking their heads, they complied. About an hour later, Paul stepped into the cell. I was, at this time, manic to say the least. I screamed at Paul as to where he had been and that a group of police had come into the cell and wanted to look at me to get an ID parade. Paul looked at me, still hunched in the corner with the coat covering me.

'Well if they don't know what you look like, how can they get your ID parade?' I saw the light. The group of officers entered again, took a good look at me still wrapped neck to toe in my coat and left. Paul also left to sort what needed to be sorted for the parade. A couple of hours later I was led to a room where the line-up was going to take place. When I walked into the space I was shocked. I looked at the line-up they'd picked for me, one of the men actually had a purple Mohican haircut. Out of the group of ten men there was maybe two that were of a similar appearance to me.

I voiced my concerns to Paul who in turn spoke to the officer in charge and told him that the line-up would not take place under the strong objection that we were not happy with the choice of people gathered. Because we objected the next option was a group ID, which meant I would be in a room milling around with the same people that I had just refused to stand in line with and the witness would identify the suspect in the informal group.

We again, under strong objection, refused the group identification on the same grounds as before. The third and last alternative was a confrontation where I, the suspect, would have to stand alone in the door frame of an open cell. The witnesses would be told, before they entered, that they were about to see the person who the police thought committed the shooting.

I was led back to the cell for the confrontation. Once inside the cell, I took off the top layer of clothing that I had on revealing a completely new outfit. The cell door opened. As I walked out there were two lines of uniformed police against both sides of the cell corridor walls. I was placed dead centre in the door frame of the cell. I swear that you could see my heart jumping through the Fred Perry T-shirt I was wearing.

The first witness for the Pheasantry Club shooting entered – a young girl who worked behind the bar of the club. She was told to face me and look me up and down. I tried my hardest to look relaxed but in doing so probably looked as guilty as sin. She looked me up and down for what felt like an eternity. She was asked if I was the person she saw that night shooting the victim – she said no. I breathed a sigh of relief. The witness gave me a reassuring smile then exited. The second witness entered: a man in his thirties who was the manager of the club. After much of the same he also shook his head. Two down and the third one went the same way. No pick out. I was put back into the cell. I just flopped on the bed, mentally exhausted by the day's events. Paul entered. 'You alright?'

'I am now.'

'At least we know where we stand.' Paul told me that he was going to elect my case to an old-style committal, which means the CPS (Crown Prosecution Service) had to put all the evidence they had up front and then the magistrate would decide if there was enough evidence to take it to trial. If they felt the evidence is shaky, I'd get acquitted there and then. The thing that was in my favour was that in all three crimes the same gun was used. The police had the bullets but not the gun which was what they were looking for when they raided my house in the first place. The three positive identifications, luckily, were from people who worked for the security service; no civilians had picked me out. How could they have picked me out so definitely when six other witnesses from the other crimes who saw the man doing the deeds at close quarters hadn't picked me out? My theory is that when the police went to my house to get my clothes at the beginning of events, they put my clothes down in front of the three security guards and indirectly let them know that these clothes were the suspect's. Who knows but, no matter how you look at it, something corrupt was definitely afoot.

CHAPTER TWELVE

I returned back to the Scrubs feeling a lot better than when I'd left. I spoke to Ted the next morning. He was happy for me. Paul applied for an old-style committal which was scheduled six weeks later in December. Then a very strange coincidence occurred.

One night my mother, feeling sentimental and nostalgic for some reason, took out a box of prison letters from the bottom of her bedroom cupboard. She still professes that God guided her to this action and who am I to argue with that? She randomly chose one letter which was from Jackio, who was in Albany Prison on the Isle of Wight. As she read the letter Jackio mentioned about what a lovely visit it was with her and Eddie and to thank him for handing in his appeal papers. She noticed the date on top of the letter – the same day that I was supposed to have committed the robbery that I had been picked out for. At the time the robbery was actually happening, I was signing in my brother's appeal papers in Albany Prison on the Isle of Wight. My mother gave Paul the letter.

Now I had a reference to the date in question, I started to remember other things about the day. I had seen a film, many years before, based on a Barbara Taylor Bradford book called *A Woman of Substance* and at the time I was reading its sequel *Hold the Dream*. I had taken it to read on the train and ferry as it was such a long and drawn-out journey. We got off the ferry and took a cab to the prison. When I got out of the taxi, I left the book on the back seat. Once the visit was over, we took a cab back to the ferry and I dashed into the cab office to see if the driver had handed the book in, which he hadn't. I flipped the island the bird and jumped on the ferry. I'd get another copy on my way home. When I told Paul this story, he put a private detective on the island.

He not only found the cab driver but the guy still had my book on his bookshelf and because I had made a big deal out of it when I went to his office, the incident was lodged in his mind. He was also prepared to come to court to say so. It was two weeks before the committal when Paul put this new information into evidence. DIs Wellend and Cherry must have been shitting themselves as there was no doubt that this new evidence was enough to acquit me. What were the chances of a cast-iron alibi like this coming up out of nowhere? Now the corrupt scuffers were in trouble. After putting me through this, I was going to make them pay. I still had to stay in prison while the police checked out my alibi. How they didn't let me out immediately was an abomination in itself but I was an A-cat prisoner and red tape was involved. Lorna also informed me that a march through Bermondsey was to happen on the day of my committal. Lois, Julie and Lorna had been busy rounding the troops and making banners with the slogan 'Eddie Webber is innocent'.

Four months of my life wasted, sitting in prison as a high-category prisoner – mind fuck or what? The date arrived for me to go to court. I'd had no contact, apologies or explanations from the police and I still had the A-cat status. Although I knew I had a cast-iron alibi, there was still a niggling feeling as to why I hadn't been released yet. I woke up on the morning of the trial and packed up all my gear, hopefully for the last time. The door opened and I was led down to reception but wasn't processed as I had been before which I thought quite encouraging. I waited for the escort inside the holding cell.

They arrived, and for the first time since my arrest they led me out to the van without handcuffs. If I was in my right mind I would have seen the positive in this but I was far from it. I was paranoid knowing that these scuffers could do anything they wanted to me.

We arrived at Tower Bridge Magistrates' Court. I could see through the windows of the van that crowds of people had congregated at the back entrance where the prison van drives in. And who should be in front holding a banner up high, none other than my old mucker Terry. He was holding a banner with my face on it and big text that read 'Eddie Webber is Innocent'. Too fucking right I was innocent and these animals that had incarcerated me for no reason were going to know it. I was taken into the cells. Bert was there as always with a cup of tea. 'I think you might be home for Christmas, kid,' he said. *Oh my cup overfloweth*, I sarcastically thought. My anger left me in no mood for talking and I told Bert so. I was stewing in my cell. No one had even had the decency to inform me what was happening let alone the fact that I was still locked up. After about an hour of copious murderous thoughts of what I'd like to do to DIs Wellend and Cherry, the cell door opened and a smiling Paul stepped in. I went crazy, shouting that I shouldn't be in here and why the fuck was he smiling. Paul told me that they had dropped all charges and it was a matter of procedure that we had to go into court. There was also the matter of the sixteenth of cannabis that they found in my flat at the time of the arrest. I was, to say the least, flabbergasted.

After all that I had been through, they were still charging me with possession of a miniscule amount of cannabis. I was led out to the court and had to wait outside the entrance before going in. DIs bellend and Cherry were already there waiting. I looked at them with hate in my eyes. DI bellend, all of a sudden, started shouting about how I was picked out in an ID and it was legitimate. My only answer to him was, 'See you in court.' Then DI Cherry piped up and that was it, I let go with both barrels calling them all the fit-up cunts I could think of and how I was going to spend the rest of my life on a mission to get them nicked for what they had done to me. The court usher opened the door and demanded we hushed, which was met with a hearty, 'Fuck off.' DI bellend reiterated that I was identified legitimately. I calmed down and said no more for fear of giving them another reason to send me back but I was angry as I stepped into the court. I was led into the box.

The public gallery was filled with friends and family all smiling and holding banners. I was furious as I stood before the po-faced magistrate. For four months I had been screaming my innocence which, every time, fell on this vile woman's deaf ears. The armed robbery and attempted murder charges were formally put to bed. Now I had to plead for the puff. I pleaded guilty to possession of one point nine grams of Morocco's finest. After all that had happened she decided my sentence for the smoke would be a £40 fine or a day in prison. I just shook my head at this woman. I could find no words except, 'Take me back to the cell.'

As I was led from the defendant box, my friends in the gallery waved the £40 fine money at me. I turned to them and asked that they give not a penny to the coffers of these uncompassionate people. I would do the day in the court cell. I was released as an A-category prisoner which was a very rare occurrence as you can imagine. I sat in the cell for about an hour. Apart from the injustice that had just happened, I felt relieved that the nightmare was finally over. I can't explain what was going on in my head. I rushed to the toilet and threw up. Paul came to the cell shaking his head. 'I've never witnessed anything like that,' he said.

I gave him a cuddle. 'Thanks for believing me, Paul.' He smiled and told me he'd be in touch and that he would start the investigation proceedings against Wellend and Cherry. I sat on the bed, looked up at the ceiling and thanked the ultimate complexity. I hadn't forgotten our deal. Bert entered the cell with a serious look on his face. My tribe outside were going crazy and were threatening to smash the court up. He asked that if they let me out now instead of spending the rest of the day in the cells would I go out and calm the baying crowd. I stubbornly told him no! He went on to say that if my friends carried on that they would start getting arrested for the disturbance. On those grounds I said okay. I didn't want anyone getting into trouble. I still sometimes think about what must have been going on in the magistrate's pitiless mind. Every week I appeared in front of her pleading my innocence and every week she would close her ears and send me back to jail.

How can the justice system let people like that have any sort of autonomy over anyone's life? I wonder if I'd been born of another class whether I would have been treated in the same way, but the real crime that had been committed was that all involved had led me to lose all faith in humanity. The rest of my life would be defined by this moment. I would never again wholly trust anyone or anything. The ol' man was right.

I exited the court to hearty cheers and much patting of shoulders. I spotted Lorna, Lois and Julie and made my way over to them to thank them profusely for their belief in me. As I stepped outside, freed from the last few months of hell, I suddenly felt overwhelmed with sadness. It hit me like a ton of bricks; it was all too much. I looked across the road from the court exit to the entrance of the Devon Mansion flat where it all had started. I walked across the road and stopped outside the flat entrance to rewind and complete a full circle.

That night I went out for a drink with a few people. Ted and Johnny made an appearance but I wasn't really all there in my head. The next few months I was in a *Count of Monte Cristo* frame of mind. The thought of revenge on these corrupt elite scuffers was all encompassing and I couldn't think of anything else.

If I hated the police before, my hate now was on another level. I shake my head still, thirty years later, with a sense of anger.

Through Paul we reported the miscarriage of justice to the relevant channels and were put in touch with a man from the internal investigation unit.

Though I'm still not a hundred per cent sure if he was a part of the foul deed or not. The unit was called A10, set up in the 1970s by Sir Robert Mark to root out corruption. They were a group of specially selected officers, taken from both uniform and detective branches, to work directly under Robert to investigate all allegations against Met scuffers.

I started having meetings with the officer from the A10 unit but things were not going as planned. All sorts of unexplainable things started happening with regards to my complaint. The security guards who identified me had since disappeared and couldn't be found, the company that they worked for had folded and all medical records of the guard that had been shot had completely disappeared without trace.

Could all this have really been a wicked piece of police theatre?

I tried to voice all of this on a TV programme called *Rough Justice* but that came to nothing. The details of what happened to me were so mad that sometimes I found it hard to believe myself.

I was in my flat one morning, a couple of months down the line, when the thud of post being delivered hit the deck. Amongst the brown letters (which always went straight in the bin unopened) was a parcel. I opened it to find a book. Inside the cover was a note that read plain and simple in capital letters, READ IT! It was signed by my brother Jackio (very *Alice in Wonderland*). The book was called *The Brotherhood* by Stephen Knight and was one of the first real exposés of the devilish art of Freemasonry.

I flicked through the pages and noticed a highlighted chapter called 'The Police'.

Stephen Knight had also written a book about the Ripper murders entitled *Jack The Ripper: The Final Solution* based on his findings that there were implications of Freemasonic connections involved in the case. He became so compelled to expose the secrets in Freemasonry that he wrote *The Brotherhood*, published in 1984. Knight was found dead in 1985 at the age of thirty-three. Freemasons claim that he died from a brain tumour but questions are still being asked about what really happened. Knight, after his intense research, had this to say about Freemasonry: 'Freemasons applaud violence, terror and crime, provided it is carried out in a crafty manner. Humour is all important and the most appalling crimes may be committed under its cloak.'

I ran a nice Radox bubble bath and got stuck into the chapter.

What I read was frightening. One in six policemen are Freemasons, Knight said, and that it is a prerequisite to become a mason to further their police careers. Many old-school police officers that reach retirement and are still in uniform are usually people that refused to enter into the crafty craft. It's a fact, especially back in the 1980s, that many Freemason lodges were full of active police officers, judges of the realm and active criminals that would scratch each other's backs. The point is that I had a DI of the A10 investigating a DI connected to the murder squad and a DI connected to the robbery squad, could there be a chance that they were all masons?

After reading this mind-bending book, I decided that bringing charges to these high-ranking police officers was fighting a battle I could not possibly win. What would stop them doing it all over again, or worse next time? I had friends who had been shot and killed by the police, why would I be any different? I started to get very paranoid. In the book, Knight is quite revealing about the intricacies of the craft. He exposed their greeting methods using phrases like 'on the square'. When a stonemason cuts a block to use in the construction of a building, it must be perfectly shaped so that it will support the other blocks that surround it. The block's sides must all be perfectly straight with no faults so that it will do its part as just one small piece of a much larger building. To check the reliability of his workmanship, the stonemason uses a tool called a 'square', shaped like a right angle to determine whether the sides and angles of the stone are perfect. Freemasons use the term to describe their trust in each other. A man who is 'on the square' is honest and reliable.

Another greeting is 'on the level'. To a Freemason it means just that, all Freemasons are Brothers who meet on the same level, regardless of their social or economic status outside the lodge. Princes, presidents, and captains of business are no better or more important than bus drivers, plumbers, and paperboys when they sit in the lodge together.

Masonry does not detract from a man's accomplishments, nor does it exalt him above his Brothers because of his position outside the lodge.

Freemasonry dates back to the first century, some say it goes further back but I'm getting away from the point. Please give the book a read, you'll find it interesting, I promise.

I waited until the A10 DI called again. I came straight to the point: 'Are you on the square?' I asked down the phone.

'Excuse me?' was the surprised reply.

'Are you on the level?' There was a silence on the other end of the phone. There was a whole world within that pause that flagged up a warning in my mind. I told him, there and then, that I wanted to drop all proceedings against bellend and Cherry, even though they wanted to put me behind bars for the duration of my youth. I told him to tell them (as if they didn't already know) that I had full case against them. I asked, in return, that they would leave me and my family alone. His answer was a chilling 'Okay' and that was the last time I heard from him.

That was it, I was getting out.

CHAPTER THIRTEEN

It was coming to the end of 1986 and due to the recent events I was completely in the wilderness. I really didn't know if I was coming or going. Tony, my old mate from the Arnold estate, had spent some time on a kibbutz in Israel in the seventies, and the stories of his exploits in the Holy Land had always resonated with me. One night, I crossed the tracks and went to see him to ask how I could get out there.

The next day, after a few phone calls, I started the jump ship proceedings.

I had to fill in an application form then go through an interview process. I waited impatiently for the kibbutz office to get in touch with a time and date for the interview. I never went outside my door until the appointment arrived.

By this time my relationship with Lorna was over but I'd like to say thank you to her for her dedication and loyalty. I would not have been able to get through those few years without her help and kindness. So I thank you, Lorna, you have a place in my heart.

In the kibbutz office I awaited my turn to be interviewed. I was sitting with a group of young, middle-class students with fine noses. After what I had been through in the last few months I found it quite difficult to find any common ground and engage in conversation with them. I was a tightly wound ball of elastic, paranoid as paranoid could be. When the interview process was finished, I had to pay two hundred pounds for visas and other bits of entry paraphernalia but that was it, I was off to the land of milk, honey and Tottenham supporters.

The kibbutz that I was allocated to was called Kvutzat Shiller on the outskirts of a town called Rehovot. I booked a one-way ticket from Heathrow to Ben Gurion airport to leave in two weeks.

When I finally arrived at Heathrow it was something else. I had to go through a rigorous security check as the situation between the Arabs and Jews was starting to escalate in Lebanon and Syria, but to me that was kid's stuff compared to walking the streets of South East London in my present state of mind. A couple of days before leaving for Israel, a massive boil appeared on the side of my neck. *Lovely,* I thought, nothing like a puss-ridden zit to create a good first impression.

The plane landed at Ben Gurion airport. I had never really been outside England except for a couple of jaunts to Benidorm with the gang, which is another book in itself.

As I stepped off the plane, Kay's catalogue guitar in hand and the humongous zit on my neck that was ready to burst at any given moment, the heat hit me. I had never felt heat like it before; it felt healing and liberating. Shalom, Israel.

After another vigorous security search, this time with men armed to the teeth with machine guns, I exited the airport. I looked around at the vista and all I noticed was young people in green army uniforms walking about with M-16 assault rifles over their shoulders. I stared, mouth agape. It took a while to compute but it seemed to me that everybody was tuned in to war. I saw an open-back truck parked at the side of the road. One of the passengers on the plane, who I recognised from the kibbutz office interview, threw his backpack onto the truck and jumped on. I followed suit. When the back was full of wide-eyed, naive volunteers from many different parts of the world, we headed off.

It was an amazing journey, driving through the biblical terrain with the healing sun on my face. Banana, avocado and citrus trees lined the road. I had never seen anything like it before. My senses were exploding with the colour, heat, sounds and smells which were so alien to my 'fresh from prison' brain. I closed my eyes and faced the sun, then the realisation hit me. I was in a country that I'd heard so much about in my Catholic-school years, a country populated by three million people and not one person knew me. I breathed a sigh of relief. I felt the baggage of the last few months all start to melt from my shoulders and it felt great. I could hopefully find myself again and what's more, my deal with the ultimate complexity made in that oppressive prison cell in the Scrubs was being upheld. We drove through the town of Rehovot and arrived at the entrance to Kvutzat Shiller.

Everyone was walking about in a file formation. They were wearing blue working uniforms consisting of shorts and shirts, very weird and Orwellian.

The kibbutz was founded as a kvutza in October 1927 by a group of twelve academics from Lviv and Galicia and their six children. This was after the group had two years of agricultural training in Kiryat Anavim. The new settlement was named after Shlomo Shiller, a Zionist activist from Lviv.

We were taken to a dining room that was full of people in the blue uniforms and pilgrims from all over the world eating lunch. There was a happy hum of contentment vibrating all around. We were told some basic facts by David, the kibbutz spokesman. I was allocated the job of picking bananas.

After the chat we were shown to the laundry hut where we picked up our work uniforms. It was all very chilled. We were then taken to our shacks, which left a lot to be desired. A basic room with three beds inside. I was sharing with two lads: Alistair from Glasgow and Jim from Surrey. We were given time to adjust to the new climate and surroundings so I took a walk. The kibbutz was full of what seemed like newly built, pristine houses where the full-time kibbutz residents lived. After a while, I noticed groups of people heading from the dining area to the shacks. When I got back to my room, Jim and Alistair were getting out of their work clothes so I introduced myself. Jim was in his late teens and Alistair early twenties; they were both orange pickers. They gave me the lowdown on how the place worked. As it was summer, we had to get up at 5 a.m. and work until 11 a.m. as it got too hot after midday. Jim was going off to the town of Rehovot and asked if I'd like to join him.

The town was a mixture of Israelis and Arabs. Coming from Bermondsey I was ignorant of the politics of the country but it was apparent who the menial workers were.

We stopped at a shop to buy cigarettes and I was shocked at the price. They cost less than a shekel (the Israeli currency) which was equivalent to about thirty pence in the UK. We bummed about the town for a while. Jim informed me that there was to be a volunteers' party that evening on the kibbutz, a traditional welcome for new recruits, so we had to buy some booze. We then stopped at a restaurant and that's where I sampled my first genuine falafel with all the extras. If there is ever such a place as heaven, this, my friend, comes close.

We picked up a few bottles of a local brew called Arak, some banana liqueur and a bottle of ninety-five per cent proof alcohol which, I was told, when mixed together was a favourite with the kibbutz volunteers.

When we arrived back onto the kibbutz it was supper time. We dumped the booze in our humble abode and headed up to the dining hall. As we entered, it had a slightly subliminal feel of prison but with the added bonus of being a million miles, or in reality 3611.239 miles, away from SE16. There was a mixture of dialects in the hall. People were speaking to each other in our great world's many tongues. I had a bright pink no collar shirt on and a huge plaster on my neck covering the puss-ridden, ready-to-erupt volcano. I noticed a couple of English-speaking dudes sniggering as I entered. Was it the plaster over the boil or the pink shirt? I now know it was both. The food was set out as a buffet. I didn't recognise most of it but I took a bit of everything anyway. I sat down with the sniggering twosome who I soon found out to be Messrs Barry and Kenny, both rascals of the highest degree. Barry was an Englishman of Jewish heritage with a snozzle to match, who was travelling the world with his beautiful wife, Sue. Kenny was a young man who had just finished university and was starting his journey in life. Kenny's room-mates were called Marc and Kim. Marc was from Jewish, middle-class, East End stock and Kim was a lad from Denmark. I was soon to find out that they were also harmless rascals. Mine was the only raw cockney south London dialect apart from Marc's refined east London Jewish accent.

I tried talking to a couple of fit-looking Swedish girls but they couldn't understand a word that I was saying; they thought I'd come from Australia. It would be a while before I mastered the art of talking much slower to non-English speaking citizens. After talking to Barry and Kenny for a while, I told them that I was a market trader. I thought that the truth – that I had just been released from jail for armed robbery and attempted murder – was not a good idea. Their mischievous auras were, as they say, right up my street.

The night arrived and everyone was getting into party mode. The theme of the party was Roman Toga, inspired by the classic National Lampoon's eighties film *Animal House*. Everyone was wrapping sheets around themselves and emptying bottles of the banana liqueur into big bowls then adding the potent alcohol to the mix. I took a glassful and *wow!* It was indeed a devil's brew but, at the same time, so moorish that I drank glass after glass until all my insecurities melted into the fading, holy light. There was a fire burning in the yard where Scandinavian maidens, toga-clad, danced round like Viking wenches, swinging their hips and drinking the deadly mead to the sounds of Brian Ferry, early U2 and other mystical world music. I viewed the scene through alcoholic banana-hazed eyes and thought that I was indeed home. I didn't remember going to bed but 5 a.m. arrived and with it, the call to the banana fields.

Jim and Alistair tried their damn best to get me up but I wasn't going anywhere, the banana mead had juiced me. The next thing I knew, a strange face with a Canadian accent was speaking to me asking if I was okay and it wasn't a good idea to miss the first day of work. Her name was Cindy and she was the volunteers' representative. With my alcoholic and bad morning breath silently wafting in her face, I told her that I had eaten a bad falafel in town the night before and was feeling too queasy to work in the sun. She smiled knowingly and left me to my inner head and physical pain.

Eventually, when I managed to rise, I dunked myself under a cold shower then, with the sun scorching my frazzled brain, I made my way up to the dining hall for lunch. I think the term is 'the walk of shame'. Then Barry and Kenny delighted in telling me of my exploits the night before, of which I was totally ignorant. After eating, I was called into the office by David, the head honcho, and he read out the riot act. I was allowed, this one time, the undisciplined action of missing work. I tried the bad falafel story but it fell on big, deaf ears. The kibbutz was a law unto itself and the work and discipline needed to keep it going was crucial for its survival. The concept of the kibbutz was that everybody shared everything they had. Managers and workers were all paid the same wage, everyone who could cook took turns, everyone took turns to do the washing and so on. It was the purest form of Zionism that you could find in Israel. The ideology was everything. A dream come true. It all sounded very familiar to what I'd learnt from the nuns in school about what Jesus was doing.

Next morning at 5 a.m. I was by my bed, dressed and raring to hit the fields.

We made our way to a pick-up point where we would all jump into an open-backed van that took us to the magic, yellow fields of bananas. There were six men in our team. Jap (pronounced Yapp), a guy from Holland who had converted to Judaism and had been on the kibbutz since the hippy seventies. He was in charge. Gabby, an Argentinian Jew who came to the kibbutz at a young age and was now an elder; Yossy a mad Finn from Helsinki; Mick, a teacher from England, the epitome of hippydom with a beard, tie-dye shirt and beads; and Abram, an old man who wasn't really all there but had a perfectly valid excuse for that. He was one of the lucky ones who had survived the holocaust. The story was when the Americans liberated Auschwitz, Abram was a prisoner who had suffered much abuse even to the point of watching all his family be brutally murdered by the Nazi regime. Abram found himself naked in the yard when the Americans stormed the place so, seeing a dead German, he took his clothes and put them on to cover his modesty. Of course the American soldiers thought he was a Nazi and proceeded to kick the shit out of him which, on top of everything, left him a little fragile in the mind. Having blonde hair and a scar on my face from my accident, he viewed me with a lot of suspicion at first, until Gabby got through to him that I was English and safe.

Picking bananas was the hardest work I had ever done in my life, especially in the forty-degree sun. We would have to stand under the bunch of bananas that weighed God knows how many kilos. They hung in a sack like every powerful bit of fruit.

We'd have to secure the weight on our shoulders and someone, usually Jap, would cut the stem with a stick that had a curved blade on the end similar to the chosen weapon of the great grim reaper. The bunch would crash onto your shoulder then you would load it onto a trailer connected to a tractor that the old fella Abram usually drove. I loved the physical aspect of the work and became fit very quickly as we were doing this for five hours a day, five days a week.

At the weekend we would all go on excursions. After about two weeks I felt acclimatised and was probably for the first time in my adult life, truly happy and without a care in the world. A feeling I've been chasing ever since but have never found, apart from when I spent time in India in later years.

We were allowed a week off from the kibbutz every now and then to travel the country that I had heard so much about in my misspent school days.

My favourite place in all the world was, and still is, the walled city of Jerusalem.

I mean fucking Jerusalem, how heavy does that name sound in the realm of the history of this world?

It was like nothing I'd ever seen in my life. In my eyes it looked and felt the same as I imagined it did in the first century: busy and volatile.

We stayed in a hostel just outside the Zion gate, the self-same one that the naive JC entered in his time of doubt and pain. They also say the hostel was built on the ground where the great swami met his end.

The city of Jerusalem was magical. As I walked the streets something clicked. This was a vast planet with so much to see.

During its history, Jerusalem has been destroyed at least twice, besieged twenty-three times, attacked fifty-two times, and captured and recaptured forty-four times. A city truly not at rest. It is split up into four quarters: Armenian, Christian, Jewish and Muslim. I relished the different cultural sounds and smells the city offered up to this SE16 lad.

I sat for a while, looking at the wailing wall. It is a relatively small segment of a far longer ancient retaining wall, known also as the Western Wall. It was originally erected as part of the expansion of the second Jewish Temple begun by Herod the Great, which resulted in the encasement of the natural steep hill known to Jews and Christians as the Temple Mount, and is the site where the Islamic Prophet Muhammad tied his steed on his night journey to Jerusalem before ascending to paradise. A fascinating historical place.

The Jewish people would place notes between the rocks of the wall. They would then hang back and start to rock back and forth, wailing in deep prayer, hoping that their God would hear their pleas and grant them, no doubt, the gift of many shekels and salvation.

I can't see any proof that they asked for world peace. An Arab friend of mine, Abed, told me one day, as we were playing backgammon and drinking strong coffee in his humble apartment, that the Arabs had built a public toilet on the other side of the sacred wall so they could all piss up it. I think Moses missed a trick there. He should have written another commandment: thou shalt not lag up holy relics. Sadly, Abed was killed by an Israeli bullet as he innocently left the West Bank a few months later.

But no matter what the politics, the essence of Jerusalem filled my brain with ancient, magic vibes that have stayed with me to this day. Every chance I got to go to Jerusalem I was there like a shot! I entered the sacred gates one day with a Welsh friend of mine, another volunteer from the kibbutz. We called him the Miner as he was always singing Billy Bragg and Pogues' songs. His real name was Richard, a true Welsh socialist and a man of the people. His mission in Israel was to pop his cherry. He was a large man and we convinced him, whilst under the influence of the magic banana juice, to shave his head. When the deed was done he resembled a Buddha.

We arrived in the holy city and all the kids were fascinated by his appearance and took turns to run up and slap him endearingly on the head. He sometimes had six or seven kids at a time slapping his canister about. It was hilarious hearing him telling the little angels with dirty faces to 'Fuck right off like' in his fine Welsh accent. The Monty Python team would have been proud of the spectacle.

Bermondsey and prison was a lifetime away as I stared at the beauty of the Dome of the Rock in the Arab quarter, which marked the spot where the prophet Muhammad allegedly ascended into Heaven. According to the Talmud, it was also close to here where God gathered the earth to form Adam. It was on this rock that Adam, and later Cain, Abel and Noah, offered sacrifices to God. Jewish sources identify this rock as the place mentioned in the Bible where Abraham fulfilled God's test to see if he would be willing to sacrifice his son, Isaac. So a lot happened in this busy ol' town.

On reflection, I still cannot understand why the conflict of Arabs and Jews has escalated so much in this modern day. It all really boils down to who can piss the highest up the wall and accusing the Jews of nicking the original blessing didn't help much I suppose. Check out Genesis 25:28 in the bible. It's a good story and explains the 'balagan gadol' (big mess) between the divided nations. I personally found the Arabs far more hospitable than the Israelis in my time there.

Everything in Jerusalem was about money and bartering. I seemed to be okay in that department, coming from the streets of Bermondsey.

I witnessed some foolish people, usually rich Americans, who fell foul to the Arabic silver tongue. It was also in this amazing city that I found a love for chilli peppers. An Arab market trader offered me one and, with too much bravado for my own good, I chomped into the raw fiery beast. The amused stall holder knowingly called his friends over to watch my guaranteed Western reaction to the fruit.

I tried to style it out but seconds later I was running around like a headless chicken, huffing and puffing like the big bad wolf, buying bottles of water from the same man who started the fire. Since that day I have been a promoter of chillies and a chilli fiend. I even have an online company called ChilliEd.

Another amazing place of history that I loved was the Dead Sea in the Jordan Rift Valley. The Dead Sea water is so salty that nothing can live in it. We used to cover ourselves in the salty mud then walk a few hundred yards where there was a natural waterfall. It would feel amazing when you stepped under it, the clean cold water washing away the cracked, sun-dried, salty mud.

Some say the location of the waterfall was where King David hid from the jealous monarch of the time, Saul. It was also the vicinity where the Dead Sea Scrolls were discovered in a series of twelve caves around the site known as Wadi Qumran. These were written by the Essene community – some people believe they give a true account of what was going on in the bad ol' days. There was so much to see in this beautiful land.

Life on the kibbutz plodded on. The volunteers had a little area on site that doubled as a social club with a coffee bar and table tennis where we would gather each night to drink and chew the fat. It was also the place where the young, naive Israelis, who lived on the kibbutz, could have their pick of the world-flavoured, female volunteers, and there were some pretty beautiful volunteers.

One afternoon, myself and a few of the gang were sitting chilling outside the coffee area when I heard the familiar sound of a cockney accent. A group of strangers approached us. One of the men went by the name of Mitch. Mitch hailed from the streets of exotic Romford but had settled out there and married an Israeli girl. He informed us that he had just opened a nightclub called The Place in Rehovot town and was putting on a weekly Thursday night where volunteers could drink beer for half price with the added bonus of a live band. I suggested a Friday night would be better as we were up at the crack of dawn and on the fields in the week and we had all run out of dodgy falafel excuses for our hangovers. I felt an immediate affinity to him, it was nice to hear a bit of cockney again. I told him that I would rally the troops and get them all down there.

Friday night came and The Place was filled with volunteers. Mitch introduced me to an imposing figure standing at the bar, an Israeli man called Benzi. He was about six foot five and looked like an Apache Indian, with long hair and pointed features – he was the real owner of the bar. Benzi thanked me for my promotional skills in filling the place then gave me a lump of hash. He told me to be careful as getting caught with kef in Israel was a big deal. I noted the warning then joined my fellow travellers of the universe. Barry, who was a big stoner, was thrilled with the hash. We went outside and covertly smoked a joint then settled back in to watch the band. The musicians were great but the singer left a lot to be desired.

The bass player was a funny-looking little guy called Erez but he stood out from the rest and was a great bass player. Erez had just been thrown out of the army due to an exemption on the grounds of con-science. Every Israeli at the age of eighteen had to do national service. Erez made them believe that he was anti-war and refused to take orders. It's a big thing for an Israeli to get discharged from the army and to have something like that on their record. It would affect a man's future in the country as far as getting a job and going forward. It stays as a black mark all their lives, but Erez, being a creature of impulse and creativity, didn't think that far ahead and neither did I for that matter so we were a match made in Hell. There were a couple of songs that Erez took the lead on that night. He sang them in the style of Robert Smith, the lead singer of The Cure, and imitated him to a T. When the band had their break, Erez came to join us at our table. He spoke perfect English, in a Robert Smith kind of way. We talked about The Beatles, Chuck Berry, Buddy Holly and other things connected to the sacred roots of rock 'n' roll music. I told him I played the guitar and sang. When the band went back on for their second set Erez, out of nowhere, mischievously invited me up to sing. I didn't have to be asked twice and jumped onto the stage, much to the delight of the kibbutz contingent. I asked the band if they knew 'Johnny Be Good' by Chuck Berry. They did. I smiled as the opening lead intro kicked in. The moment I started singing the whole place erupted in cheers. I swear Erez had a smile on his face as big as a Cheshire cat.

When the song finished Erez asked if I knew any songs by The Doors. I think my answer was, 'Is the Pope Catholic?' To which Erez dryly answered, with a puzzled look on his face, 'Yes.' The band started to play the opening to 'Road House Blues'. 'Keep your eyes on the road, your hands upon the wheel'. I looked over to Benzi standing at the bar and I saw the shekel signs rolling in his eyes. At the end of the night a good time was had by all and my road to somewhere had begun. I walked on air as we made our way back to the safety of the kibbutz.

CHAPTER FOURTEEN

Barry and Sue were involved in amateur dramatics back in their home town in England and had decided to put a show on for the kibbutz residents. The kibbutz had its own well-equipped theatre. Barry wrote a sketch about the London kibbutz office process and asked me if I would play a part in it. I had never done any sort of acting before but threw myself wholeheartedly at his directorial mercy. We started rehearsing the sketch. I was to play was a rebel-type character who caused a bit of chaos in the office. I was typecast, it was such a fun night. I also wrote a song for Miner recalling an incident when we caught him sucking a drunk American floozy's unwashed toe. The song was called 'Randy Old Taff', sung to the tune of 'Dirty Old Town' by The Pogues. Miner performed the song in bondage clothing and a pair of speedo swimming trunks – a vision I still shudder at.

After Miner's show-stopping performance, it was time to start our sketch. I remember feeling physically sick before my entrance onto the stage. I entered stage left in a black leather jacket with the collars up and faded jeans, doing my best James Dean impression. I probably looked more like Peter Dean than James Dean but I entered to a round of applause, my ego thinking that I could get used to this. The sketch went down a storm. I told Barry afterwards that I enjoyed it so much I wouldn't mind doing something like this for a living when I returned to Blighty. He laughed of course.

Friday night at The Place started to become a ritual and Benzi and my relationship progressed. I would find myself in his establishment each day after finishing work on the kibbutz.

I liked Benzi – he was a lovable rogue that had many fingers in many pies out there. He'd started his life on a kibbutz up north but was always looking for a way out of the monotonous day-to-day regime. He caused so much havoc that they paid him a handsome sum to leave. With the money and in his early twenties, he headed for the hippy drug-driven paradise of sixties America where he got heavily involved in the Ken Kesey and Timothy Leary tune-in, drop-out culture. Somehow he found his way into Jim Morrison's (The Doors) immediate circle. Though eventually he returned to Israel after getting a bit too heavily into heroin.

I loved sitting outside his club, basking in the holy sun and eating chicken, fresh off the barbie, listening to his stories about Andy Warhol and The Factory. He even told me he had slept with Edie Sedgwick, Warhol's unfortunate muse at the time. I had no cause to disbelieve him.

Benzi was a fan of anything that was anti-authority. I started to teach him cockney rhyming slang and we would go up to gambling clubs in the town where I would sit behind the other players and tell Benzi what they had in their hands in London slang. You can take the boy out of Bermondsey but you can't take Bermondsey out of the boy, eh? The confused faces on the other card players were classic as the words 'bottle of glue' meaning two and 'cock and hen', ten, were banded about.

Benzi used to bung me a few shekels after we left. How I never got killed by these war-hardened four by twos (Jews), I'll never know but, hey, I was in the sun and 3611.239 miles away from grey, oppressive South East London.

One Saturday a month a new batch of volunteers would arrive at the kibbutz. This one Saturday they came from Finland and, apart from my friend Yossy who hated his race and country and classed himself as English, I had never met another Finnish person, but he well and truly set the bar. Yossy had dated a girl from Manchester for a few years and had adopted elements of her Mancunian dialect which left him with a northern twang in his Finnish accent. Yossy would get all emotional and become a mass of contradictions when he had a drink, and boy could he drink.

Like a true Viking he would sup vodka straight from the bottle, Odin looking down at him with pride, I am sure.

He told me a funny story about how some Vikings, back in the day, after a heavy night of mead drinking and rape, decided to get into a boat and invade Rome. So they set off from Norway in two boats to conquer the biggest empire in the world. With heavy hangovers and morsels of wild boar and God knows what else in their beards, they made their way to the coast of Italy. Approaching the shore, they saw light from the villages inland. They covertly landed the boats and stormed into a local village like maniacs. They did their rape and pillage thing then returned to their boats with whatever treasure they could muster. Thinking they'd pulled the numbers on Rome, they returned home and were held as conquering heroes. Lucky there was no Internet in those days.

With that story at the front of my mind, we greeted the modern-day Vikings with complimentary spiked banana juice. They were nice people, totally crazy but, hey, who wasn't in those days? One of the group was called Marjetta. We bonded right away; she was a bit older and wiser than the rest of the group. As the days went on, I found myself wanting to be with her more and more but was also aware that I didn't want to jump into any kind of relationship after just finishing the heavy one with Lorna and the fuck-up of prison still lingering inside my nut. She was keen but I resisted. It nearly happened one banana-intoxicated night on the roof of our hut when we were lying there looking at the star-blanketed night sky, but it didn't. Sometimes in life the heart speaks louder than the prick.

News filtered through that Bob Dylan was touring Israel and was coming to Jerusalem. Being fans, the kibbutz organised tickets to his show. I couldn't believe it, Bob fucking Dylan in the Holy city. As a bonus, Dylan had recently converted back to Judaism from Christianity and this was his first concert in Israel since the U-turn. We all piled into the kibbutz van and headed to the valley, residents and volunteers alike. As we entered Jerusalem the excitement was palpable. Arabs and Jews were all coming together in the name of music for the event. The moment transcended politics. Tom Petty and Roger McGuinn were the support acts and were sensational. Then the moment came, Dylan ambled onto the stage wearing a yarmulke and stood there just looking at the crowd for about a minute. Then came the word 'Shalom.' The crowd erupted. Dylan launched into 'Tangled up in Blue'. Oh my days, for the next couple of hours he played an energy-filled set of his classics. I was spellbound and blessed to be there.

Dylan wasn't the only star we were exposed to at that time. Back on the kibbutz, a rumour was spreading about a film extra casting in Jaffa for the third *Rambo* movie that was to be shot in the desert. They needed a stock of Russian soldier extras who, in turn, were to be slaughtered by the miniscule muscle-bound, lisping, Vietnam vet.

We all made a day of it and went along to try and get on the set as extras and earn a couple of hundred dollars for the work. We lined up outside an office in Jaffa. There were about twenty people from all parts of the world all vying for the work.

As I was smaller in height than the line in front, I stood on a curb to try to get an extra head above the rest. A door opened and, bosh, the legend that is Sylvester Stallone appeared. I remember thinking how small and prefabricated he looked. He walked up and down the line picking the biggest of the bunch and because my head was above the rest I was chosen. I stepped off the curb and immediately lost five inches of height. Ol' Syl looked a bit confused and promptly changed his mind about me. Later I asked one of his crew why he reneged like that. I was told that because he was small, he liked to pick big men to fight in his movies to make him look like the giant slayer he portrayed (fair enough) but five hundred dollars for a week's work, I should have worn Cuban-heeled army boots like him. I was gutted.

Yossy's time was nearly up on the kibbutz so we decided to go off to Egypt for a couple of weeks and he would leave the land of milk and honey from there. It was around my twenty-fifth birthday. The evening before we started our travels, we had a joint birthday and leaving party. It was a great night of boozing which ended with us all sitting around a fire singing and me getting my ear pierced as Yossy convinced me it would be a great gesture to Odin to keep us safe on our travels. Marjetta had bought me a little gold earring and someone put a cork on one side of my ear and pushed a pin through the other. Luckily I was anaesthetised by the dreaded banana juice.

With no sleep, the Viking and ex-prisoner made their way to the bus station, both fiercely hanging in the midday sun.

I fell asleep the moment my bottle and glass hit the seat. Next thing I knew we were off the bus and sitting on Mount Sinai on the Sinai Peninsula, the self-same mountain where Moses witnessed the forging of the ten commandments and the burning bush. There was no burning bush but plenty of burning kef. I wondered if the father of the Israelites was partial to a puff as well having spoken to a burning bush. I smoked a joint on the holy landmark as I listened to my old faithful Sony Walkman whilst looking over the desert. The location was timeless. The Eagles' 'Hotel California' was blasting in my ears. 'You can check out anytime you like but you can never leave'. All I can say is that it was a moment.

I bet the nuns from school would have been turning in their graves as I sucked on a large joint on this sacred ground.

We crossed the Sinai border and headed to the quaint little fishing village of Dahab. We were armed with a stash of coffee, pilfered from the volunteers' social area of the kibbutz. When in Dahab, we swapped the ill-gotten coffee for a couple of cigarette boxes full of weed, as ya do.

Our mission was to find a spot on the banks of the River Nile for the night where we could smoke the weed at sunset, watching the surrounding mountains turn to golden brown, but what ensued was a battle with the indigenous bugs that were every westerner's nightmare. They congregated on the stagnant surface of the Nile. After much swotting and cursing, we rolled out of our sleeping bags, built a fire and smoked another offering to Odin.

I had my guitar with me and I started strumming. A little caravan of Bedouin stopped nearby and started setting up their tents. One of them moved towards us. I whispered to Yossy that we might be in a bit of trouble. When he got close enough for us to hear, he lent forward and spoke the soft throaty words I'll never forget: 'You play "Hotel California"?' Synchronicity or what? I started playing the tune and he beckoned us over to his caravan. We nervously complied and I sat and played guitar. We broke bread with them. Every now and then my eyes would meet with Yossy's and we'd smile at the unfolding scene.

In the morning, with the backdrop of the mountains of Jordan, Yossy said his goodbyes and we promised to stay in touch, but we'd had our moment and if we should ever bump into each other again it wouldn't be down to a phone call, the universe would make it happen. Shalom, Yoss. The couple of weeks we spent in Egypt together is in the memory bank.

I returned to the kibbutz, minus the Viking and a shade wiser, or so I thought, and headed down to Benzi and The Place. I'd now been in Israel for over a year and Bermondsey never really featured in my head at all. One day, hit by a wave of nostalgia, I thought I'd phone the folks back home and let them know that I was okay. Plus I wanted to say hello to the ol' man as he'd been released from prison that year. The phone system on the kibbutz wasn't up to scratch and you had to reverse the charges if you wanted to call outside the country. So I dialled our home number and waited. My dad's voice came on.

'Shalom, Dad, how are you all?'

'I'm alright. You in trouble?'

'No.'

'Fuck me, how much is this call costing?'

'I don't know.'

The phone went dead. Nothing changes.

Sitting in town with Benzi one day, he lazily informed me that there was somebody he'd like me to meet. We trotted off to another part of town that I'd never been to before and didn't recognise a lot of the language that was being spoken; he told me it was Russian. He led me into a baker's shop and introduced me to a skinny man with rat-like features – who we will call the Russian – sitting around a table with a group of men who looked like they had just jumped out of a gangster movie. Benzi introduced me by my full name. The flat-nosed group were filling their faces with cakes and drinking coffee and didn't take much notice of me, which I duly appreciated as I felt a bit out of my league. I found out later that the Russian, who by the way, stank of malice, was the head of the mafia outfit based in the town and operated out of the baker's shop.

Benzi explained that the Russian was interested in changing dollars for shekels, undercutting the bank rate and would I want to be his man on the kibbutz. I was running out of money so I agreed. As we were leaving, the Russian called me by my surname and brought a bag out from under the table. He took a block of cannabis out.

'You sell this as well.'

Alarm bells started ringing in my head but what harm could it do, selling pot to hippies. I took the puff.

He threw another box to me full of Pastila and Ptichye Moloko Russian deserts. I thanked him.

'You have forgotten something, Webber?'

'Have I?'

He took a bundle of shekel notes and threw them at me.

'You get me American dollars.'

We left the shop.

'Fuck, Benzi what you getting me into?'

'You need money, now you have.'

I found out the bank rate and set about undercutting it and started to change dollars and sell puff on the kibbutz, idiot that I was.

I'd pop into the baker's a couple of times a week, each time with a few hundred dollars that I had changed. Barry and another couple of people were buying the kef and I started getting maybe sixty quid every now and then. It doesn't sound a lot but it kept me going. What I forgot was that nothing stayed low on the kibbutz. The communal nature of the place meant that no secrets could be kept and loose lips, sooner or later, really do sink ships. One day, whilst I was picking bananas with Gabby, he turned to me and got straight to the point.

'Webber, you must stop what you are doing.'

I'd become close to Gabby and his wonderful family to the point where he would invite me to his home on the kibbutz and his beautiful wife, Tammi, would cook food, which was a rare thing for a resident to do.

They never strived to build relationships with volunteers as our presence there was so transient.

'What, you want me to stop picking bananas?'

'Where are you getting the shekels to swap for dollars?'

I was taken aback. Do I lie or tell the truth? I decided on the latter. 'You stop now, these people are *lo tov.*' No good.

We carried on with the work but a vibe was apparent. I felt, for some reason, that I had let Gabby down. The next time I went to the baker's I told the Russian that I was stopping the money changing. He didn't like it but he was a rat and untrustworthy and Gabby was my friend.

I told Gabby I had stopped. He was pleased and our relationship got back on track.

I had organised an evening at Benzi's place, just me with an acoustic guitar as some members of the house band couldn't do the gig due to army commitments. The night started great. I was on a chair on the stage and people would come up and do songs like Simon and Garfunkel's 'The Boxer' and 'Rocky Raccoon' by the Beatles.

In the break the drummer of Erez's band, a guy called Hadad who was in the audience, joined me outside to smoke a joint. We fired it up and, after a few minutes, all hell broke loose. I was jumped on by a plain-clothed, Israeli part-time scuffer who threw me over a parked car and cuffed my hands. Another did the same to Hadad. The scuffer reached into my pocket and pulled out the kef. I'm fucked, I thought.

I had watched a movie when I was in the UK called *Midnight Express* all about the consequences of smuggling cannabis resin in these sorts of countries. They try to show the world that they are making an effort to halt drugs in their country. My thoughts shuddered as I remembered the outcome of the film. We were thrown into a police car.

'Le'an atem lohim otee?' Where are you taking me?

'Atah medaber anglit?' Do you speak English? I stuttered.

His only reply was, 'Sheket.' Be quiet.

He drove us to the local police station and I was thrown into a cell. Well, when I call it a cell, my true meaning is a shithole. There were two sets of rotten bunk beds and three of them were occupied by Arabs. Shit. I'm either going to die here or get used as an old rag doll. The death thought was the most appealing. Another country, another jail, was this going to be my life? What about my deal with the ultimate complexity, surely it didn't end here? I was forced to make another one with it. I pleaded to the cell's filthy ceiling with my tail between my legs.

The Israeli government liked to make examples of foreigners who broke the law. I had about half an ounce of puff in my pocket. I was thinking, surely I can't get more than two years for it. The thing that was most heartbreaking about my predicament was the thought that the Israeli scuffers would go onto the kibbutz and search my room, finding my little stash of kef and dollars that were tucked neatly under my bed. I also had a bong in the room. Gabby would definitely find out. The door to the cell opened. An officer ordered, 'Yatsa.' Out.

He took me to the front desk and told me to 'Shev' and 'Sheket.' Sit down and shut up. My friend Jim had seen the unfortunate incident outside the club and grabbed another friend Amir, who was an Israeli resident of the kibbutz – they were there waiting at the desk. The cop started to converse with Amir. I feigned a smile, unconvincingly.

Over time I'd been teaching Surrey Jim the art of cockney rhyming slang.

'Jim, listen to what I'm going to say.'

He nodded attentively.

'In the shovel and broom (room) under my uncle Ned (bed), there is some huffpay.' Jim stood thinking, mouthing the words.

'Uncle Ned?'

'Jim, listen mate, I could be in the process of getting shagged by Arabs here, not to mention going to prison.'

The cop began to get aggressive because I was talking to Jim. 'Sheket.' Be quiet, the cop demanded.

'Jim, take no notice of this big-nosed cunt,' I countered, knowing he never spoke my language. Jim and Amir laughed at this.

'Do you understand shovel and broom, Jim?'

'Sheket achshav!' Be quiet now! The cop was revving up. The penny dropped with Jim.

'Uncle Ned, bed,' he shouted.

'Go Jim, before they get there.' I didn't have to ask twice as Jim headed for the door. Amir was talking in Hebrew to the cop as Jim dashed past him.

The cop directed the next words to me. I asked Amir to translate. 'He wants your passport.' The cop nodded his head.

Amir chose now to inform me that he thought I was in big trouble. I told Amir not to say anything else to the police, especially that I was staying on the kibbutz, but the cop already knew. I was taken back to the cell. Was it the rat Russian? Was this his doing because I had stopped changing money and selling puff for him? I laid down on the bottom bunk, deflated and feeling very alone. Then I remembered someone once told me that Arabs were a bit dubious around mad people because they believed that their madness was a gift from Allah.

I jumped up from the bed, puffing my chest and making all sorts of grunting sounds. I fell to the floor and manically started to do press-ups and beat my chest like a gorilla, then I got back on the bed laughing out loud. I think they got the point. One of the Arabs could speak a bit of English and he introduced himself as Abdel. I told him my apprehensions regarding our fellow cell mates. He laughed and spoke to the other two in Arabic who also laughed. In the early hours of the morning, before the cock crowed, I lay there, staring at the well-worn slats of the top bunk. I felt dirty and ashamed and all down to a poxy bit of puff. I'd fucked it all up again. When would I learn?

The only means of washing in the cell was an open pipe that protruded from the wall. The toilet was a hole in the floor which smelt disgusting. I lay on the rotten bed and closed my eyes.

The only thing stopping me from bursting into tears was showing face in front of my hardened cell mates. I spent two days in the cell. The only good thing that came out of the experience was the little, broken English chats I had with Abdel about God and the country's politics. After much soul-searching the cell door opened and I was ordered out. This time, after some processing in an office, I was told that I should go and never come back. I couldn't believe my ears, the ultimate complexity had come good again. I found out later that the town's chief prosecutor was Hadad's father and he had made some sort of deal for his son to be released for fear of embarrassment. In releasing his son, they had to release me. What a divine bit of muzzle (luck). I was saved from entering the divine comedy once more. But, I must say, these deals with God were thought-provoking.

I took a taxi back to the kibbutz. Marjetta was crying and mumbling that she thought she had seen the last of me. After my shower, Jim told me that when he'd arrived back from the police station, he found my stash and threw it away in the banana field. Mick, the hippy teacher, had taken care of the bong. He had broken it up into little bits and scattered it all around the banana field. The vision of this six-foot odd, lanky hippy bounding through the field breaking up and scattering the bong made me laugh. I loved him for that.

Then I got the call which I was dreading. David, the head honcho, wanted to see me in his office. It was like being back at school again but this time it was serious. He told me that I must leave the kibbutz immediately. I didn't argue.

I asked if I could have a couple of day's grace to try and organise some money and a ticket home. He said no, I was to pack my stuff and leave immediately. I understood. I spent that night in Benzi's bar, sleeping amongst the rats and bugs.

The next morning Erez came to the bar. I told him what had happened and he invited me to his mother's house for some food and a wash. I accepted with a grateful heart. As we walked into Erez's family home, his mother took one look at me and started screaming. Fuck me, I thought, I'm not that ugly. She was screaming at Erez to get me out. I noticed that there was a numbered tattoo on her arm. She had also been a prisoner of the Nazis. I had to accept that my Aryan looks were disturbing to certain people in this country, so I left. Everything I owned was in a rucksack and a case. I told Erez that I had no money to buy a ticket home and all he said was, 'Join the band.' Genius! But where was I to live? He suggested I move in with Gersham, the keyboard player. Eureka! Gersham and Hadad, who I had been arrested with, shared an apartment. Not a good idea, I thought at first but soon found out that Hadad had been moved by his parents to his aunt's in Ashkelon, so Gersham was on his own. So there it was, life was picking up again but I was becoming weary of my self-inflicted stupidness. Maybe they were right in school and I was just a plain and simple fool. I had just been miraculously released from what could have been the fifth level of Dante's masterpiece and for the first time in Israel, I had no plan of action.

We found a drummer called Omri and he moved in with me and Gersham. We started rehearsing at Benzi's gaff. It wasn't long until we had a set together and our first gig, which we did for free for Benzi.

The only thing that I was worried about was if the police found out I was still there.

Our first gig was momentous. The Place was full to the brim with native Israelis and kibbutz volunteers. I was playing an old electric guitar that Erez managed to cadge off someone. It was hard work but it did the job. That night, Erez and I went home with a couple of Swedish girls and swapped rock 'n' roll for an evening with ABBA.

After a few more gigs I got sick of playing the shit guitar that Erez had borrowed. Back in England, I had a vintage Fender Stratocaster and I decided to go home and bring it back. I borrowed one hundred and fifty dollars from a Danish friend, Holger, a volunteer and another true Viking from the kibbutz. It was really big of him to do that as he had no way of knowing if I was ever coming back again and it was a fair sum in those days. Thanks for the trust, Holger.

I said goodbye to Marjetta as she was going back to Finland in the next few weeks. I felt my nose grow bigger as I promised that I would go see her in Valhalla. A couple of days later, I bought a ticket and headed to the airport. I was nervous as I headed towards the security point at Ben Gurion airport. I was sure my puff escapade would be on a police file so I was expecting a strong pull but it all went swimmingly and I walked straight through.

I sat on the plane with a tingling feeling of anticipation at the prospect of returning home.

I pondered on the mad chain of events that had led me on this journey. It was the first time that I was able to reflect objectively on life and its strange occurrences.

CHAPTER FIFTEEN

M e, my earring and my new-found hippy mentality landed back in the UK at Heathrow. After my time in Israel, the weather and temperature in the UK was a shock.

I didn't tell anyone that I was coming back; I thought that I'd surprise them.

I made my way by tube to London Bridge then got on a bus (sound familiar?). The world that I grew up in looked so grey, wet and unchanged. I was a little excited at the thought of seeing my tribe again.

I arrived at my parents' flat and took a breath before opening the door. I stepped in and met the ol' man in the passage. He looked at me, noticed Marjetta's gift in my ear lobe and said, 'What the fuck have you got in your ear, you silly bastard. All them front-wheel skids [yids] have turned you into an iron [poof].' Hello to you as well, Dad.

I never got back into the vibe of England, I just wanted to get me and my trusty Fender back to Israel ASAP. I buzzed about for a bit and got some money together. Socialising with anyone didn't interest me at all, I had tunnel vision. I got myself a couple of grand then booked the plane back to Israel. I phoned Erez (from a phone box, the ol' man would be pleased to hear) and a couple of weeks later, with the trusty Stratocaster over my shoulder and a friend of mine's brother, Bob, who was at a loss in the UK, headed back to the future.

We took a cab from Ben Gurion airport, arrived at kibbutz Shiller and covertly sneaked in. The first thing I did was pay Holger back his money.

'I bet you thought you'd never see that again.'

'Why would I think that?' came his unexpected reply. 'You're my friend.' The sentiment wasn't wasted on me.

I left Bob at the kibbutz and went to meet Erez in town. We then slipped over to Benzi's club. On the way Erez informed me that we had our first gig in Jaffa the following Friday. Off to Jaffa again, this time no movie stars were the incentive, just pure rock 'n' roll.

Jaffa is the oldest part of Tel Aviv, an ancient port city also known as Yafo in Hebrew. Yafo nicked its fame in history for its association with the biblical stories of Jonah, Solomon and Saint Peter, as well as the mythological story of Andromeda and Perseus. A nice place to start the new adventure I thought. Through Benzi I rented a room in an apartment in Rehovot that was owned by a wretch of a hunchbacked Arab called Maliki, who looked like he would rob his own grandmother. The room was situated on top of the town's bus station. I unpacked and had a cup of Maliki's coffee, for which he charged me a shekel, then took off for a band rehearsal. At the end of the rehearsal, we had to come up with a name for the band. Many names got bandied about, one of which was The Locusts, a nod to the Beatles and our biblical setting. I laugh out loud as the memory kicks in. We decided on the name The Others. Erez got it but the other members of the band couldn't get their heads around it.

That night a few of my old friends from the kibbutz came to my new room for a party and a smoke. Maliki was hovering about like a weasel, checking and smelling out the mix of western girls. He was starting to make them feel uncomfortable so I told him politely to lech tiz-day-en (fuck off). He looked at me with daggers as he left the room like a wounded Nile mosquito.

In the morning I informed the leftover stragglers about our gig in Jaffa and they all promised to come. I stayed in bed all day accompanied by Ulrika, a Swedish girl who was as mad as a hatter in all departments and a bit of a rock chick to boot. My first and only groupie.

Friday arrived and we packed up a van with all our stuff then headed to Jaffa. As we passed through Tel Aviv we were stopped by the police. Erez and the rest of the band were quite rude to them as I cowered down in the back. When the police left I asked, 'How could you speak to them like that?'

'Fuck them,' Erez retorted. 'They are only people like us just doing a job. Anyway, we have no kef, so no problem.' I reached into my pocket and pulled out a slab of gear. 'Chara,' (shit) said Erez. We got away with that one. The rest of the journey was full of pseudo-philosophical conversations on the writings of Friedrich Nietzsche and Immanuel Kant, of which I knew and understood nothing.

We arrived at the bar we were playing at. Ulrika, my new-found groupie, and a few other friends from the kibbutz were already there and they helped us unload and set up. We were to get a hundred dollars for a two-hour set.

The crowds started coming as the promoter had worded the posters as if we were a famous English band, except he spelt it The Udders. Ten o'clock and we were ready to go on. We plugged in and Avid, the lead guitarist, launched into the 'Johnny Be Good' intro. The crowd loved it and for the next two hours we played songs from The Doors, The Beatles, Janice Joplin, Jefferson Airplane and by the end of the night the whole joint was jumping. When the gig was finished the owner, who spoke perfect English, paid us our money and, with dollar signs in his eyes, asked us back the next week. I said I'd let him know. I wasn't going to do it again for a hundred dollars, he'd have to come up with another fifty, so I took his number. As we were packing the van, I saw two Israeli lads bullying a small Arab lad. I ran over and stood in front of the Arab and informed the aggressors that if they wanted to punch him they would have to punch me first, so one of the Israelis did. A right-hander straight on my chin. I fell back onto a wall, dazed. I gathered my thoughts then returned the compliment. I caught him with a blinder and his friend ran away. We were fighting when Erez, Ulrika and the owner broke it up. 'What the fuck are you doing?' Erez exclaimed. 'He's only an Arab.' I was ready to punch Erez as well. The bully Israeli who I was fighting started cussing at me. I didn't understand what he was saying but certainly understood the intent. I punched him again. This time he ran off and Erez informed me that he was swearing holy revenge.

The van journey home to Rehovot was tense to say the least. I was angry at Erez.

We had a heated debate about the politics and anger between Arabs and Jews. All down to a story about two brothers in a fictional book. When the van stopped in Rehovot, I steamed off with Ulrika at my heels. It was around 1 a.m. We headed for Benzi's place. He was closing up but when he saw me and Ulrika he opened the door and we went in for a night cap.

I told him what had happened but he had no sympathy for my story. He explained to me about the Hezbollah, a Shia Islamic militant group who were sending videos over to the Israeli intelligence showing their soldiers biting the heads off live puppy dogs and informing the Israelis that the same fate awaits any Israeli soldier they capture. I saw his point. The next day I shook hands with Erez and we agreed it would not be a good idea to go back to Jaffa. For the next few months we played at Benzi's. He gave us food, drink and a hundred dollars a gig.

One evening, Ulrika and I were just chilling in my room when the door burst open and a group of Israeli uniformed police entered. It was like the raid on Entebbe. Two of them jumped on me, another grabbed Ulrika, who was screaming like a Nattmara (Swedish Banshee). *Fuck it, here we go again,* I thought. They searched the room from head to Ulrika's toes looking for kef but they didn't find anything. The whole situation stunk of my landlord, Maliki. After checking my passport and papers the police reluctantly left but not after telling me, in no uncertain terms, that I was not welcome in the town or the country anymore. Fucking déjà vu.

I told them I was in a band and we had gigging commitments, that I had four months left on my visa and when it had run out, I would leave the country never to return. As they found nothing incriminating in the room, the deal was struck.

As they left I saw the landlord cowering as the police were chastising him.

I packed up all my gear and left the apartment. I crashed at Gersham's again but in my head I was coming to the end of my time in Israel so I started processing the thought of going home.

I'd spent almost two years out there. I'd been involved in mafia business, changing money and selling puff, banished from a kibbutz with no money or ticket home, locked up in a police cell with the prospect of prison and joined a band. I think my cup had well and truly overflowed. I plodded along with the band but my heart was not really in it. It was time to leave Israel for good. I told Erez I was off and promised that I would get something together back in England and call him over to play bass. We had a final gig at Benzi's and what a gig. Everyone, including the Russian rat, turned up – it went on all night.

Benzi and I had formed a nice relationship; I told him that he would be welcome in England any time.

CHAPTER SIXTEEN

I landed in Blighty a changed man, purged from the reason I went out there in the first place, and moved back into my flat in Casby House.

I didn't have a clue what I was going to do, so after a couple of months finding my feet again, I set about looking for like-minded people to start a band. I found two brothers that lived up by the Thames called Rob and Geoff Killick. Geoff was an all-round musician, there was not a musical instrument he couldn't set his hand to. His brother was a drummer. To keep the wolf from the door whilst gathering minstrels, my other line of work was fly-pitching. An old school friend that I hooked up with called Tony and I used to go to Berwick Street in Soho and buy dodgy tin, gold-coloured earrings. We'd buy the earrings, boxes and a strip of nine-carat gold stickers then spend the night putting the product together. Each box would hold a pair of earrings on a red velvet tray in a small case. In the morning we would head to a market like Petticoat Lane and set up. We'd have a little table where we'd sit the case on, two look outs, who would scan for the market scuffers, and a rik. The job of the rik, usually a girl, would be to buy the product first.

When all was ready we would open the case and scream at the top of our voices, 'Nine-carat gold earrings, stolen property for sale, a pound a pair,' then we'd go into the spiel of how 'they never fell off the back of a lorry, we bleeding well got up and took them ourselves and buy them quick because if a man in blue comes that way, we'll have to run the other way as fast as our little legs can carry us.' We said it was stolen so people would believe they might actually be nine-carat gold. Then the rik would step forward and buy a couple of pairs.

Seeing that someone had bought the product gave the public confidence and they would all be slinging pound notes at us, thinking that they were buying real gold. We didn't really think that we were ripping anyone off as you could buy the same earrings in Ratner's jewellery shop for £2.50. The lookouts would be scanning the market for the boys in blue and if one came along they would shout a hearty, "Ave it up,' which meant a scuffer was heading our way. We'd then smash the case shut, no matter if a hand was in it or not, and scarper down the lane to a café where we'd have a cup of coffee until the coast was clear and set up again. Some days we'd earn five hundred pounds. We'd travel all over the place – Brighton promenade, Hastings – wherever crowds gathered. I'm sure we were responsible for a lot of people walking about with green ears in those days.

Erez flew over from the Holy Land and moved in with me. We started getting it together with Geoff and Rob. After about a month of solid rehearsing we started putting a few local gigs on. We had a great set and great musicians; Erez, Geoff, Rob and I were gonna conquer the world. We started to include songs like 'London Town' that I had written into the set. Our first gig together was at the Bermond centre, the self-same one that housed Lois and Julie, who were instrumental in putting the 'Eddie Webber is Innocent' march together at the time of my fit up. On the afternoon of the gig, we set up our amps and stuff not really knowing if anyone was going to turn up but we had nothing to worry about. It was a full house. We played a stonking set and the tunes went down a treat. I think it was the first local gig of its kind. As far as I know, no one in our Bermondsey circle had formed a band then put it out there.

Over the next few months we started to play all the pubs around the area. I loved it but my criminal friends found it all a bit confusing.

Back in my flat, it was getting a bit intense with Erez and me both living there. All he'd do all day was sit and smoke puff, and it started to drive me mad as I didn't seem to have any space with someone there all the time. I insisted that he get a job. I went down to the local café

Rosie's on Jamaica Road, and asked if they had any vacancies for a hobo Israeli. As luck would have it they did and Erez became the café's new dishwasher but I don't think he liked it very much. Hey, sometimes a travelling 'four by two' has to do what a travelling 'four by two' has to do. It was quite funny, though, as Erez developed a taste for bacon, a swinish no-no for most Israelis but Erez most definitely was not like most Israelis.

I started to sell a bit of puff again to make some money, not in a big way, just to friends, but life was good, we were on the road to stardom.

One afternoon I was in my flat when the phone went. I put the receiver to my ear and heard a familiar voice saying, 'Webber.' It was Benzi. He wanted to come to the UK and stay with me for a while. I thought about the implications of having two Israelis staying with me for a moment but then welcomed him over. When I told Erez later that night, he shook his head and told me I was mad to have him here.

Benzi landed on our fair shores three weeks later. I picked him up at the airport. It was his first time in the UK.

I thought that I would take a detour through Peckham on the way home, which was a very different place in those days. Benzi looked a bit anxious as we drove through Peckham Rye.

'Webber, I thought we had problems in our country, this looks like Harlem.'

I laughed.

We arrived at Casby just as the human dishwasher finished his shift in the café. In we went and while having a joint, we decided then and there to go to Amsterdam, as Benzi had always wanted to see the place. Two days later, Benzi and I jumped in the car and were heading for the Harwich ferry. Seven hours later, we disembarked at the Hook of Holland then promptly headed to the Sodom and Gomorrah that was Amsterdam. We found a seedy hotel that was run by Arabs which we booked for a couple of days. Benzi asked me not to mention he was a Jew, so when they asked where we were from I told them that he was an Apache Indian. We parked our belongings in the room and headed for a café to eat. The menu came, full of Dutch delight and we ordered a couple of joints, some cake and a coffee then looked through the window at the colourful passing trade. When we were sufficiently stoned we went for a wander. Two dark-skinned fellows emerged from a crack in the wall. Emanating demonic vibrations they slid up to us and offered to sell us a bit of coke. I told them we weren't in the market for any but Benzi insisted, having not tasted the devil's marching powder since his jaunt to the States in the seventies. One of the fellows pulled out a wrap and handed it to me. I opened it, took a bit on my finger and rubbed it. It felt coarse, like powdered glass.

They laughed as I told them to fuck off and they promptly pulled out another wrap, this one feeling silky and oily. We paid the men and returned to the hotel room where we both indulged. It was like rocket fuel. A few minutes later I felt the old feeling of principles and morals departing.

'I want to fuck an African,' Benzi declared, out of nowhere. Well, we were in Amsterdam. We put the coke in a drawer and off we trundled to the red-light district where paying for a brass was totally welcomed by the clog-wearing powers that be. After browsing the windows checking out the women, Benzi made his exotic choice. Only downside was she looked like a rough Winifred Atwell.

'You sure?' I said scrunching my face. Benzi flew into the gaff like a builder on his lunch break in a pie 'n' mash shop. I wandered around the seedy square for a bit, waiting for Benzi and Winifred's duet to finish and stumbled into a blues bar where a band was playing Muddy Water songs from his album 'After the Rain'. After about an hour I suddenly thought, *Shit, Benzi!*

The music was so good that I had forgotten about him. I dashed back to Winifred's gaff and she was back in the window. I surveyed the vista in the hope of seeing my six-foot-odd Apache Indian's head above the rest but alas there was no sight of him. I navigated my way back to our hotel in the hope that he was there. On entering our room, there he was, bent over a table hoovering up the rest of the oats and barley. He looked up with a trail of powder stuck to his nose. 'I love Amsterdam, Webber, let's stay for a week and buy some more cocaine.'

We went in search of the demons, bought another gram and spent the rest of the day and night drinking and talking bollocks. It was daylight when we returned to the hotel after another wait in the red-light district whilst Benzi and Winifred made some more music together.

When I eventually got to bed, I remember thinking, *What the fuck am I doing here?*

I felt a bit off orbit. When I awoke, after having about two hours of wired sleep, I looked over at Benzi who was snoring like a happy khazir (pig).

Fuck all this, I'm going home, I told myself. I was missing my life. My head felt like an elephant had pissed in it. I ran to the bathroom and was promptly sick as a pig, waking the big fellow up in the process.

'I'm going home.' Benzi tried to convince me to stay but my mind was made up. He decided that he would stay for a bit longer, no doubt Winifred was on his mind but I was off home.

A week later I got a call from him asking me to wire some money to a bank for him as Winifred and the like had robbed him. I wired him the money the next morning and he booked a flight back to the UK. When he arrived at Gatwick, he looked like a shell of a man. On the way home he told me he had taken heroin out there and could I get him some here. That was it for me…time to go home, Benzi boy. Later that day Erez shook his head at me. 'I told you,' he said. Benzi tried to protest but I wasn't having a scag head wrapped round me and told him that, in my experience, they cause nothing but trouble. The next week Benzi went back to the Holy Land and I haven't seen him since. Mazel Tov, Benzi.

It was now time to talk to Erez about him getting his own space. He had no choice but to go over to north London where many Israelis had settled. Erez met some people that had a room going so he took it and got a job as a taxi driver.

The band was fading fast as the other band members started to drift off the idea of becoming rock stars.

Mum with her hands full
Mum, Dad and me

Jackio and me in an obligatory school photo
A sanctuary for wasps

Me all dressed in pink after a gypsy told my parents I was going to be a girl

The first time I ever received a conscious shock: getting stung by a wasp!

My grandad on my dad's side. He was a Navy man

My grandparents on my mum's side

Me rocking out in my apartment in Israel

With Erez, Geoff and Rob rocking the Bermond Centre

My first ever show entertaining the troops on the kibbutz

Part 2: Alison

Chapter Seventeen

I was on that road again with no direction other than the desire to be involved in the arts in one way or another. Someone told me about a theatre company in Rotherhithe called the London Bubble. It was a company whose ethos was to bring theatre to those who would not normally visit the theatre. It sounded right up my street and a good place to start.

I entered the building, walked up a couple of flights of stairs and entered an office. There was a man who looked like he had some authority talking to a group of young people, who were all sitting drinking tea and eating biscuits. I approached him and got straight to the point: 'I want to be an actor and I was told to come here.'

He smiled and said, 'Well you've come to the right place then.'

He introduced himself as Adrian Jackson and invited me to join the evening's workshop. We all went up to a big hall at the top of the building. Adrian scattered the group and started a warm up playing drama games. I felt a little self-conscious and asked if I could sit at the side and just observe. I sat on a chair and watched as the group formed a circle and started an improvisation game.

One person would stand in the middle of the circle and another would step in, then they two would start to improvise a scenario. When everybody had taken a turn it was back to the games. I suddenly had the urge to leave the place as this was not what I was expecting. I raised my hand to get Adrian's attention and asked if I could use the loo, with the full intention of hightailing it out of the place never to return. I had the notion of being a movie star, not playing what I thought were childish games. As I was halfway down the stairs with the exit door in sight, Adrian called to me from the top of the stairs and asked me the magic question, 'You are coming back, aren't you?'

This knocked me a little off whack and I turned and stuttered, 'Y-y-yes, course I am.' Kicking myself, I entered the toilet, gave it a minute and returned to the group.

Adrian gave us all a short play written by the German dramatist Bertolt Brecht called *A Respectable Wedding*. He assigned each of us a character from the piece; my part was the father of the bride. We spent the next hour reading and talking about the play. At the end of the session, Adrian informed us that he wanted us to start working on it with a view to performing it in a theatre. After taking a big gulp, I took the play home that night and read it again. This was it, the real deal and the start of a new exciting journey. Doubts and fears of performing live theatre filled my mind.

I had never read a play before, let alone one by Bertolt Brecht, but the farce seemed to resonate. I loved the way Brecht ruthlessly laid into the apparent perfection and false morality of the aspiring working class.

The play reaches its peak with a wedding that dissolves into chaos. I actually related to the oppressed bridegroom whose special day turns into a nightmare. It was reminiscent of my life so far.

I couldn't wait to get back to the Bubble to start rehearsing. Adrian was very clever at getting his perspective of the play across. We started to improvise scenes and in the process I started to learn some of the convention of theatre and how to shape up a character. Adrian would tell us to work on finding an aspect of truth within ourselves that we could wield onto the character.

I felt at home at the London Bubble and with Adrian, it was a little creative oasis, smack in the centre of Bermondsey, unique for me at that time. We performed *A Respectable Wedding* at, of all places, The Bermond Centre.

It was a fun show. I wish we'd had access to a video camera in those days as no footage exists of the first show I ever did and I would love to see it again and cringe. After that show we put on an improvised night in the Bubble's tent. This was a huge tent that used to go up in parks and other green pastures of London.

After a year at the Bubble, and with a few more productions under my belt, it was time to progress on my road to stardom. I went looking for another acting course. I found one and the one I found changed my life forever and a day.

Someone had mentioned a drama course at Morley College in Lambeth. I made some enquiries and found out that to get into the course you had to audition. The auditions were being held on the Thursday and Friday of that week.

Sod it, in for a penny, in for a pound, I thought. I jumped on the oxo cube (tube) and crossed the tracks from SE16 to SE1, doing the Lambeth walk, heading for 61 Westminster Bridge Rd. As I neared the college building I was met with a queue that nearly reached around the block. *Sod this,* I thought. *I must be able to get to the front somehow.* So I slowly started walking to the front and tried to slip in, nonchalantly.

'Oi!' someone shouted, in an alien posh voice. 'There's a queue you know.'

I thought about my response before putting my hands up and, with tail between my legs, made my way to the back of the line. It seemed to take forever to move so, me being me, I decided that Morley College wasn't for me. Flipping the bird at the universe, I headed back to the mean streets. That night I remember going through torment as I lay in my bed. *What's the matter with you?* I thought to myself. *You want to be an actor, get back down there tomorrow.* I sometimes wish I hadn't listened to the reasonable voice of torment. It would have saved me a lot of future gut-wrenching heartache and poverty.

I decided to go back the next day and suffer for my peace of mind. As I approached the college, though, all was different. There wasn't a queue in sight.

I entered the building and asked at least three different people the way to the drama auditions and still got lost. Two years finding my way around Israel and here I was lost in a building in Lambeth. I couldn't help but chuckle to myself. After a while and many directions later, I found the hallowed ground of the drama department. As I entered through double doors I found a group of people gathered on some stairs. They were all busy mumbling to themselves, giving their audition speeches a last polish. I was drawn to a guy who was sitting on his own on a step with what seemed like a constant smile on his face. ''Allo, mate, is this where the drama thing is?'

'Hee hee,' he responded.

I sat down next to him. 'My name is Eddie.'

He introduced himself as Michael Parle and we shook hands. 'So, what's the coup here?'

'Fuck knows,' Mick replied, 'I think we have to do an audition speech.'

'Audition speech?' *What the...*! I didn't have one. 'What speech are you doing?' I asked.

'One from the film *Dirty Harry*,' Mick answered.

'What scene?' I enquired.

'You feeling lucky, punk...'

'Ah that one.' I was impressed.

We chatted about the London Bubble. I told him to come down there, then the double doors opened and, all I can say is, an entity entered. It was like a thunderbolt hit me as one of the most beautiful women I had ever seen glided through the door, all blonde and classy. She parked herself on a step. Her creative, independent aura was spellbinding. Mick's name was called to go in for his gun-toting audition.

I had tunnel vision as I moved towards what I can only describe as perfection. I sat down next to her.

'Hello,' I coyly spurted out. 'My name is Eddie, are you here for the audition?' *Silly question, I suppose.*

'Yes.' Her voice was soft and, dare I say, very posh.

'And your name?' I enquired.

'Ali.'

'As in Baba?'

The witticism fell on deaf ears. 'No, as in Alison.'

I heard my name called to go in and entered the theatre to face a three-man audition panel sat behind a table looking very reminiscent of the three wise monkeys: Peter, Brian and Roy. I was directed to a chair in front of them.

'So, tell us about yourself,' one of the panel said.

How long you got? I thought to myself. I told them a little about what I was doing around that time, keeping it quite tame of course, touching on Israel and ending up with the fly-pitching market work.

Peter asked what audition speech I was to do. I told him that I had just done a production of Brecht's *A Respectable Wedding* with the London Bubble and could give them a bit of that if they so desired.

Peter, who I warmed to immediately, asked if he could hear my fly-pitching pitch. I stood up and launched into my nine-carat gold, stolen property spiel. I think they must have thought I was crazy as they didn't say much after I finished. As I stepped out of the door, Ali asked what happened. I, apparently, so Ali says, spoke for about five minutes without answering her question. I said goodbye to Mick and with Venus in my head I strutted back to Bermondsey. I felt good about doing the audition but for some reason couldn't get Ali out of my head.

I returned back to the Bubble and carried on learning the craft from Adrian.

A few weeks later the letter tumbled through the door. I picked it up and silently registered the Kennington postmark. I ripped open the letter. I'd got in! I felt proud. Next time I was at the Bubble I told Adrian; he was happy for me. With the addition of Mick, who had taken me up on my invitation, we started working on a production of William Shakespeare's *Macbeth,* which Adrian renamed *MacBeff* and gave me the lead role. Now it was getting serious. Mick was cast as the heir-apparent Malcolm. I went over to French's book store in the West End to get a copy of the play, having no idea about Shakespeare. I vaguely remembered hearing about him between dozes in a history class at school. That night I ran a bath and got my nose stuck into the play. The beauty of the pictures created by the writing was so cinematic.

Besides, this Duncan hath borne his faculties so meek, hath been so clear in his great office, that his virtues will plead like angels, trumpet-tongued, against the deep damnation of his taking-off; And pity, like a naked newborn babe, striding the blast, or heaven's cherubim, horsed upon the sightless couriers

of the air, shall blow the horrid deed in every eye, that tears
shall drown the wind.

Wow, great imagery.

We started rehearsing and Adrian translated the text to us perfectly. A black girl called Pauline was cast as Lady M, which was great casting. Especially for Bermondsey in those days.

At the same time, I started the Morley theatre course. On the first day we all found ourselves sitting in the rehearsal room. We were an eclectic mix to say the least, Mick included. I scanned the place, no Ali. Oh well, some ya win and some ya lose. A week later, the door opened and in stepped Venus. I smiled to myself and whispered to Mick, 'I'm going to marry her.' Our eyes met; I'm sure I was more affected than she was but game on.

Morley was a great course. The teachers were real and all working actors or writers. As the months passed, Ali and I started to become good friends and one day I invited myself around to her flat in Clapham. Armed with a dozen red roses and my trusty acoustic guitar, I jumped into my beat-up VW camper van and headed to the posh side of town. I remember the butterflies in my stomach as I knocked on her door. We spent a comfortable afternoon playing the guitar and me singing odes to love.

Ali told me she was a born-again Christian and was a regular churchgoer, a definite hurdle I had to overcome but, as they say, slowly, slowly catch the monkey. When it was time to leave I was on cloud nine and in no doubt that I wanted to be with her. Only trouble was, she was in a relationship with a geezer called George from Greece, a hiccup to say the least.

Back in Morley College we had to pick a scene to perform in front of the class. I chose one from David Mamet's *Sexual Perversity in Chicago*. It was the scene where the character Bernard Litko is trying to hit on a girl. God indeed works in mysterious ways as the female character's name was Joan Webber. Who would I ask to do the scene with me? No brainer. I was in my flat in Casby House looking at the telephone, heart racing as my finger shakily dialled her number. I toyed with the thought of putting the phone down but then Ali answered.

I can't believe how nervous I was. I stuttered out my request and she said yes. I put the phone down and punched the air. Step one out of the way, as I knew we would have to spend time together rehearsing the scene. Art was indeed imitating life. The next time we were at college, we had to stand in front of the class and explain the scene we had chosen. Ali and I stood side by side and I remember doing the talking. Brian asked what the motivation was behind my choice to work with Ali as Joan wasn't posh. I muttered something stupid and a knowing giggle erupted from the class. Now, Brian was an amazing teacher but was sometimes void of necessary tact.

'I know the play,' he said. 'You want to get into her knickers.'

'Eh?' I'm not usually stuck for words but his statement stopped me dead.

'Your character. He wants to try and get into Joan's knickers.'

Another ripple of giggles. I looked at Mick who was grinning like a Cheshire cat. I could almost hear the 'hee hee'. Ali was oblivious to the sniggers as she was only there for the scene. So we got to it – the scene that is. I had to grab her when I could as she had a busy life. It was a really nice world when I was with her and we shaped a nice little scene which we performed to the class, apart from the sound of a cockney attempting an American accent. Ali invited the class to her 21st birthday party at her flat, so after college we all piled into the camper van and headed to the far-off shores of Clapham. When we arrived, there were a few of Ali's friends scattered around. I walked into the kitchen and there she was talking to her boyfriend. I said a cold hello and lied that I was pleased to meet him. It was a great night apart from the fact that my heart was punching me like a boxer. At the end of the night we said our goodbyes, though I can't remember if I bade farewell to George.

It was getting to the point where I'd turn up to Morley and if I didn't see Ali's car, my heart would drop. As the months rolled by, we were getting closer and closer. George had returned back to Bubble land which was a touch. I was walking up the stairs to the rehearsal studio one day and Ali was by the door. She asked if I would like to go to the theatre with her. I had never been to a theatre before and without a moment's thought I said yes.

Sod the theatre, it was a date with the person I had fallen in love with hook, line and sinker. We were off the next week to see *Les Misérables*, whatever the hell that was. When the day finally arrived, I borrowed a nice car from a friend and couldn't wait to spend a whole evening with Ali. I picked her up with a bunch of flowers in hand and off we went to The Cambridge Theatre in Shaftesbury Avenue. I sat through the production in awe, it was another world. When the show had finished I couldn't stop talking about it.

On the way home the conversation moved to religion and she said she would find it hard to get involved with anyone who was not a born-again Christian. Well I knew God through our past deals with each other. I took her home, said goodnight and walked away with the warmest feeling I had ever felt.

We started to speak a bit more often on the phone. One night I asked her if I were to let Jesus in my life, would he come? She said yes, so I did and began to read the Bible. I admit, my initial interest in Christianity was because Ali wouldn't go out with a non-Christian but after a while, I started to see something in Jesus' message. We arranged to meet and talk about it and it was sealed. We started going to St. Michael's church together in Victoria. St. Michael's was full of middle-class, healthy, wealthy young career people. I often felt uncomfortable sitting in this alien environment but I would have sat in a vat of shit as long as I was with Ali.

A brother of a good friend of mine, Paul, owned a restaurant in Fulham and I organised a night out for me and Ali.

We got to the restaurant and Paul sent over a bottle of wine on the house but all I could see was Ali.

I thought I'd be flash and order a carrot and orange soup and complained to a laughing Ali when it arrived cold. As we were sitting there, Ali pulled out a piece of paper. She had written a poem and asked if I would write some music to it. I read the poem which it began with, 'There's a warmth deep in my heart when two worlds come together'. I read on and realised it was about us and love. We left the restaurant and at the end of the night I struck up the courage to give her a kiss, and that was that.

The next night I had composed music for the song and sang it down the phone to her. One night we watched a whole movie together on the phone, me at my house, she at hers. I felt so comfortable being around her, we fitted together perfectly.

The next time we were in Morley, we announced that we were an item expecting total surprise from our fellow thespians but all they said was, 'It's about time.' They'd all seen it coming for ages even though we thought our feelings had been so hidden.

We were going great guns at the London Bubble with our production of *MacBeff*. Learning the lines was a nightmare as I'd never read Shakespeare before but once I got to grips with the text and images, it became a pleasure to delve into his creative and inventive use of the English language.

At the same time we were deciding what play to do at Morley College for an end-of-term production. I was cast in the role of Wilson in Joe Orton's one act, radio play *The Ruffian on the Stair*. The play is set in London in a bedsit occupied by an Irish rogue and an ex-prostitute.

My character had been having an incestuous affair with his brother who had, unfortunately, been run over and killed by a van. So it was quite an intense piece and coupled with the madness of *MacBeff*, I've got to tell you, there wasn't much room in my head for love thoughts. I grew a beard for *MacBeff* and had to shave it off for Wilson. I had to find a way to separate the two maniacs.

I remember being in the Casby lift with Ali one day. My hair was growing wild and I had bags under my eyes. 'You look mad,' she said. When we got to my flat, I looked in the mirror and she was right, I did indeed look mad. Maybe I was taking it all a bit too seriously.

We opened *MacBeff* in a venue next door to what used to be The Crunchy Frog and, if I may say so myself, with the guidance of Adrian (who was awarded an MBE in 2017), we did a fantastic job for where we were at in our development as actors. The play was a really good interpretation and was directed at the local people who weren't too au fait with the bard. I remember, one night on stage, I was blasting out a soliloquy when I caught sight of my little nephew Frankie in the audience. I started to show off and lost my focus. At the end of the speech, I turned around and there were actors on stage that I should have dismissed much earlier on in the speech. When I turned I saw the look of terror in the other actors' eyes. Luckily, I had my back to the audience or they would have seen the fear in mine but I calmly told them, in character, to go off and get back to work. The rest of the play went smoothly. A good acting lesson learnt.

I loved the London Bubble, it was a good training ground and I met some life-long friends. It was a massive influence on my future career.

CHAPTER EIGHTEEN

Now it was onto the next play at Morley College and the genius of Joe Orton's *The Ruffian on the Stair*. We started rehearsing but as Ali had just got into the Guildford School of Acting and was to leave Morley College, she couldn't commit to acting in the production so she became our stage manager instead. Roy Kendall was to direct us.

One Saturday, Ali informed me that her family had invited me up for Sunday dinner; this was the next level – meeting the folks. So I slung on my best Joe Orton tight white T-shirt, a pair of 501s and Adidas trainers. We drove up the A3 past Guildford and took the Thursley slip road. What a mad coincidence, it was the same one we took all those years ago on that crazy night in Frensham when we went night fishing whilst tripping. Eventually we came to Ali's family house. Every house we passed looked like a mansion to me. We turned into a drive and there it was, a massive house with a swimming pool and tennis court. I turned to Ali. 'Why didn't you tell me you had a house like this?'

'Why would I?' she innocently replied. The car pulled up at the front door. Ali's mum and dad, Jane and George, stepped out to greet us. I had never had much to do with the middle class up to then so I was a bit lost as to what to say and immediately turned into a chimney sweep stereotype, feeling well out of my depth.

We went into the living room where there was a small gathering. I noticed a little old lady quietly sitting in a chair who resembled the hedgehog Mrs Tiggy-Winkle from the *Beatrix Potter* books. She was Ali's grandmother. I then started talking to a nice old upright fellow called Edward, who was an ex-army surgeon and an elder of the village and, to my saving grace, also a Christian which was at least one thing we had in common. Ali's parents were lovely people despite their culture being so alien to me. George was a maritime arbiter of Lloyds and Captain of the London Division of the RNR, with a CBE for his services. Jane was the daughter of a Lord and herself an Honourable, whatever that meant. We all adjourned to their dining room; a nice roast beef was on the menu and I was starving. The food was served out very civilly around the table. I picked my knife and fork up and began to eat.

'You're left-handed?' Jane said.

'No, I'm right-handed.'

'Oh, you are holding your knife in the wrong hand.'

I swapped it over but it didn't feel comfortable so back it went. Then it happened, I coated a nice, crispy roast spud in gravy, lifted it to my mouth and, bosh, it fell off the fork and rolled down my nice white T-shirt. No one said anything but all my efforts of sophistication were lost in that moment. Ali laughed and I nearly died as I finished the meal with, what looked like, the path to Oz on my shirt. I can't remember if I changed it or not but I must have.

After lunch I had a nice chat with Ali's mum about God, as she was a real Christian on fire for the Lord, and was until the day she died. I miss her still, she was a lovely, caring lady who always thought of others before herself and gave the two of us so much support in the coming years.

When we were driving home I reflected on the day and was a little confused. If I wasn't aware of how the other half lived, I was now. I felt so far away from where Ali's family was that I was concerned our infant love was doomed.

Over the next few months I met Ali's two sisters who could not have been more different. Sarah is the eldest and a bit of, what they called back then, a 'Sloane Ranger'. Over the years we have had many enlightening, intelligent and sometimes heated debates about different religions. I have always found Sarah to be a beautiful, generous, fragile soul who, like me, is a seeker looking for some eternal answer. Jo is Ali's middle sister and one of the most beautiful and intelligent souls I have ever had the pleasure to meet in my life – a total original. She was a single mum with a lovely little boy called Ben. We clicked immediately. She was studying to be a doctor and had spent a year training in India and it showed. I love her and her now-partner, Paul, very much, and also Poppy and Tom, their other two kids. I will take the time now to thank her and Paul for all the support they have given to myself and Ali over the years. I'm blessed to have met you both this time around.

Ali and I carried on attending the church service in Victoria but the nice clean environment and the posh congregation continued to grate on me. I always seemed to feel a little unworthy around these people, I'm sure due to my education and environment. I had been emersed into this different world so fast…too fast. How could I speak about my life to these people? How could they understand my journey? The majority of people we were hanging about with were very brainwashed by the western concept of Christianity and posh public schools. Even those we knew that did come from my world aspired to be something that they were not.

But Ali and I were getting closer and closer, we were so comfortable in our own company and we were always laughing. I felt, for the first time in my life, totally at peace with another person, a most definite first for me, apart from Sue all those years ago. I gave my love and trust unequivocally to Ali and with her, God.

I was still selling a bit of dope to make a living and told Ali I was very lucky at Bingo to explain my supply of money. She didn't believe a word but never made a big deal about it. Opening the doors to Christianity made me aware that I was doing something wrong. Concept, mistaken for reality, is a pretty powerful influence. It knocked me onto a different orbit, so I stopped.

I had a haircut, got a bit of sun and shaved, and I was ready for *The Ruffian on the Stair*.

It was great coming from one play and jumping straight into another. We rehearsed for a couple of weeks and I loved every moment of it. Life couldn't get any better; the transition I was going through seemed natural. I was acting, I was in love and, for the first time in my life and most importantly, I had a philosophical direction.

On the opening night of *The Ruffian on the Stair*, I remember being quite nervous but I had God and Ali on my side, what could go wrong? The first half of the play went well. The set looked great – the space was divided into three rooms: a kitchen, a living room and a bedroom. We even had a real goldfish happily swimming around a glass fish bowl. At the end of the play my character gets shot and I fall onto the table housing the fish bowl (spoiler alert) which then falls to the floor. No one wanted to hurt the fish, and rightly so, so Ali covertly swapped the fish for a slice of carrot at some point in the play. The audience never noticed the seamless change. The scene came and I crumbled onto the table and the fish bowl went flying. As I was lying dead on the floor, I heard a piercing scream from the audience and felt someone clamber over me. I couldn't understand what was going on as this had never happened in rehearsal, but obviously I couldn't look up. She was cursing and using the word evil as she tried to save what she thought was the goldfish, until she grabbed the hydrated piece of carrot. Silly cow thought the goldfish was still in the bowl. I can't imagine what she felt when she realised her mistake. The incident certainly added a bit of spice to the production and has given us a story to dine on for many years.

Time passed and it was time for Ali to start her three-year drama course at GSA.

I decided that, although the course wasn't finished, it was time to leave Morley College and get an Equity card as, in those days, it was a requirement to go forward in acting. The only trouble was that to get a card you had to prove you were somehow earning money in the arts. It was a catch 22, as you couldn't work without an Equity card and you couldn't get an Equity card without professional work. I got to know the owners of The Ship, a pub we used to use when at the Bubble. We did a deal that I would perform every Saturday for no money, just a fifty pounds Equity contract, which was the minimum requirement.

Equity would need seven past contracts, one present and seven future ones. The owners of the pub, Steve and Nina, agreed to back date seven and give me what future contracts I needed, an arrangement that suited both parties perfectly as there was always a good crowd when I played. I spoke to Peter Attard, one of the teachers at Morley College, who agreed to take some headshots for me, and when I acquired my

Equity card, he then would suggest me to Stage Centre Management, the acting agency co-op that he was part of.

Everything was going to plan and Ali and I were falling deeper and deeper in love day by day, hallelujah.

One Sunday at the church service in Victoria, I stood up and splurged out my life story and about being fitted up by the police and how that journey had led me to God and acting.

After the service I was talking to one of the happy clappy crowd and he told me about a Christian mission he was involved with that was working with young Muslims in North London and would I like to be involved. Day by day I was getting more and more brainwashed by the Christian philosophy of doing for others, so I agreed. As I was leaving the church, a woman got my attention. She introduced herself as Susie Parriss and told me she was a casting director and to give her a call. I had my Equity card on track and I thought that there might just be something in all this God stuff after all.

I started playing guitar and singing old covers at The Ship every Saturday. I'd also managed to secure some mid-week gigs in some other local pubs, which helped in the Equity contract department.

The gigs in The Ship were turning out to be quite a success and, with the help of my ol' mukka Mick, and Ali, who would join me on stage every now and then, I'd play to a full house every week. I'd sent in my Equity contract requirements, the rest was in the lap of the gods. I was totally immersed in art, love and religion, all dissolving happily into one, what could go wrong? Three months later the elusive Equity card landed on my carpet and I was accepted into Stage Centre Management. I was thrilled – that was it, I was a professional actor.

I called Ali and she was ecstatic and told me how proud she was. I hadn't heard those words too often in my life and I'm not afraid to say they caused an emotional lump to mysteriously appear in my throat.

It was at that time when I started working with the Muslim kids in a youth club in Victoria. I loved it. I seemed to be able to talk to them a bit better than the happy clappy Eton Rifles. After a couple of weeks I got to thinking about the kids in my home village of Bermondsey, who were going through the same experiences as these kids I was working with. It started to become a little bit of a dilemma, so, like every good

Christian soldier, I decided to pray and ask the governor upstairs for a bit of guidance. God had spoken and somehow communicated to me that I should start up our own church service in Bermondsey, and he didn't even need a burning bush.

A couple of months after my new epiphany from the Lord, I went to the curate of St. James's Church in Bermondsey, which was coincidently a stone's throw from where Tommy Steele used to live. The curator was none other than Snowy Davoll, the head honcho of the CUM youth club I'd attended years before. He was quite surprised to see me. The last time we'd been together was about fifteen years earlier and I had probably pulled up in a stolen motor vehicle or caused some sort of havoc with the in-house holy folk. Our bizarre conversation went something like this:

'Snow, I think that God is telling me to start up a church service for young kids.'

Snowy looked at me for a minute and said, 'Okay, when do you want to start?'

'This Sunday.' It was Wednesday.

Snowy told me that it might be a tad impractical for it to happen that quickly.

'Okay, Sunday after next then?'

Snowy said that he would have to run it past the church's PCC committee (whatever that was).

'But Snowy, God is telling me to do it.' He invited me in for a cup of tea and I told him the events of the last few years and how I'd been led to this point. We decided that I would come to church on Sunday and announce my fiendish plan to the congregation. I was now about to affirm my faith to a lot of people that had known me and my family for years as reprobates, but I was on a mission, literally from God.

Sunday came and I mooched up to the altar and talked to the dropped-jaw congregation about how God had told me he wanted me to start work with the young people of Bermondsey. At the end of the service, a vicar by the name of Bob Mayo approached me.

He had taken over from Snowy as the new director of CUM. 'I'll start the service up with you.'

That was the beginning of our work together for the next couple of years.

A couple of months later and after many hours of prayer, Bob and I opened the doors of the church to the kids on a cold, February, Sunday evening.

I was so excited at the prospect of working with local kids that knew nothing about Jesus and his message. A few weeks passed but no kids came. I was becoming frustrated that the only people turning up were adults from the church. Could God have forgotten to do some calling? The following week, as we walked through the church grounds, we saw a group of young people on park benches laughing, drinking beer and smoking joints. I approached them and invited them into the church for our service.

'You're Eddie Webber, ain't ya? You know my mum and dad. What the fuck are you doing involved in God shit?' *Good question.*

'Come into the church and I will tell you.' One of the lads held his drink in one hand and a joint in the other. He indicated to them both as if he needed an excuse not to come in.

'Bring it all in, I'm sure God won't mind a bit of booze and mother nature, eh Bob? We'll be in the church until 10 p.m.'

Bob looked at me a bit warily but, fuck it, in my universe we were out to save souls. I believed, at that time, that if you didn't acquire salvation from the Lord you were on the road to Hell.

Bob and I went into the church. A while later some of the group stumbled in with cans of beer in their hands. We welcomed them and started talking about the message. At the end of the service the kids said that they would come back the next week. After a few self-indulgent pats on the back, we closed the church, happy.

The service started to grow and so did our need to brainwash these wayward young Bermondsey folk. After about six months the service was thriving. Ali was three quarters into her first year at drama school and I had started to get acting work through Susie Parriss and Stage Centre Management. Stage Centre, as I mentioned earlier, was a co-op agency so each of its actors had to spend a day in the office calling casting directors and trying to hustle work for the other actors on the books. It was a great learning curve in finding out how the business worked and, thanks to Susie Parriss keeping her word, I made my TV debut in *Birds of a Feather*. My first ever line on TV was, 'Double Glazing. Double egg and chips more like.'

CHAPTER NINETEEN

Then it happened; my world was turned upside down. Ali decided to broaden her horizons and jumped into a relationship with another guy from drama school. I was devastated. When Ali told me the news sent me sideways. I didn't know if I was coming or going. It was like being in a misty dream where I couldn't wake up. A stake had been driven straight through my heart. How could someone, who I loved so much and who professed to love me, do something like that? I really didn't see that one coming. I questioned everything that was happening in my life at that time.

Under the anaesthetic of religion, I just stumbled through the next few months, blocking everything out. Ali and I had a massive heart to heart and decided to split up after realising that she had a bit more living to do before she could settle down. And rightly so – she was twenty-one and I was twenty-eight. I could vaguely see her point but only vaguely.

Looking back now, I probably expected a little too much of her. I had lived life and made many, huge, wrong choices. She had come from a very protected, all-girl boarding school environment with a heavily influenced Christian upbringing and had not seen too much of real life.

Despite understanding this now, at the time I was so angry with myself for letting my guard down and, truth be known, with God who I had given my life to but, hey, what can you do? I was blinded with love.

For the next few months I was in a daze. The thing that really helped me through that time was the work we were doing with the Bermondsey youth. They were the ones who really needed the guidance. The middle-class, CUM helpers who were involved in the service, including Bob, didn't have a clue about these kids or, in my opinion, the true message of the human Jesus so I didn't want to walk away and leave the kids to the class ignorant helpers. Bob offered me a full-time job at CUM, being paid by the Church of England, what else could I do but accept? The job title afforded me was Gifted Youth Evangelist. *Who would have thought?*

I started work at the club with half the fallen fish scales returning to my eyes and started a drama class there. We enacted elements of what the Swami Christ and his naive disciples had proclaimed in the Bible. We also took the kids on camping trips to islands in Surrey. It was a nice time on the surface but inside I was dying twenty-four hours a day not having my soulmate anymore.

The kids loved the adventures Bob and I took them on. As I write now I am preparing to go to the funeral of one of the kids who came to the service, Rocky, who was violently stabbed to death in Southwark park a week ago…very sad.

The service was going from strength to strength and I was falling into the comfortable, middle-class, Christian mindset as I needed something to latch onto. I just couldn't shake Alison out of my head.

The whole time we were apart I was only half-present and my heart was in pain. It was a bad time.

After six months in the deserted desert of deserted love, I decided to send Ali a Valentine's card, not knowing what her situation was. Next thing I knew, I was sitting in my flat in Casby House when the phone rang. I answered to hear Ali's voice. My heart started beating faster and then out of nowhere, she asked me to marry her – it was 29 February, a leap year.

And so we resumed where we had left off but this time we committed ourselves to a life together, though, subconsciously the recent negative history was banked in my hard drive.

Ali and I became inseparable once more, like a right and left arm. We decided to get married after she had finished drama school. I carried on working at CUM and Ali started to get involved as well. The kids loved and accepted her immediately, how could they not? She was beautiful and caring.

We decided to have a holiday and headed off to Limassol in Cyprus. When we arrived at the apartments we were met with hanging electrical wires and unfinished walls – we looked at each other and laughed. A porter took us to our room. We were dreading to see what it looked like inside, but we didn't have to worry, it was perfect and in full decorative order.

After a couple of days chilling we decided to hire out a trusty stead in the form of a Suzuki 125 motorbike in order to explore the place in a bit more depth. Dressed in shorts and a vest we headed for the hills, destination Troodos.

We didn't know anything about the place, it just sounded interesting. It was amazing just me and my beautiful girl in our world of magic love. Nothing else mattered. The sights were amazing – we drove through deserted villages and up mountains. Ali wanted to have a go at driving the bike. At this point we were a few thousand feet above sea level. After explaining how to work the gears, she took off. As she went over a hill, the noise of the engine fell silent. I started to run towards the hill thinking the worst, had she driven over the edge? Dreading the sight to come, I reached the top and there was the love of my life, caked in mountain dust trying to pick up the bike. It had stalled and fallen on top of her. I really thought that she had driven over the edge – we pissed ourselves laughing.

We resumed our journey and after a while we entered a quaint, little mountain village and stopped to buy some water. When hydrated again, we got on the bike but alas it wouldn't turn over. As I tried to kick-start it again and again, I was met with a pathetic putt, putt, putt. God knows where we were and how we'd get out of there if the bike was broken. Not being mechanically minded, I asked a local van driver if he could help but to no avail. By this time a group of black-clad women from the village had gathered around us and the bike. I tried to start it again but it was dead to the world. As the women didn't speak any English, I mimed that I needed to use a phone. They pointed in the direction of the shop then all headed for a little church. I called the bike hire place and after five minutes of arguing that I had tried everything they mentioned a reserve fuel tank switch.

I told them it was more serious than that and that I knew about bikes but they kept on insisting that I tried the reserve tank switch. I thought I had better give it ago. After returning to the bike, I turned the switch on, gave it a few minutes then kicked it over, boom, it fired up first time. *Phew*! Then, all of a sudden we were met with cries of 'Madonna, Madonna!' as the group of women ran out of the church, elated. A miracle had occurred from their prayers to the Holy Mother. After giving a compulsory donation to the church prayer box we got off on our way, heading for the mountains of Troodos. As we travelled up the mountain we started to notice people coming down dressed in thick Parka coats which we thought quite strange. We travelled a few more miles and bosh, we hit snow which we were definitely not dressed for. As we reached the village of Troodos we were frozen. Sometimes, when in times of trouble, we humans can say the most bizarre things. I turned to Ali, who was now quite blue with the cold, and said, 'Don't let them see we're cold, we're British.' We forced smiles at everyone who caught our eyes – they must have thought we were bonkers dressed in our shorts and vests. We decided to head back down the mountain, still smiling at the bemused strangers as we stiffly glided through the village. When at last we reached warmer air we fell off the bike and had to thaw out.

That night, after a hot bath we went to a restaurant and, as Israel was only a stone's throw away, I started regaling stories of my time in the Holy Land.

Most of the stories were of my adventures with Yossy, who I had last seen six years ago partying with the Bedouin on the banks of the Nile. We were sitting at a table outside and my back was to the road and at one point, for some reason, I turned around.

'Yossy!' I yelled. Ali thought I had gone mad. There, walking past the restaurant was the Viking himself. If I had turned a split second later, I would have missed him.

We stared at each other in shock and I then introduced him to Ali. He was in Cyprus working as a holiday rep for a Finnish tour company. We had a mad little chat and he went on his way. Just shows you what a small world it really is and somehow we are all connected somewhere down the line.

When we returned home it was now time to do the right thing and ask Ali's dad for her fair hand. We jumped into the car and headed down to her leafy country home. I have to say that I was a bit nervous at the thought of getting down on bended knee. Halfway through the journey, Ali hit me with a little bit of additional information.

'We have a custom in our world'—we used to refer to our cultures as 'our worlds'—'when one asks for a hand in marriage one has to quote an old English script.'

'Eh?'

'We have a sixteenth-century script that all potential husbands have to recite when asking.'

'What?' I nervously said through an even more nervous laugh. 'What does it say?'

'Oh you know, things like "I asketh permission for the hand of your maiden daughter etc, etc". You'll be okay, you're an actor, you'll smash it,' she said convincingly. I sighed. Could it get any fucking worse?

'Okay but you could have warned me earlier so I could have looked over it a bit. Come on then, give me the text.'

Ali started to laugh. Of course there was no script. I can honestly say she well and truly got me on that one. We arrived at Ali's house and the afternoon went well despite my nerves. Jane and George gave me their blessing...*phew*.

We set a date for our wedding – we were getting married. Gulp!

There was only one thing left to do: our families had never met. I strung it out until a couple of weeks before our wedding but could string it out no longer. My mum was fine but how could I let the old man or my brother, who had just been released from a twelve-year sentence for armed robbery, loose on Ali's family? Jack had had it bad in jail and had fallen foul to a few mental health issues, and who could blame him? Those years in the Machiavellian prison system of that time would make or break anyone. I just couldn't get my head around our families meeting. I told Ali my fears but she said I was being silly and it would all be okay.

The last lunch was arranged for a sunny Saturday afternoon in June.

We were to spend the afternoon at Ali's family home; a nice swimming pool, a game of tennis, what could go wrong?

The afternoon started well, my family had found the house, and that's where it ended. Jane, Ali's beautiful mum, had laid on some nice food and wine.

I decided to emulate Dustin Hoffman in *The Graduate* and submerged myself in the swimming pool for the duration of the afternoon. My head rose every now and then, like a turtle, to breathe and earwig what was going on. Sarah, Ali's sister, and her husband-to-be, Andrew, had come down as well. When I came up for air, I'd take stock from my watery womb. Jack was in one corner of the garden talking to Sarah and the ol' man in another chatting to Andrew, all, I might add, with ample glasses of the finest vino in their hands. Could Ali be right about my silliness? I submerged again to ponder the thought. The next time I came up for air, I heard a familiar sound:

'Ladies and gentlemen, we have stolen property for sale, nine-carat gold earrings, a pound a pair.' Did my state of mind cause a flashback to my market days? No such luck. Ali's sister had asked Jack what he did for a living. He was fly-pitching in the markets at that time and had a case of earrings in the boot of the car so proceeded to drag Sarah and Ali's mum to said boot and began the spiel. I remember seeing Sarah's confused face and Jane scrutinising a box of earrings before saying, 'Oh aren't they lovely.' I dived down deeper this time. I hated being in this position. The next time I ascended for breath I caught Ali's eye, she smiled, I went under again.

Hours seemed like days. At last the afternoon had dwindled and it was time for the outlaws (excluding Mum in that comment) to journey back from country gardens to the mean streets of Bermondsey.

I exited the pool to say my farewells only to hear the ol' man asking Sarah and Andrew about their wedding which was going to be a big society affair taking place at the Temple Church, London later on that year. His response was, 'Where are our invitations then?' Which caused much stuttering from Ali's family. He then proceeded to grab Ali's dad and planted a kiss on his lips, which freaked him out totally. Arbiters of Lloyds with CBEs and a Harrow education just didn't do that sort of thing but everyone was smiling which was good. Ali and I went home, relieved and full of the joys of family and life.

The next day I went to work at CUM, had a great holy session with the lads then made my way back to Ali's flat. I should have known something was up as I spotted a few little clues on the journey. As I left the tube station and walked over the common, I remember it was a cold evening. I saw a fellow, obviously down on his luck, sitting on a bench drinking cider out of a bottle. So with my holy cap on, I sat down and started talking about how Jesus could make a difference to his life.

'So you are a Christian?' he said.

'Yes,' I piously replied.

'Give me your jacket then, I'm cold.'

I had a beautiful, expensive, brown leather jacket on. I didn't know what to say except for no.

He rightly told me to fuck off. I did, with my tail between my legs but I learnt a valuable lesson that day: one needed to be sincere to walk the path of Jesus.

I should have given him my jacket, I would have felt much better but the way I feel about Christianity now, I'm glad I didn't.

As I entered the flat, Ali was on the phone in tears. She looked at me and a feeling of doom washed over me. Had someone died? Had Jesus come back for a second crack at the whip? Did she burn the dinner? The latter was probably the most likely.

'What's happened?'

'That was Mum, it was about yesterday and our families meeting. They think that I am marrying into the London mafia.'

The ol' man had been lulled into a false sense of security whilst talking to Andrew and, thinking that scullduggery would impress, he spent the whole afternoon telling fictional stories about how he was this and how he was that, all revolving around crime and bigging himself up as a gangster. That same evening, silly Andrew repeated all that my Walter Mitty father had said to him and, coupled with the stolen property rhetoric from Jack, they all put two and two together and came up with a million. I was furious with all parties.

'So what about our marriage in two weeks?' I nervously asked.

I didn't get the answer I was expecting. Ali told me she would find it hard to walk down the aisle without her parents being happy about it. It was time to lay my cards on the table with them.

Next morning we jumped into the car and headed down to Surrey. When we arrived Ali's dad was standing around the swimming pool. I nervously approached.

'George,' I blurted out, 'about yesterday, that is my family, it's not me. I love your daughter and want to spend the rest of my life with her.'

George thought for a moment. 'No need to say anything. I know you love Ali and I have no problem with the two of you getting spliced. We will have a wonderful day next week.'

A ton weight lifted off my shoulders at his words. Next stop the wedding!

I took some time out to reflect on my journey so far. Growing up on the streets of Bermondsey, prison, police fabricating evidence against me, Freemasonry, living in Israel, getting involved with the Russian mafia and then getting locked up, forming a band, acting and going to drama college, meeting Ali, becoming a Christian, working as an Evangelist back in Bermondsey, the different cultures of our two families, splitting up with Ali and now here we were getting married.

What the fuck does the future hold?

Chapter Twenty

Our wedding was a crazy day. I didn't have too much to do with it as all the arrangements were put together by Ali and her family. I was in a bit of a quandary as to who I was to invite; apart from my new Christian and acting friends, all my old buddies were either armed robbers or bang at it in some other way. Ali's aunt, who was to be there, was a high court judge at the Old Bailey so I was a bit worried that she might recognise some of my tribe and vice versa.

My old pal Charlie Nunn stepped in as best man. We were to be married in St. John's Church in Surrey. Charlie was a London Cabbie so we thought it a good idea that he would bring Ali to the church in his cab (bringing a bit of London to Surrey and a practical vehicle for a wedding dress). So on the day, there I was at the altar, dressed in suit and tails, absolutely terrified. The music started – a classical piece chosen by Jane and Ali. If it had been up to me, Ali would have walked in to 'Working Class Hero' by John Lennon. She glided in with her dad and looked stunning. I had to look away as the sight and connotations were far too big for my poor overworked brain.

The service went without a hitch. Bob, the vicar from CUM, married us and Peter, our teacher from Morley College, read a Shakespeare sonnet. Then, as quick as you like, we were husband and wife. Our congregation burst into rapturous applause. Some more chosen music kicked in as we left the church. After the proverbial photos of family and friends, we headed off to a nice polite reception at a quaint little barn in the village. I don't remember much of it except we had a pianist playing groovy jazz piano (our choice). My Aunt Kate was ready to hitch up her skirt and start a good old cockney sing song. In retrospect I wish she had. The whole thing was Ali more than me, I just wanted to get away and start our life together. Ali's godfather spoke first and rambled on a bit too long in my book.

I have no idea what he said. Then it was the turn of my best man Charlie with the quickest best man speech ever recorded. It went something like, 'I agree with everything everyone has said about them both,' then he dashed away. He told me afterwards that he couldn't think of what to say because all of his memories of us were about being up to no good. We both burst out laughing. I can't even remember eating or what the food was; banoffee pie was the dessert, I remember that. I kept a watchful eye on my brother and the ol' man, cutting into their conversation whenever I thought it was going bandy or they were chatting with someone they shouldn't really be talking to: a judge, a lawyer or really any of Ali's guests.

I earwigged the ol' man talking to a posh air force pilot and telling him that he used to fly planes in his national service – it was one of the most stressful times in my life and I've had some, as you've read. Despite my anxiety the two cultures mixed perfectly and a good time was had by all. The stress was finally over, we got in the car and that was that, we were married. My head was spinning as we headed for a gaff called The Manor House in Castle Combe near Bath, a wedding present from Sarah and Andrew, leaving all the eclectic class madness behind. It was just me and my beautiful wife – the memory of Ali, at that time, evokes a strong emotion as I write. I remember my love for her was and is eternal.

We had told everyone that we were going on our honeymoon the next day but, in truth, we were going three days later, so that gave us a couple of days of anonymity in London as a newly married couple before we jetted off to Sri Lanka and the Maldives. It was the happiest time, just the two of us in London alone. A couple of days later we flew off to our honeymoon. The first week in Sri Lanka was just us having fun. One day we were walking outside the hotel looking for a bank. A jolly, head-wagging Sri Lankan, who spoke perfect English, approached us so we asked him for directions to the nearest bank. He motioned us to follow him. He took us down a dirt track which led into the jungle. When questioned if this was definitely the way to the bank he just nodded enthusiastically and waved his hand onwards. We walked on through the vegetation and he said we were near his village and did we want to see it. It was an opportunity to witness another culture and we said yes. We visited a school and met some villagers. He then took us to see these amazing temples and we bought lots of sweets and dished them out to the village kids. We then reached a river and he called over to someone in an old traditional wooden boat. He beckoned for us to get in, so we obliged. We were on the river, exotic birds and other water beasts were gracefully and noisily making their presence known to us. It was beautiful even to the point where we were all singing holy songs from each of our cultures. It was an amazing day full of new experiences – we were with this guy and his pals for hours.

As we drifted on the peaceful river, Ali and I could not have wished for a better start to our life together as husband and wife.

When at last we reached the shore, we bid the kind stranger goodbye but as we turned to leave he put out his hand and demanded we give him a hundred quid. 'Excuse me?'

He started to explain that he was a tourist guide and the fee for the day was a hundred quid. Now I'm not an unjust person but anger rose within me. We had shared an amazing experience with him, giving each other our souls, or so I thought. I started to laugh and my Bermondsey side erupted and I told him to do one. A hundred quid! The normal wages out there, I was told, were miniscule, something like sixty pence a day. I shook my head and gave him twenty quid, which was a fortune for a day's work and we took off with him close at our heels demanding the rest. He had more chance of the monkey god coming down to make him a cup of tea than me giving him any more money. I was annoyed that I had fallen for his old bollocks and made it clear that if he didn't leave his boat would be inserted somewhere where the beautiful Sri Lankan sun don't shine. Licking his wounds with his twenty quid in his pocket, he sauntered off. We never found the bank.

Another day we went to visit a temple where you had to walk up a thousand steps that were carved into a granite hill. The movie *Cliffhanger* was all the rage at that time and Ali and I had gone to see it at the cinema before we jetted off.

Halfway up the one thousand steps, I decided to do my Stallone impression and go off track and instead of climbing the stairs, climb the rock face. Our guides looked at me with curious tilted heads as I jumped over the railings onto the sheer rock face. After about half a second, I got stuck and couldn't move a muscle, to the delight of the guides who were now pissing themselves at the silly Englishman clinging for dear life onto whatever he could. I started getting somewhat dizzy as I looked at the five hundred foot drop below and feebly started to cry for help. They left me hanging for a while, I suppose to teach me a lesson, before hauling me back to safety. The other tourists plus Ali were all shaking their heads at my silliness but, hey, that's me.

When we reached the top it was all worth it. The vista was biblical, a full three hundred and sixty degree view of everything. 'Bow before me and all this could be yours' sort of thing.

After a week we flew to an island in the Maldives. Stunning was not the word for it. I'd never in all my life witnessed anything so beautiful, such a clear, blue sea where all sorts of colourful fish would sporadically pop up and see what the coup was. It was absolutely stunning. We walked into our accommodation, which was a grass hut with all the mod cons and the bed had been sprinkled with rose petals. It was paradise.

After our first night on the island I started to feel a twinge in my jaw. I was reading an eye-opening book about Malcolm X, which took my mind off the twinge, that had now progressed to my ear, for a while. The book and its topic fascinated me.

A bit later we went for a swim and, as the day progressed, the twinge became a pain. By the end of the next night, my face felt like it was a balloon. I had developed an ear infection. There we were in a place which I'd settle for being heaven and I was in pain. I couldn't even get into the water. I styled it out for another day or two but it got to the point where the pain was too much and my face too swollen. We were leaving in a couple of days and had six take offs and landings to get us home. The only doctor was on the main island so we had to hire a speedboat to take us there in order to be able to get it all sorted before our flight. The doctor gave me a course of antibiotics and syringed my ears out but that was it for me and our idyllic honeymoon. The flights were manageable and we arrived back in the UK, tired and me with a swollen face.

Bob had been taking charge of the service whilst I was away when an incident occurred one Sunday. The kids were feeling a little over-energised and had decided to have a little tea bag war in the church. Because there had been other vandalism to the church that year (nothing to do with our kids), the PCC decided that this was their chance to shut the service down. They had never really taken to what we were doing and had complaints from the six old ladies who used to attend the service before ours that they felt intimidated walking out of the church when the kids were waiting to come in for their service. Whatever the motive, despite our protestations, they closed it. From that day on I became detached from their God and their Christian system. I was still working for CUM but that was it for me.

We had upset their tidy middle-class hypocrisy and they took the coward way out by smiling as they killed our creativity. To say I was furious was an understatement. So began the rot between me, conceptual Christianity and the middle-class mindset.

Ali took the view that it was human failure and not about God but to me it was another outright major betrayal. I had put myself on the line, in an area that I had been brought up in, preaching the word of the Christian god. All my mates had thought I was crazy and I don't blame them either.

Help came by way of a phone call from Stage Centre. They had got me an audition for a play that was to feature at the Edinburgh Festival Fringe. It was an adaptation of an autobiography written by a member of the Kray twins' firm, Tony Lambrianou, called *Inside the Firm*. They wanted someone who could play the guitar and had a reasonable singing voice. I went to the audition and met the producer and writer, Jon Ivay. I sang my self-penned song 'London Town' and got the job. Ali had also got her first acting job with a theatre company based in Norwich called Tiebreak. That was the beginning of a busy year for us both. I handed my notice into CUM and shook the holy dust from my shoes, never to return, and started rehearsing the play at the top of a pub in Streatham. It was the start of a great adventure and, better still, life-long friendships. I met the cast: Jimmy Puddephat (Ronnie Kray), Aran Bell (Reggie Kray), Ben Martin (Jack the Hat) and Mark Pegg (Tony Lambrianou). All rascals in their own little ways.

I took to the show and cast like a duck to water and, as the days went on, I felt the bullshit God thing dissipate.

CHAPTER TWENTY-ONE

The journey up to Scotland for the Fringe festival was like a film in itself. Phil, one of the producers who was also in the cast, had a London Taxi as his private car. Myself, Ben and another member of the cast, Paul, bundled into the cab and laughed and smoked weed for the next six or seven hours until we arrived, bleary eyed, in sock land. The producers had rented a big Edwardian house for us in Henderson Row.

Edinburgh was like nothing I'd ever experienced. The whole city stopped for the festival as the creatives of the world descended onto it and our little firm was at the centre. We would put on our costumes (1960s suits) and become the real Kray firm, handing flyers out in the streets and at night invite other artists back to our digs to party. I had taken my guitar with me and Phil played the blues harp. We'd drink, smoke weed, laugh and then laugh some more. Ben, Martin and I clicked immediately, our humour and thought processes were very similar. Dinner time in the house was always fun as everybody loved cooking, and the kitchen, like all good households, was always the place to be. The album of choice was Paul Weller's 'Wild Wood'. It's crazy how music has the power to transport you back to a time and place. Every time I listen to that album I get the smell of that kitchen in Henderson Row. Another album we played to death was Nirvana's 'Nevermind' and the track 'Smells Like Teen Spirit'. It would be on full blast as we all danced and cooked in the kitchen. Very pagan.

We had been up in Edinburgh for two weeks and finally it was time for the show. Charlie Kray, Tony Lambrianou and other members of the old Kray firm came down for the first night. It was quite comical as all these old so-called gangsters moved into the flat with us. It was very surreal but fascinating at the same time as we listened to all the old stories. It seemed like they had never left the 1960s. Though I noticed that they all had one thing in common: their eyes had a dull sadness in them. I'd seen that look before in every long-term prisoner I had ever met. Dead, cold, emotionless eyes.

Our set consisted of six separate boards, each standing about ten-foot high, which we had to assemble in ten or fifteen minutes before we performed each night. The show had a very complicated lighting plot which was full of gobos and light trickery. We arrived at the theatre for our technical rehearsal and, after about two hours, the show was all cued, and it had all gone swimmingly.

So there we all were, in the dressing room after putting the set up, ready to start the show. There was a buzz about our first night due to the infamous old villains sitting in the front row. The BBC was covering it and all the mainstream press were there. The show started with Ben's booming voice in his Jack the Hat character. The lights went down and the play started.

'Ronnie, you're a fat poof – you're nothing but a fat poof,' blasted out of the venue's speakers. God knows what Charlie Kray was thinking on hearing this. We were all pissing ourselves with laughter in the dressing room.

As we all entered the stage from the wings as the Firm gang, we noticed something was wrong – the lighting was completely different to the tech run. We started the performance and all the lighting states that we rehearsed never happened. There was a scene where Tony Lambrianou and his brother, Chris, drag me on stage in just my underpants then kick the shit out of me in a garage. The usual lighting state made the scene moody and sinister but now, without it, it was just a plain bright light. After kicking the shit out of me, the scene fades to a blackout but, of course, nothing was happening in that department. Mark and Jimmy, who were playing the Lambrianou brothers, left the stage, leaving me, lying unconscious in the centre of it. I was waiting for someone to drag me off but, alas, no one did, so I just stood up, in my underpants and made my own way off stage. It was so embarrassing. God knows what the infamous front row thought. We made our way through the rest of the show and, at the end, there was an almighty row with the producers. Our lighting technician declared that the lighting board had been sabotaged by a rival company. *As if!*

That night we all got pissed in the Festival Club Bar. At closing time, we decided that the night wasn't over yet and headed out, with all the old gangsters in tow, onto the mean streets of Edinburgh to find another place to end what was a bit of a disastrous night.

We found a seedy little club tucked away down a side street. There were two big bouncers on the door and they wouldn't let us in so Charlie Kray and Lambrianou stepped up with the 'do you know who I am?' bollocks. The bouncers told them 'no they didn't know who they were' and 'fuck off'. How times had changed, eh?

A few days later I was walking up Princes Street and a flustered Tony Lambrianou approached me and asked if I could lend him fifty quid as his car had just got clamped and he had left his wallet back in the flat. I reluctantly took fifty quid out of a cash machine on the proviso that he would pay it back later. I then found out that he had arrived by train and he didn't have a car up there. I never saw the fifty quid again. Once a gangster, always a gangster.

The rest of the run went great and we had some fine reviews. It was our first year of marriage but I was up in Scotland and Ali was doing her thing in Norwich. We were on the phone every day but were missing each other. After Ali had finished her show, she and Rossy, the wife of Aran Bell who played Reggie Kray, came up and joined us. It made life so much better. Rossy and Ali clicked immediately and the four of us shaped up a life-long friendship. After a couple of days, Ali and Rossy went home and our madness inside the Firm resumed. During the last week of the play, Ali called to say that the company she had just finished working for were doing another play and the lead character had dropped out and would I be interested in taking the part. It was work so I said yes.

The last night of *Inside the Firm* was a good one. Ali had come back up for it and we had a great wrap party. Ben's friend, the singer

Michael Ball, also came down for our last night. I have a great video somewhere of Tony Lambrianou and Charlie Kray trying to sell him a racing greyhound...you couldn't write it!

After a week back home with Ali and I getting back into our life again, I was off up to Norwich. But as soon as I arrived I started to wonder if it was a good idea. I had arranged digs before I got up there and they were awful.

The landlords were a couple from Yorkshire. They opened the door when I first arrived, both sporting long greasy hair in ponytails and wearing Iron Maiden T-shirts, heavy rockers through and through. The house was freezing as they never had the heating on. They said it was because they were from 'up north' and didn't feel the cold. Well I wasn't from up fucking north and I did feel the cold. The bathroom was filthy with hairs everywhere. I set about finding some more digs. When Ali had been working up there, she had stayed in a place owned by two lovely, creative people. So I got the address, hoping that they still had a room to rent. It was a beautiful Victorian three-storey house. I knocked on the door and it was answered by a beautiful petite woman called Debbie. I introduced myself as Ali's husband and asked if she could rent me a room. Her partner, Chedgey, entered the kitchen where we were having a cup of tea. We chatted for ages. It turned out that Chedgey was an artist who had studied up in Liverpool and had been a friend of John Lennon's in art school. That was it for me, surely the stars had led me there. Then came the kick up the bollocks, there was no room at the inn. I was gutted, compared to the place I was staying in, it was a palace. As I was about to leave, Chedgey suggested that if I was out doing the show all day, I could rent his studio at the top of the house every night. I jumped at the offer.

The show we were doing was a theatre-in-education thing called *The Invisible Boy*. The subject dealt with panic attacks and the exploitation of a young kid, who was played by a thirty-year-old, thirteen-stone actor.

My character was a Bill Sykes type who made the kid believe he was invisible then got him to burgle houses under the threat of violence. It certainly wasn't Shakespeare by any means. The woman playing the mother role was a fiery actress who was quite strange.

We would all take off in the morning, cramped up in the back of a van, ready for whatever school or community centre we were performing in that day. I just wanted it to end as soon as possible. I hated it and, to top it all, the other two actors, who were both in relationships, decided to embark on an affair.

It was hell on wheels. I just wanted to be with my new beautiful wife and make babies. Ali and I grabbed the odd weekend together but basically it was terrible and, to add to it, one weekend when we were together Ali received a phone call that her dad had been rushed to hospital. We jumped in the car and headed straight there.

We were the first of Ali's family to arrive and when the nurse came in, I feared the worst by the look on her face. Ali's dad had died of an aneurism – quick as that. It was terrible. After everything we'd been through, to be taken like that before he had the chance to see our life progress was tragic. Ali and her family were in bits, as you can well imagine, and I don't think she has ever gotten over it. RIP George. You have two beautiful grandsons who you would have loved.

I had to go back to Norwich and the schools we were performing in were quite unruly. Because my character was a violent one, some of the kids would be growling at me and giving me wanker signs whilst I was performing on stage.

Sometimes it was all I could do not to burst out laughing at their angry little faces. I must have been doing my job well. This went on for three months then, when the production ended, Ali got another play and it all started again. In between we buried George. We'd been married for a year and had maybe seen each other for about two months of that. Coupled with the tragedy of Ali's dad passing, it was a pretty awful first year of marriage.

When Ali finished her production, we decided that enough was enough and we wouldn't accept any more work for the time being. We booked a well-needed holiday to Playa de Las Americas, Tenerife. It was a great time. We hired a little open-top jeep and started to investigate the island. We covered as much of the place as we could. We swam and lay in the sun, letting the hard work and the tragedy of the year melt away. One early evening, we were walking along the beach paseo when we saw a man doing the three-card trick. He had three cards on a table and was asking people to guess where the queen was. I thought I'd give it a go and promptly lost two thousand five hundred pesetas. Ali was in stitches and taunted me that Mr Bermondsey, street-wise Charlie potatoes had lost our money. I must admit, I did feel a bit of a fool.

The next day was cloudy and we were walking down the same paseo when a young girl accosted us and offered us a scratch card with a chance to win a free two thousand five hundred pesetas. Having lost the same amount the day before, I thought why not. I scratched the card and, of course, it was a three-star winner, the only catch was, that to claim the money, we had to spend a day looking around some time-share urbanisation. It was cloudy so why not.

We were whisked away to an urbanisation somewhere and spent the day being grafted by a geezer who wasn't very good at his job. After about six hours of ear-splitting bollocks, we declined the offer of buying into it. I asked for our bounty and it then started to get a bit nasty. Two suited men came over to the table and started a real hard sales pitch with an underbelly of threat to it all. After another half hour of this, we started to get angry and they realised there was no point in pursuing this sale. We got our money and took off. I can see how many are intimidated by these people, especially the elderly. It was a heavy few hours but we had got our money back.

That evening we decided to spend our booty in Los Cristianos. We started at a restaurant where I tried snails for the first time – that wasn't a bit of me, truth be told. Then we hit a karaoke bar. We got chatting to a nice Welsh couple, Sandra and Gareth. We clicked straight away and had a great night singing songs, including a rendition of Eric Clapton's 'You Look Wonderful Tonight', then an embarrassing duet of, 'You're The One That I Want' from *Grease*.

The next day we planned to venture to the volcano Mount Teide. Its 3,718 metre summit is the highest point in Spain and the highest point above sea level on the islands of the Atlantic. We got up early, jumped into the jeep and took off for the adventure. It was an amazing journey, seeing the different terrains from green to scorched. We arrived at the volcano and got the cable car up to the top. I'm not very good with heights so I spent the journey sweating profusely and clinging to my wife for dear life.

When we reached the top it was amazing, we were actually above the clouds and the silence was tangible. We spent about two hours up there, even though the advice was to spend an hour maximum in the thin air, but we took some amazing photos. When we had had enough, we entered the cable car to return back down. After about ten minutes descending, out of nowhere Ali slumped on my shoulder then fell to the floor – she had fainted. People parted like the Dead Sea. I fell to my knees to tend to her with the confused faces of the other passengers looking down. Ali told me later that all she heard was my voice telling the people, 'Don't worry, she does this all the time.' It was the first time she had ever fainted. When we got to the bottom, she was ushered into a room and checked out. All was fine and we went our merry way. What we didn't know at the time, was that Ali was pregnant, so the thin air and lack of oxygen must have affected her.

We found out that we were to become parents once back in the UK. We were both thrilled at the prospect of a little baby.

Through mutual friends, we met a couple who lived on the road behind us, Michael and Annie Stephens. Annie was also pregnant and our babies were due almost at the same time. I just want to give a shout out to these beautiful souls and their amazing daughter, Amber. Annie has since tragically passed and Michael has found love again with another amazing woman, Sian. Love, love, love to you both and thank you for your friendship and support over the years.

Around this time, Jackio decided to buy a pub and asked me to run it. As I didn't have a job and Christianity was a thing of the past, I agreed. So started another mad adventure that would drag me back to those pre-Christianity days.

CHAPTER TWENTY-TWO

We named the pub The Crunchy Frog after the hippy club I mentioned earlier. Jackio just gave someone a few grand and they gave us the keys, no licence, no legal paperwork. To say it was mad is an understatement. On our opening night we were full to the rafters which was hard going as there was only myself and one barmaid. A lot of the people that turned up were from the local criminal elite with obvious bulges under their jackets and vast amounts of cash in their pockets. We got a young DJ called Scott, who was one of the lads I had worked with at CUM, and we were off. Money was flowing over the bar hand over fist. Jack had taken care of the business side of things so God knows what the dotted i's and the crossed t's looked like but, hey, it was making money. We decided that we would need another worker behind the bar so I approached Bob the vicar. When we opened up the following Friday night, there was Bob, proud as a peacock, in his dog collar pulling pints.

One guy came up to buy a drink who was foaming at the mouth having taken a bit too much of the marching powder.

'You a real vicar then?' He dribbled, teeth bared like a cartoon.

'Yes I am.'

'Well fucking bless me then.'

Bob gave the foaming fiend a blessing and the guy turned to his mates and said, 'I'm getting a fucking blessing from a proper pie and liquor.' Bob made the sign of the cross and the foaming wretch took out a packet and offered Bob a line. Bob declined and the wretch went back to his mates happy. It was the talk of the town for weeks. I'm sure the holy Bob still dines out on that story.

After a couple of weeks, we were going great guns. I used to open the pub at midday and usually close about 4 a.m. It was hard work but the pay was good. It was at this time that I started having a bit of cocaine again to get me through the day. Ali was about six months pregnant and one night she decided to visit the pub. People were dancing on the pool table and everyone was full of merriment. Then all of a sudden the pub went unnaturally quiet and people started hitting the deck. As I went around to the other side of the bar, I saw a friend of mine waving around a 44-calibre handgun wanting revenge on another friend who had insulted him. It was like the wild west. No one was moving, then Ali entered the bar. She was immediately pushed to the floor by my brother's girlfriend.

I moved cautiously towards the man speaking quietly and slowly as he continued to point the gun around the pub, then calmly reached out and took it from him. The gun was cocked and ready to fire and I didn't know how to uncock it so I asked for help. Another friend of mine came to the rescue and sorted it. What had sparked all this off was that he had been told that he was probably one of the ugliest men the insulter had ever seen. The next year the insulter was found stabbed to death. He was a nice fella outside of drink and he left a young family in the wake.

I used to let certain friends stay for late drinks at the weekends. Sometimes I wouldn't get home until 7 a.m. This one night a group of people who were fired up wanted to carry on drinking after last orders. I'd had enough, so at about 2 a.m. I threw my old mate Jimmy the keys to the pub and told him to make sure that someone was here at 10 a.m. with them so I could get in again. I ordered a cab and went home. The next morning someone was there with the keys and when I walked in, the bar was spotless and there was a pile of money left on the side.

I noticed four holes in the wall which hadn't been there the night before. Someone who was in the pub that night came in and I asked about the holes. He told me that there was a geezer who had no connection to anyone, who was passed out drunk on the bar. One of our regulars and another man dragged him over to the seat by the wall, placed a vodka bottle on his head and started shooting at the bottle.

How they never killed him, I just don't know. I shook my head in horror, *What the fuck am I doing here?*

Everyday a girl from the area would come in and sit at the bar and I started to develop a sort of relationship with her. She was intelligent and modelled for a living, and she looked like it too. She was beautiful but I was married so she was a no-go but it was nice to chat to a girl that came from the area and had a creative passion. She also liked a bit of Charlie and she made it quite clear she had a liking for me but, perish the thought. Then it happened.

As I said, I had started to have a line or two of cocaine every now and then. This particular evening I was, I suppose, feeling a little amorous due to the coke and she invited me upstairs for a line. We went up to the room above the bar and racked a couple and, out of nowhere, she started to put her hands on me. The coke opened the door for the devil and I was receptive to her advances but, before anything happened, a guardian angel in the shape of my brother Jack entered the room.

He made it quite clear that I was out of order and was not thinking straight. Ali was six or seven months pregnant and he was right. He told the girl to go and banned her from the pub. There is no doubt that I would have taken it further if Jack hadn't come in at that time. How could I even think about doing something like that to Ali and our marriage? It shook me to my core. I was slipping into my old ways and I didn't like it. When I went home that night I felt so guilty. I should have told Ali but I didn't. In retrospect, I wished I had never ever set foot in that pub from the start. I'm sure life would have taken a different road if I hadn't.

One afternoon, myself and a few friends were in the bar when three uniformed police officers walked in asking for the manager. No one wanted to come forward. The police were confused to say the least.

'Who's in charge?' The question was met with shrugs and the shaking of heads.

'Where is the barman?'

Again the question was met with silence. The police left but we were all sure that was not the last we would see of them.

The next Friday night the pub was banged out again. At midnight the doors flew open and a dozen of the met's finest ran in and raided the pub. The music was shut off and pockets were covertly emptied; the floor looked like a bad night in a Columbian coke lab with packets scattered everywhere. One police officer came out of the toilet with a bag of cocaine wraps. As there was only myself and one barmaid on duty that night, we were approached and asked where the manager was. I told them I had no idea and that I just worked there. The police emptied the pub and I was told to tell the manager to report to Rotherhithe police station in the morning. I told them I'd leave a note but that was enough for me. I went home never to return again.

My TV acting work started to pick up with the help of Susie Parriss. I had been at Stage Centre Management for a couple of years and felt it was time to progress. I asked Susie if she could help me get a more conventional agent. She put me in touch with an agent called Barry Brown. I met him at his office and he agreed to put me on his books.

Ali was nearing the due date of our first baby. She went into labour on 6 October 1995. This was it, all our expectations were now going to be realised. When the reality set in that we were having a baby, it was mind-blowing and very scary. For the last four months we had been placing a CD player on Ali's tummy, playing music to our unborn child, who we'd named Chunky due to the size of her stomach. She was outrageously huge. I had read somewhere that playing music to an unborn baby helps to bring some continuity from inside the womb to out. We played all the music that I had listened to as a baby: The Beatles, The Stones, The Who, plus modern-day bands like Oasis, Ocean Colour Scene and Blur. The main tune we played was the theme tune to *Twin Peaks*.

Once the contractions were coming thick and fast, we jumped into the car and rushed to St George's Hospital. I remember asking Ali if she could hold on another day as 9 October was John Lennon's birthday and I would have loved him or her to be born then. You can imagine her answer. When we arrived at the hospital they took us to the birthing room. Ali had decided that she was going to give birth without any form of drugs, which I thought was silly as drugs are drugs and have a right to be used under these circumstances, but she was adamant. She tried the gas and air but it didn't agree with her. After twenty-eight hours of contractions and the constant loop of the *Twin Peaks* theme tune, she relented and elected to have an epidural. I immediately got on the gas and air – well it was rude to waste it. It was 1 a.m. on the morning of 8 October and the anaesthetist was called to administer the epidural.

A man staggered in looking the worse for wear as he had been working twenty-four hours straight and had just put his head down when he was called to us. He had just rolled out of bed and he looked like it too with ruffled hair. His name was Manuel.

'You are not going anywhere near my wife,' I said.

And he just waved me off saying in his Spanish accent, 'I get a coffee, I be fine.'

I felt helpless as I looked at the woman I loved trying to squeeze out a human baby whilst screaming in pain. I found it all very daunting, and my only contribution to the event, apart from the obvious, was to tell her she was doing well. At 5 a.m. on 8 October our beautiful boy was born to the sound of the now worn-out *Twin Peaks* track. The name we chose for him was Alfie Kenneth Webber. Kenneth was a shout out to Ali's dad and my Uncle Kenny. He was so beautiful I felt tears of joy trickling down my face. When the nurses passed him over to Ali, I looked at this little off-coloured bundle of life and my exhausted wife and was instantly filled with so much love for the two of them that I thought my heart would burst.

We were taken back to the ward and given a bed. As soon as Ali's head hit the pillow she crashed out and who could blame her, what I had just witnessed was incomprehensible. I climbed into bed with her and just squeezed her tight, kissing her and thanking her. I was so relieved that there were no complications and Alfie's perfect fingers and toes were all accounted for.

I closed my eyes to savour the moment and maybe get five minutes of kip as it had been a long couple of days, when a lovely West Indian nurse popped her head around the curtain. When she saw me in bed with Ali she said, in her beautiful accent, that sleeping with patients wasn't allowed. 'But I've just had a baby,' I protested. The nurse laughed and let us be.

Throughout the day people came up to visit. Sarah, Ali's sister, was the first. She asked what we were going to name him. 'Alfie,' we both said with pride and love.

'You can't name him Alfie,' she said, 'what if he wants to be a banker?' I couldn't believe what I was hearing.

'What if he wants to be a wanker,' I came back with. I was a bit put out with her comment to tell you the truth. The ol' man came up and asked the same question. He was also a bit put out as Eddie had been the name of the first born for generations of his family, but having the same name as one's father carried complications, I found. I was always called little Eddie and I hated it, so it was to stop here.

'Alfie is a common name,' he said. I shook my head in wonderment at people's insensitivity. When all the visits stopped, my beautiful wife and I, now parents, just sat in silence looking at our manifested love in his cot. It was too much that this beautiful little life had been made by us.

We arrived back home, put Alfie in his baby bed and stuck the *Twin Peaks* track on. As soon as the music started, his eyes closed and we never heard a peep out of him.

For the next few weeks he would wake up for food then, with constant music playing in the background, would just drift off to sleep again. Ali was resting up and our flat was filled with so much love and peace. Nappy time was a bit of a mission but I'll leave it there so as not to embarrass him. A memorable moment is when we first took him out in his pram. Ali felt so overcome with the bigness of the world and the desire to protect our little Alf that she started to cry. It was a beautiful moment for me to witness – it was the purest form of love that I had ever seen.

After a few months we decided that we would look for another place to live as the flat, although beautiful, was a bit small. So with Alfie in his newly acquired Mothercare car seat, we went a hunting. We drove around Dulwich, which we thought would be a good place for schools, but couldn't see anything that floated our boat. As we were driving back home, we turned into Clive Road in West Dulwich and there it was, number 139 with a 'for sale' sign outside. It looked perfect so we drove to the estate agents and they took us to view it. As soon as we walked in we both fell in love with the place and decided to buy it there and then.

All went well with the sale and we moved in a couple of months later. Number 139 Clive Road was built for us: a three double-bedroom Victorian house with a massive kitchen and living area. It was a great start to our new family life.

Alfie came into his own. He started to adopt an endearing mischievous, anti-authoritarian disposition (wonder where he got that from!), especially when he learnt to say the word no.

The little rascal relished in the power of the word but didn't like it when we said it to him. He climbed everything before he could even walk and we had to have eyes in the back of our heads. One day Ali and I were in the kitchen and we heard a rustling in the passage and a little distressed call. We rushed out into the hall and there was little Alf climbing up the outside of the banister dressed in a Spider-man suit. Funny how superhero history repeats itself.

It wasn't long before another wonderful lightning bolt struck. Ali told me she was pregnant again, which was a bit of a surprise, as Alfie was only nine months old.

He was settling in as our number one son and up on his feet. Our second beautiful boy, Barney, was born on 13 May 1997.

We went through the same procedure at St. George's Hospital and Alicia, who had helped deliver Alfie, was there at hand again. No one who visited mentioned anything about Barney's name this time. I'm sure they knew better of it. So there we were, a four-piece family centred in love.

Barney was completely different to Alfie; you didn't even know he was there. He was smiling all the time even with his older brother's incessant tormenting. Could history be repeating itself with the first and second born? It looked like they were going down the same road as me and Jackio with Barney stealing Alfie's thunder.

I was ticking along with the odd bit of TV work. One of the jobs was a TV adaptation of the film *Lock Stock and Two Smoking Barrels*. It was being shot at 3 Mills Studio using the same set as the TV series *Bad Girls*. I walked onto set and my mind went back to prison days. It was a perfect replica of a prison wing. It resurrected feelings of times gone by but with some differences; this time I was being paid to be there and the walls were made of cardboard. I was working with a great actor called Richard Graham who taught me a huge amount about TV acting. We struck up a great friendship which has lasted the years.

Everything was on track but, for some self-destructive reason, I started covertly using again the occasional line of coke and binge drinking. The come down from these demon substances caused a lot of grief between Ali and me; she had no idea of the extent of my addiction.

I realise now that my relationship with drink and drugs have never really been compatible but, like everything in life you come to regret, the realisation came a bit too late.

We now had two beautiful boys who we loved more than life itself and a beautiful house but, due to my weaknesses, I was on the road to nowhere. I became verbally abusive to her which, in turn, caused her to turn off and hide her love away for her own protection of sanity. I was becoming a bit of a monster and certainly not the man she first fell in love with at Morley College. Looking back at it all now, it was probably me getting angry at myself for not making the grade and taking it out on her, but it was going to get worse long before it was going to get better. My head was all over the place, only now we had two kids to grow, so I had to try and find something to make a living as acting wasn't enough.

One day I had to go to Bermondsey for a meeting. I had an hour to burn so popped into a pub. There was a live band playing made up of five local kids called 'Eusebio'. It was the nineties and the Britpop Indie scene was thriving with Oasis and Blur leading the way. I noticed that the guitarist was a cut above the rest. When their set had finished I had a chat with him. His name was Rob and he told me that he was thinking about leaving Eusebio to form another band with his cousin Kevin who was over from Australia. I gave him my number and told him to keep me informed.

A couple of weeks later I got the call that would take me down another road in life and another destructive adventure. I popped into one of their rehearsals and was blown away by their music.

I introduced myself to the rest of the band whose names were Pugsy and Dinesy. I told them there and then that I'd have a go at managing them if they put in the work and rehearsed every day – they all agreed. Rob and Kevin were quite prolific song writers and before long the band, who called themselves The Sound, were ready to get out into the world. Their first gig was at a pub called The Finish Arms in Bermondsey and it was packed out to the rafters. They had been rehearsing every day for about five or six months and were totally on top of their set. They smashed it that night. On the strength of that gig and a merciless PR campaign which took the shape of me putting posters up all over the place day and night, more local gigs started coming in and before long the band was gigging every week to full houses. I started developing a working relationship with a lovely guy called Dave Clarke who owned the local Southwark and Bermondsey newspaper *Southwark News*. He would take photos and give great reviews of every local gig. A few more local bands entered the mix and Dave and myself named the scene *Bermondsey Beat*.

I threw myself into the promotional side of it hook, line and sinker. In time, a few more bands that weren't from Bermondsey were added to the stable: Coloride led by my good friend Ian Jefferies, and Hubble Deep Field, named after the powerful space telescope. Their keyboard player, Harry Waters, was the son of Pink Floyd's Roger Waters. They were a great little psychedelic rock band. Harry incorporated a lot of his dad's original Pink Floyd synthesised sound into the band's set but most importantly they were all proficient musicians.

The other band was called Glyda. It was made up of sons and nephews of established rock stars. Tramper Price, son of Jim Price (The Rolling Stones); Will Boyd, nephew of Patti Boyd and Eric Clapton; and Jessie Wood, son of Ronnie Wood (Rolling Stones). Glyda was a great little blues rock band, again all great musicians and man did they kick. Will was heavily influenced by Eric Clapton, obviously, and his lead guitar was impeccable. They outshone The Sound in musicianship, but definitely not in the charisma department. All in all the ingredients were there for the kicking little music scene that was now developing.

Another good friend of mine Paul Hallam was promoting the prestigious 100 Club in Oxford Street at that time. I asked if he would give The Sound a gig there and he agreed.

The 100 Club gig was something else. I hired out a red double-decker bus to transport the fans from Bermondsey to Oxford Street and sold tickets. It was a sell-out in no time. The night of the gig the bus turned up at the designated meeting point and we all piled on. It was a mad journey. The bus driver didn't know how to get to Oxford Street and turned left down the Old Kent Road instead of right towards the Elephant and Castle. When I told him he was going the wrong way, he stopped the bus and illegally U-turned in the middle of the Old Kent Road to much cheer and merriment from the now-inebriated passengers. Rock 'n' roll.

We got to the 100 Club, fell off the bus and all filed in. The band rocked the club that night and the fans relished in the festivities to the point where Jeff, the owner, informed me that he had run out of booze an hour before the gig finished. Apart from a couple of scuffles, the night was a success.

The same night Paul introduced me to a friend of his, a photographer called Darren Russell who was photographing bands all over the world. You can see his work in a book called *100 Nights in the 100 Club*, I recommend you check it out. Darren was impressed with the band and said that he'd take some glossy snaps to make up a portfolio. We made arrangements for the shoot. Darren organised a clothing company to dress the boys and Vidal Sassoon to give them haircuts. I must say, they brushed up lovely with their new barnets (hair) and dressed in the fashion of the day. We shot some great publicity stuff. It was then we decided to get into the studio and record an album. We used a studio in Greenwich that was owned by a producer called Mick who I had met in Edinburgh when doing the Kray twins play. I borrowed some money from my mother-in-law and off we went. It was a fun time and we made a pretty good album, which we named 'Mrs Blue'. I asked my Aunt Kate if she would be on the cover as Mrs Blue and she agreed. Russell the Wise was now a fish stall holder in the Blue market place so we shot it in front of his stall.

I had another gig at the 100 Club with Hubble Deep Field and Glyda. We even incorporated Ali playing her bassoon live in one of Hubble Deep Field's songs. It was a star-studded night of sixties royalty.

Ronnie Wood, Mike Rutherford of Genesis, and Keith Richard's ex-wife, Anita Pallenberg, all turned up.

I must admit I had a bit of a giggle to myself as I looked around and reflected on my crazy life as all these mega stars walked through the door. It was very surreal (I hope they all paid). The bands did me and their families proud and put on a fine performance.

To promote The Sound's debut album, and with the Sex Pistols in mind, I hired out a pleasure boat and did the necessary PR. Like the 100 Club gig, the tickets sold out in a couple of days. I called a few people that were in the music business and invited them to the evening. A guy called Morris turned up who worked for a record company, owned by a couple of brothers, that operated out of a famous boxing gym in the East End of London. After the band performed he was pretty impressed. That was it in my eyes, I was sure it wasn't going to be long before a deal was put on the table. I was elated, at last the future seemed productive again. The Sound had been on the road for over a year at this point, playing all the prestigious and shit venues that London could offer. Ali and I were loving this dip into the music industry. It was exciting times.

I got a phone call from Rob one afternoon to say that the band wanted to have a meeting. I headed off to Rob's house in Bermondsey. I knocked on the door, Rob answered with the rest of the band standing behind him and, then and there, I was unceremoniously fired! They made some silly excuse that I wasn't doing my job and they wanted to go it alone. *Wasn't doing my job?*

I had been out all hours of the night pasting posters up all over the place, rain sleet or snow. I was funding the project out of my own pocket. I had made it possible to record an album, put on all sorts of promotions including getting them on show in the 100 Club, my home life was suffering, I had two little babies all whilst trying to maintain an acting career. I was flabbergasted – a year and a half of my life wasted and inches away from a record deal. I was furious and told them so in quite an aggressive manner. I stormed off with tears of anger in my eyes. What the fuck had happened? It all seemed like it was going well.

Over the next few days I found out what had happened. Morris, the record producer, had approached the band behind my back and convinced them that he could take them further than I could. Unbelievable! I'd given my heart and soul to these boys and to be sold down the river like that was unforgivable. I found out that the brothers who

Morris worked for were friends of some people I knew and, through them, I arranged a meeting. I stormed over to the gym and told the brothers that going to The Sound behind my back was a liberty after all the work I'd put in. They didn't have a clue what I was talking about. Morris had done it off his own back. They assured me that they would talk to Morris and would have nothing more to do with the band. I felt a bit better and somewhat vindicated. If the band and Morris had been upfront with me and not so duplicitous in their actions, I'm sure we could have worked something out, but fuck it, fire has to be met with fire, right or wrong. Morris backed away and the band split up. The damage had been done once more, the guard had come down and being fucked over again was the price. When was I going to learn?

Trust was a dangerous game, a game that I was finding totally out of my league. What was the universe up to? Every time I went two steps forward in life I always seemed to end up taking three steps back. I didn't know which way to turn at this time. I had no spiritual philosophy. At least when I was a Christian I had a soft comfort blanket but now my blanket seemed to be made of barbed wire. I was lucky I still had my acting or I think I would have imploded. But acting wouldn't be enough to provide for my family. The cultural divide between Ali and me was starting to raise its ugly head. I went into a crazy state of mind and Ali, to my shame, fell into despair. I just couldn't see any way out. Was it time to do another deal with the man upstairs? I think not, me and the top man were at war and he could go fuck himself as far as I was concerned. The mist inside my head was too dense to make head nor tail out of anything. I had lost my way again but instead of communicating, myself and Ali turned off to each other. The kids were still babies and I was lucky that they were young enough not to be too badly affected by my frequent, atrocious behaviour and shouting bouts. I look back at these times with a great sadness as I was unreachable. I think if Ali and I could have communicated a bit more, we could have stopped the rot that was setting in. I'm truly sorry Ali but I know you know I did love you and always will.

I carried on promoting Hubble and Glyda but without any conviction. My heart wasn't in it anymore. I had invested too much time and energy in The Sound and had been brought down with an almighty thump.

Fuck it all was my attitude.

CHAPTER TWENTY-THREE

I made a crazy and impulsive decision to open a bar in Spain.

I spoke to Ali and we decided this change of circumstances could be what we needed to get our family life back on track. I decided to forget the notion of becoming a film star or a rock band manager. So the next Tuesday, I packed my bags and headed off to what I again thought was a sunny future. I was going to get things sorted and Ali and the kids were to follow. I touched down in Malaga airport with a new perspective. I spent the next couple of weeks acclimatising to my new environment and was happy to find a few friends from Bermondsey that were living out there, one of them being Lee of 'Hells Angels on the heath' fame. Home from home so to speak.

Marbella is a funny place and has a sort of false romanticism about it. In the 1980s, British elite criminals exploited the no extradition law between the UK and Spain and settled out there to enjoy their ill-gotten gains and start a drug-smuggling production line that touched the whole of Europe. The bonus being it was all done in the sun.

It seemed Marbella belonged nowhere in the world. The majority of ex-pats out there were either successful retired businessmen or people on the run for one thing or another.

After a month, the bar was ready to open and what an opening night it was, packed out to the rafters with a mad mix of heroes, villains and the roads in between. What could go wrong?

After the success of the opening night we were all patting ourselves on the back. The coffers were full and the future looked like the weather out there: bright. It was long before the euro and it was cheap to live as the pound was strong. More importantly, for some people there was a great black money micro economy that kept the country above water. Every transaction was usually cash and void of any bank dealings.

I set about finding a school for the kids and we settled on Aloha College which was situated near Puerto Banus, a glitzy harbour by day and Sodom and Gomorrah by night. To someone like me with a booze habit it was like pouring petrol on a fire.

You could drink twenty-four seven (which I did a few times in the coming years) but I was okay at that moment as I was on a mission. I kept the demon brew at bay whilst in the bar, at first.

The kids were accepted into the school. They were still in the UK and not due to come over for a couple of months but the school headache was out of the way.

One night after I finished work in the early hours, I had had a drink but instead of getting a cab, I decided to drive home. As I approached a roundabout, to my horror I came face to face with a Spanish scuffer road block. They pulled me over and breathalysed me. I was well over the limit. The officer looked at his breathalyser machine, looked at me and shook his head and asked for my passport. As I handed it to him I whispered the magic words, 'Sin factura' (without ticket). He looked at one of his cop friends and called him over. They started chatting and looking at me between words. When his friend left, the officer nodded, gave me a wink then gave me a price – three hundred pounds to turn a blind eye to my silliness. Trouble was I had no cash on me. I told him of my predicament and he had a solution. As he waved over a waiting police car I thought, *Fuck it, now I am in trouble*. Drunk and driving and trying to bribe a scuffer, here we go again. I tried to talk my way out of it but my Spanish left a lot to be desired and it came to no avail. I resigned myself to the fact that I was nicked and sat in the back of the car. But his solution was to drive me to a cash machine to draw out the three hundred quid required.

He took the money, led me to the police car and drove me back to my car where I was told to wait awhile, drink some water and then basically, fuck off. I drove my car up the road and parked it up as I was paranoid that the police would probably pull me over again and go for another three hundred quid or, worse still, arrest me. It was a lucky escape and, as you can imagine, I never drove whilst drunk again... except for a couple of times.

I found it a very civil way to learn a lesson. It could never happen in the UK like that. I would have been banned from driving or even given a prison sentence. Not to mention bribing a cop as well. Lesson learnt, that night the universe was truly with me (to my shame).

I was introduced to a little ex-timeshare family firm who were starting to make movies out there and for the next few months I would visit their offices and just generally chew the fat with the son, Darren. The timeshare label should have flagged up a warning but they seemed nice people and their employment history was irrelevant to me at that time. Darren, who had just finished his degree course in film school, had started to shoot a few ads for companies out there and wasn't a bad filmmaker. We would talk about movies and stuff which was nice as it seemed to keep me in a creative loop instead of talking bollocks to drunken and sometimes broken, shady characters.

The bar was ticking by and the week before Ali and the kids came over, I found a lovely apartment that overlooked the sea in San Pedro.

The house in Dulwich was to be rented out so it would generate a bit more income which paid for the school and covered the rent of the apartment. I was getting a good wage from the bar and apart from my few demons raising their heads now and then, all was, as they say, hunky-dory.

Ali and the kids arrived, we moved into the apartment and the kids started school. Aloha College was an international private school so everyone there spoke English. The kids loved it and made some nice friends. When they finished school they would come home and we'd all play around the swimming pool or have a walk down the beach. It was very different to the lifestyle they had led up to now and they excelled. What kid wouldn't – sun, sea and sand every day. We found a couple of nice restaurants inland and a few friends and our new life had begun.

I was working all the hours under the sun in the bar. The cliental were from all walks of life. There was a hooky doctor that was used by the locals to remove the odd misplaced bullet every now and then, London criminals on the run from the UK and Europe, girls that earned their money on the streets. I used to survey the surroundings sometimes and shake my head and think if the devil could cast his net. I started drinking more and more to alleviate the boredom of standing behind the bar. I personally couldn't wait to get out of the place at the end of the night as working behind the bar killed any creativity that I had left, listening to drunken people telling their sad life stories.

It used to drive me mad, as every bar person knows, when people are drunk the barman or woman becomes their best friend and confidante. You are a captive ear and there is no sanctuary behind a bar.

Everyone I knew from London used to pop in when they were over on holiday, which was nice as it was a chance to catch up.

One particular guy, who we will call Fred, used to frequent the place. He used to pop in every night and, to tell you the truth, was a bit of a loud mouth nuisance, and a big cocaine user. When he was out of his nut, he would upset a lot of people. I tried to make him see sense but the booze and drugs took all his rationale away. When behind the bar, you would sometimes be privy to covert conversations from the punters. Another guy who drank in the pub didn't like Fred at all, and one night put one on Fred's chin and knocked him spark out. When Fred came to, he started threatening the man who had chinned him, saying things like, 'I'm going to shoot you and after I shoot you, I'm going to shoot your family.' The guy who hit him just smiled as Fred left the bar, still threatening and shouting his mouth off. I never saw Fred again.

It was all going crazy once more. Sometimes I would sit and think if all the grief of working in the bar was worth it.

Ali had no idea what was going on as I really wanted to keep her out of it all. So I would hide the fact that I was drinking more and taking some coke just to get through the monotonous days and nights. My behaviour was getting worse as I had a hangover most mornings. I became distant as all I seemed to be doing was getting up, going to work and drinking every day – there didn't seem to be any middle ground to be with my family. After a year or so running the bar and sliding deeper and deeper down the abyss, I made the executive decision leave the place. I had uprooted my family from the UK on the strength of this job and had failed abysmally down to my addictions.

It was at this time that I made a mistake that I have regretted all my life.

We decided, well I convinced Ali, to sell our beautiful family house in Dulwich, as I thought that we would be staying in Spain forever. It made sense to buy a house instead of throwing money away on rent. Ali was always adamant that we shouldn't sell our house unless we were getting an income but me being me – an addict and a fool to boot – didn't listen. Plus the person that was renting the house had started to mess about with the rent. So it started to become aggravation and we did the deed and put it up for sale.

We went house hunting, found a house on an urbanisation in Estepona and we bought it, without too much thought. The urbanisation was lovely, it had a massive swimming pool for the kids and the majority of people that lived on it were Spanish. Ali never had a good feeling about it, but again I convinced her that it was okay. I was probably suffering from another hangover at the time. We were never really happy there, which I'm sure added to our internal strife. Again, I'm truly sorry Al.

Ali had met a lovely classy, creative Indian woman by the name of Yasmin and they both decided to try and introduce a bit of culture into the creative dry lands of Marbella and get some kind of an income at the same time. Yasmin was the wife of a successful clothes designer called Farouk, both very nice people. The match of these two classy ladies was made in heaven. They started up a youth arts festival called Fuente, which concentrated on dance and performance incorporating all the Spanish international schools and conservatoires. In the meantime I had to think of getting some sort of living out there. I couldn't uproot my family again and we had no house in the UK anymore. It was a scary time.

There were lots of offers to help me out but it meant moving to the wrong side of the tracks again. I had chosen a new way of life and had promised Ali, myself and her family that no matter how financially bad off we were, I would never go back to that way of life. Don't get me wrong, it has been so tempting over the years but as the great swami Jesus allured to, temptation resisted is a true measure of character. Pity

I never put those wise words into effect with regards to how much alcohol I was drinking at the time. I would have to try to get us out of this situation the right way and trust the ultimate complexity.

As I was walking along a beach one day, pondering our circumstances, I bumped into Darren. He told me that he was putting a movie together called *Oh Marbella!* and there was a lead part for me if I wanted it. I said yes immediately. They had set up a film company called Versatile Films and were in the process of trying to get the funding.

I told him that I would try and help on the casting side. So I got in touch with a couple of good acting friends of mine back in the UK, Tom Bell and Geoff Bell (no relation). Tom was the father of Aran Bell, who played Reggie Kray in our Edinburgh play and Geoff was an old friend from the South London streets and Morley College. They both jumped on board feet first. The funding process for the movie started to move quite quickly.

The part I was going to play was a timeshare victim – *ding!* – called Dave. The plot evolved around four different stories and perspectives of Marbella which would all somehow intersect at the end of the movie. My character, Dave, and his wife Tina, who was to be played by a fabulous UK actress called Cathy Murphy (*EastEnders*), are out on holiday in Marbella and get fleeced by a timeshare operator.

Rik Mayall was to play the timeshare salesman who fleeces the trusting couple of everything, even Tina's fidelity.

Rik was a hero of mine. I was a huge fan of the ground-breaking TV series *The Young Ones* and the eighties new alternative comedy scene that Rik was paramount in bringing to the fore. Rik had had a bad quad bike accident the year before and was seriously hurt so this was his first film after mending.

The other members of the cast included Mike Reid, a great seventies old-school stand-up comedian who also had a recent tragic past and was one of the leading characters in *EastEnders*. Tom Bell, Geoff Bell, Craig Kelly, from the TV series *Queer as Folk*, David Gant, my old Bermondsey light ale (pal) Roland Manookian, Lara Belmont and Sara Stockbridge, a one-time muse for Vivienne Westwood, and last but by no means least, Jake Abraham from Guy Richie's *Mean Machine*. It was to be directed and written by Piers Ashworth, a Hollywood writer who had also settled out there in a little village inland, and his writing partner, Nick Morcroft, a lovable rogue who hailed from the mean fields of Essex, who I became great friends with. Darren's parents, were producing the movie. I'm sure that their timeshare education and spiel helped a lot when pitching for the money. It wasn't long before the movie was fully funded but I thought the producers were playing with fire as they took money from some pretty dubious people who saw it as an opportunity to clean up a bit of black scratch (money).

Cathy Murphy flew in from the UK and I picked her up from the airport. We spent some time chatting about our characters then I took her to the hotel where all the cast were staying. My friend Tom Bell was arriving the next day. I told the producers I'd pick him up but they declined the offer because as Tom was quite a bit of a name in the film business, they wanted to lay on the glitz and pick him up in a limo. A limo was so not Tom and I warned them but they weren't having any of it.

The next day I was in my house, it was late, when the phone went. A manic French accent at the other end started pleading for me to come to the hotel as Tom had arrived drunk and was beginning to get a little out of control. When I got to the hotel there was pandemonium. Tom had arrived drunk and Darren's mum rushed up to him all excited and started the sycophantic stuff, 'Oh Tom, I am a big fan, I am so pleased you are a part of this movie,' to which Tom replied, 'Who the fuck are you, you fat French cunt? Where's Eddie?'

I managed to calm him down then guided him to his room. On the plane over he'd managed to polish off a good few vodkas as he was one of those old-school sixties actors that liked a drink – think Richard Harris and Peter O' Toole. I started pissing myself laughing at the sight of Darren's mum in a frenzy, almost having a breakdown caused by Tom's insults. When Tom was safely tucked up in his room, I shot out to get him some food and water as he hadn't eaten or drunk anything, apart from vodka that is. When I came back he'd been at it again, round two.

Later I was told he had mercilessly verbally abused everyone in authority concerned with the film. I got him to his room again and forced him to eat a nice bit of paella and drink some water then left him to rest. The blind leading the blind comes to mind. I hung around for a bit in case his inner demons decided to arise again but that was him chucking out zzzz for the night, phew.

The next problem with Tom arose when he found out he'd be working with Mike Reid. In Tom's eyes he was a stand-up comedian and should have no part of being a film actor. 'Fooking stand-up comedian, fooking *EastEnders*, you taking the fooking piss.' Tom and Mike eventually found an equilibrium after Mike told him of the recent tragic suicide of his son. Although Tom was a bit of a rascal, he also was a creative and his heart and empathy for the downtrodden was always in the right place. Mike was a big fan of his also. So in the end it all worked out and they played some pretty funny scenes together. Try and get hold of the movie to see the three great men who are no longer on this earth. They don't make them like Tom, Mike and Rik anymore and I still miss Tom dearly. Rest in peace my old cocker and God help them fooking officious angels up there when you arrived.

Oh Marbella! was my first lead role in a film and I was determined to do a good job. The first day of filming was at Malaga airport and the whole cast was involved as it was the start of every characters' journey in the film. Ali, Alfie and Barney came along and it was a wonderful day's filming – the kids and Ali were also incorporated as extras which was a bonus for me.

The first day was in the can. It was an intricate scene where all the characters passed each other at some point in the baggage hall.

Rik arrived that evening to do our first scene the day after. I felt a bit nervous but I had nothing to worry about. As soon as we met we gelled. We would spend the next three weeks chatting and laughing and talking about everything sacred: *The Young Ones*, the effect that his accident had on his life, the start of the alternative comedy scene, nothing was out of bounds except for booze. He couldn't drink alcohol due to the brain damage from his accident. When exposed to booze it caused a chemical reaction which sent him into some sort of epileptic fit.

One night, we were all sitting in the hotel chatting after the day's filming. I piped up for a joke, 'Fuck this, this is the last time I do a job like this for a hundred grand.' Everyone laughed.

The next day on set the director called me aside. 'What did you say to Rik last night?'

I shook my head not having a scooby (clue) what he was talking about. 'Nothing untoward. Why?'

'He asked should he know you as an actor.'

'Why the fuck should he know me?'

'Well he couldn't believe you were getting a hundred grand for the film, knowing how much he was being paid.' Classic. Another one who I bet gave the angels a bit of jip when he arrived at the heavenly comedy club.

It turned out to be a good little movie, though it was a shame the producers ended up not being very competent souls as the movie never really saw the light of day. It was a shame especially, in retrospect, for the actors that are no longer with us but I met some life-long friends in the film's stills photographer Johnny Gates and the film's PR man and now international radio DJ Giles Brown.

CHAPTER TWENTY-FOUR

We screened the film in London. After the screening I met a woman called Kate Staddon who was an agent for Curtis Brown, a prestigious talent agency in London and New York. After seeing my performance she agreed to represent me. This was definitely a step up. I went back to Spain elated. I started to get work again in the UK and had to start commuting, sometimes twice a month. I used to fly out of Gibraltar, fill up with boxes of cigarettes at the duty-free shop and sell them back in the UK, which would cover my expenses to and fro. Getting work again in the UK was weird as I had left not intending to carry on my acting career. I had parts TV shows like *Doc Martin, The Bill* and others, I just couldn't shake acting off. Every time I decided to give it up, I'd get more work. I'd stay at my mum's in Bermondsey which was sometimes hard work as she had got used to living on her own after having enough of the ol' man and chucking him out a couple of years beforehand...not before time, in my book. He had abused her love and kindness for long enough and a good woman scorned and all that, sooner or later runs out of forgiveness.

Back in Spain, Ali and Yasmin's company started taking off. They were putting on some great extravaganzas of dance and performance in some great venues in Marbella, which led them to take shows to Paris and London. They worked all the hours God sent and it was paying off.

I loved the shows. Dancers would come from all over Spain and

Europe and would perform Flamenco, Classical, all styles right through the card. They had managed to get the Spanish superstar dancer Joaquin Cortés to be the patron of their company which was a huge coup de grâce and no mean feat for two British girls moving in a Spanish hierarchy.

We decided to take the kids out of Aloha College and put them into a Spanish school in central Marbella as we thought it a good idea for them to learn the language. They hated it. Especially Alfie. He was so unhappy being uprooted again and it showed, poor love, but we took the stance of sometimes you had to be cruel to be kind and a new language would stand them both in good stead for the future.

My photographer friend Darren, who did The Sound photos back in the day, called up and asked if he could visit. I hadn't seen him for a while and welcomed him with open arms. We met at Malaga airport and as we crossed the road to get to the car park, a car nearly hit me. I started shouting at the driver when suddenly Darren shouted out a name and went to talk to the driver in the car. The driver was a friend of his that had relocated out there as well. After talking about what a small world it was, we swapped numbers for the purpose of meeting in the next few days. On the car journey back Darren told me the driver's name was Paul Newman who was part of the big mod revival back in London and was a great blues guitarist to boot. I took Darren out to a bar that night and he met a few of the unsavoury characters that drank there.

He took his camera out but I told him it wouldn't be a good idea to take photos as some of the people in the pub would not appreciate it. The camera went back in its case faster than it came out. The next day we all went to Gibraltar where Darren took some amazing family photos for us that still have pride of place on our walls at home.

A couple of days later was New Year's Eve and we ended up at a big party. Darren pulled out his camera and was promptly told to put it away once more. The booze and merriment flowed all night, and it was most definitely one to remember.

The next day was a nightmare, though, as the hangover from hell was upon me. I stayed in bed the whole day which annoyed Ali as she probably wanted to walk up a mountain or something crazy like that, but I was out for the count.

Darren arranged to meet Paul the day after and we met in a bar just outside Marbella. At the end of the meeting Paul and I had decided to put a blues band together and promptly advertised in *The Sur*, an English newspaper out there, for a bass player and a drummer. The ads were answered by a bass player called Terry and a drummer, who didn't look unlike Mike Reid. We nicknamed him Bo Dollar on account of him always talking about what possessions he had. I took a dislike to him straight away but he was a good drummer so I suffered him.

We started rehearsing in a little studio in Fuengirola and before long we had knocked together a kicking little authentic Chicago blues set. Paul was, and still is, an amazing guitarist and a blues man to his soul.

One of my great musical heroes growing up was Lonnie Donegan, who was responsible for bringing Skiffle music to the UK in the fifties. Skiffle was a music genre with jazz, blues and American folk influences, usually using a combination of manufactured and homemade instruments like washboards and wooden boxes with broom handles and string for the bass. Lonnie had also been a great influence to John Lennon and The Beatles. One day, as the band were rehearsing the Peter Green version of 'Sugar Mama' in the studio, the door opened and who should walk in, none other than the man himself. He was rehearsing for a show in the room next door. You could have knocked me down with a feather. Paul's lead guitar playing had drawn him in. I stopped the rehearsal and spent the next half hour in rock 'n' roll heaven as he told us stories about his early days getting it together in fifties England, playing the devil's music and meeting the greats like John Lennon, Chuck Berry and Muddy Waters. He asked us to play some more and we obliged with Muddy Waters' 'Hoochy Koochy Man'. I've never been the sort of person to be in awe of anyone but that night goes down as a tick on the ol' bucket list. I feel blessed that it happened as the great man passed not long after. If I'd had the presence of mind, I would have got him to sign my guitar but we have a saying where I come from: 'If my aunt had bollocks she'd be my uncle' (sounds like a Lonnie Donegan song).

Our first gig in Spain was in a little club in Fuengirola. I don't think the audience really got what we were doing. We had a great blues set: Little Walter, Sonny Boy Williamson, Jimmy Reed, Muddy Waters, Tommy Tucker to name but a few. There were lots of white socks, sandals and football shirts from the UK who kept asking us to play 'Wonderwall' by Oasis. Don't get me wrong, I love a bit of nineties indie but this was definitely not the place for it. We got paid at the end of the night and we were happy.

Art is such an organic thing, I find. From nearly getting run over by Paul at the airport, here we were performing together and getting paid. We started playing little clubs up and down the coast. We didn't get a lot of money but we were being productive. It was the same path as I had been treading in Israel all those years back. Time had stood still.

People started recognising me from *Oh Marbella!* It was the first time I was being acknowledged by strangers for my acting work and I must say I got a buzz from it. At the end of each gig we would hang about in the venue and party.

My favourite drink at the time was Spanish Brandy, a powerful brew. I shudder when I think of how much I was drinking at that time and what it did to my life but I couldn't see any way of stopping it. Then, from out of the blue, a human was sent to help me.

After *Oh Marbella!* Darren and his family started putting together another movie about the sex slave industry. It was originally going to be called *Wish You Were Here* but was later renamed *Slave*. It was written by a lovely lad called Bret Goldstein. They wanted me to play a convert to Islam named Salim. Okay! Why not?

Two established American actors, Sam Page and Natassia Malthe, and Roger Pera, who was Spanish, were cast together with ex-pat Michael Maxwell, and my old mate from *Oh Marbella!* David Gant. It was an interesting little piece. I was asked if I knew anyone in the UK that could play a club owner. It was a nice part. I got in touch with another friend of mine who knew Howard Marks, who was quite a notorious drug smuggler back in the day. He had written a book called *Mr Nice* which had become a bestseller. He agreed to come over and do it.

Darren and his family were made up and looked at Howard's involvement as a coup. Howard and I had a mutual friend in Spain who Howard was to stay with whilst over here. It was fascinating to be with him in Spain, apart from hearing all his stories about his many years spent in the American prison system. Everyone seemed to have read his book and it took ages to walk anywhere when you were with him as everyone wanted a photo.

We started shooting the movie and it came to the time when we had to spend a few days filming on a massive yacht which was anchored in the middle of the Med. We would all be sleeping on it as well. About two o'clock one morning I couldn't sleep so I thought I'd look for some drink. I walked around the boat opening cupboards looking for a lonely bottle of brandy that would give me peace. I entered the kitchen and Michael Maxwell was sitting there alone smoking a fag. I bade him well then carried on my search for the elusive bottle of booze. He just watched me in silence opening and shutting cupboards with a knowing, thin smile on his face.

After a while and no luck in the booze department, I piped up, 'Where the fuck can I get a drink on this poxy boat?'

Michael laughed. 'You don't need a drink, have a cup of tea.'

'Fuck tea, I need brandy.'

'No you don't.'

I sat down with him and found out that he was a recovering alcoholic. He gave me his number and said to ring him anytime if I'd like to speak more about it. I laughed and denied I had a drink problem (as you do). We left it at that and I trundled off sober to bed to wrestle with my demons for the duration of the dawn.

Slave could have been a good film but once more the producers for some reason never made the grade. After the film had wrapped, we had a party and our blues band was the entertainment for the evening. Every time I swigged back a shot of brandy and met with Michael's eyes, some kind of guilt connection would happen which made me a little self-conscious. I told him this and he just laughed knowingly again and said, 'Well, you have my number.'

The film never really saw the light of day. I don't know if that was a good or bad thing but it was my second movie and I had shaped up a good character in Salim, so I'm told.

Over the next few months I returned to the UK to do some more TV work but I had the buzz for movies and wondered when I'd get the chance to do another one. Life in Spain carried on as normal with Ali and me struggling to make ends meet.

One particular argument left me angry and Ali in tears and this time she gave me no quarter. She was leaving me and taking the kids back to the UK. The sincerity in her words left me in no doubt that she meant it, especially when she said I had become a monster and she didn't love me anymore. It was like a ton weight falling on me that shook me to my soul. I pleaded with her not to go and decided that I would have to do something about my behaviour. She stayed and I picked up the phone and dialled Michael's number. We arranged to meet the next night and go to an AA meeting. The meeting was in an old church in the old town of Marbella. We entered a room where there were twenty people sitting in chairs, some of them deep in thought, shouldering what seemed like an eternal sadness in their eyes. All these people had, at some point, reached their rock bottom. Some had lost everything that was dear to them, wives, kids, homes. The meeting started with the serenity prayer.

> *God, grant me the serenity to accept the things I cannot change, Courage to change the things I can, And wisdom to know the difference.*

The words resonated with me. It was about asking God to help again. A few people stood up to share their stories, Michael being one of them. I sat and listened and was sometimes shocked at the words spoken. A lot of these people's rock bottom moments made mine look like a kid's story. I chose not to speak but was profoundly affected. At the end of the meeting myself, Michael and a couple of others went to a little café and drank coffee.

These were brave people that had reached their limits and wanted to face their demons, I was inspired by their bravery.

I realised that this was not going to be a quick fix, it was a day by day thing. I was encouraged to introduce the mantra 'I won't drink today' into my life. I felt a ray of hope about the future. I started to attend regular meetings and joined a gym. Ali went to Al-Anon (for family and friends of alcoholics) and was pleased that I had made a start on the road to recovery and put her threat to leave me on hold. Being clean and getting fit in body and mind started to feel good. I also had to change my social circle but the alternative of losing my family made every decision easy.

We started to get back on track. I still got angry from time to time but it wasn't because of a hangover. I began to look for work and decided that I would have a go at selling a health product called Herbalife.

It worked like a pyramid system, the more people you turned onto it, the more money you earnt. I started incorporating the product into my new fitness regime and, I must admit, it worked for me. After a couple of months I had dropped as many stones. I made a little money but not enough to maintain our family so I knocked that part of it on the head but carried on using the product.

Ali and Yasmin's company was well established by then. Every year they would put on their event in the main theatre in Marbella. They had full support from the Ayuntamiento (town council) of Marbella which was a feat in itself for two foreign nationals. They were working so hard to make it all work and began a national dance competition too.

I feel another cap doff coming. Ali and Yasmin had established a life-long friendship that I'm sure had a lot to do with maintaining Ali's sanity whilst putting up with me. I started to see the world in a different perspective and the hangover free mornings were a blessing. I kept the meetings up for about nine months. AA had a twelve-step programme that I couldn't really get my head around. Step 1 was about the only one I could relate to.

(1) We admit we were powerless over alcohol – that our lives had become unmanageable.

(2) Come to believe that a Power greater than ourselves could restore us to sanity.

(3) Make a decision to turn our will and our lives over to the care of God as we understand Him.

(4) Make a searching and fearless moral inventory of ourselves.

(5) Admit to God, to ourselves and to another human being the exact nature of our wrongs.

(6) We're entirely ready to have God remove all these defects of character.

(7) Humbly asked him to remove our shortcomings.

(8) Make a list of all persons we have harmed and become willing to make amends to them all.

(9) Make direct amends to such people wherever possible, except when to do so would injure them or others.

(10) Continue to take personal inventory and when we are wrong promptly admit it.

(11) Sought through prayer and meditation to improve our conscious contact with God as we understand him, praying only for knowledge of his will for us and the power to carry that out.

(12) Having had a spiritual awakening as the result of these steps, we try to carry this message to alcoholics and to practice these principles in all our affairs.[1]

The only trouble for me, at that stage, was that I could not equate the concept of any higher power after my disastrous born-again Christian era. It left me very suspicious of any sort of religious concept. It would be years before I found any kind of spirituality again, though find it I did in India. So I decided that I would have to be strong enough to go it alone, with the knowledge that if I fucked up again, Ali and the kids would be down the frog and toad (road).

---

1   Alcoholics Anonymous The Twelve Steps of Alcoholics Anonymous

Chapter Twenty-Five

A few months later came a stroke of luck. Ali and Yasmin were at some sort of networking party for Fuente one night. When she got back that evening she told me she had met an actor from South London who was involved in a film that was to be shot over here, about London gangsters in the eighties. She told him that I was an actor from Bermondsey and would be perfect for a project like this. He gave her his number and told her to get me to call him ASAP as he was going home the day after tomorrow. His name was Tamer Hassan. I gave him a call in the morning and arranged to meet him at a Chirinquito in La Cala that afternoon.

I entered the Chirinquito with a CV in hand and there was the unforgettable Tamer looking like a movie star, sitting around a packed table with his entourage. Our eyes met and he invited me over. He told me that he was involved with a director/writer called Nick Love and they were working on a movie called *The Business* also starring Danny Dyer. He went through the plot of the film. I started to get a bit excited about the content. When he told me the other actors involved I laughed. My ol' pals from the flats and *Oh Marbella!* Roland Manookian and Geoff Bell. I handed Tamer my CV and a DVD of *Oh Marbella!* and he promised to lay it on Nick.

'You got a good boat [face] for this,' he said as we shook hands. I left the beach feeling really good about the meeting. I then text Roland

and Geoff to ask if they could stick my name up to Nick Love as well. Roland got back and said he had already done it. I had a tingle in my belly over the next few days, something seemed very right about the project. At the end of the week I got a call from Kate, my agent, with an audition for the film in North London. I booked a flight and spent the next few nights sleepless with excitement.

I landed in Gatwick the day before the audition and phoned Roland. He told me that it was looking good as Tamer had also piped me up. I arrived at Vertigo Film's office and Nick was there to meet me, dressed head to toe in Fila clobber and with a grin like a Cheshire cat. He came across as a nice confident fella, 'one of your own' as we say. We went into a room where Geoff and Tamer were sitting. When I walked in, it was all cuddles and smiles.

I'd never felt so relaxed at an audition before. We started to improvise a couple of scenes from the film and ended up in fits of laughter. And after we all went out for a bit of brady bunch (lunch). Nick and myself had a few mutual friends that lived out in Spain and in the UK, which gave us some common ground. I left the meeting walking on air as I couldn't have done much more in the audition. Usually after auditions I'd walk back to the tube station thinking I should have done it this way or should have done it that way but I was totally at ease. Now the hard part: the wait to see if I had secured the job.

I flew back to Spain and after a few days called up Geoff fishing about trying to find out if he had heard any feedback. He hadn't. Another couple of days went by, still nothing. It had been a week since the meeting and not a dicky bird. I was gutted. I really thought I had nicked the job. I put it out of my mind and carried on with sober life. I was sitting in my house feeling a bit depressed when the phone rang. I answered and it was Nick.

'I thought I'd call you myself to tell you the bad news, Webber.' My heart dropped.

'Okay mate, I appreciate it, if you could keep me in mind for any other parts in the film I'd be grateful.'

Nick started laughing which I thought a bit odd. 'Course you got the job, you cunt, you were bang on.'

Did I hear right? 'Eh?'

'You're in, I thought I'd just let you roast for a bit.'

'Ah you cunt, I've been pulling my hair out here.'

He laughed and told me he'd send the script and be in touch, then ended the call. I tell you the last week had been a stressful one and now I could relax.

The script arrived and I spent the next hour or so reading it and belly laughing at the familiarity of the writing. Kate called and it was official, I was to play Ronnie in the film. Nick called and told me he was coming out for a recce and could we meet. Could we meet? Is the pope Catholic?

The next week I met him in Puerto Banus. He came back to the house and we spent a lovely day with Ali and the kids by the pool chatting. It ended up us having a few more things in common as I told him about the demons that I was trying to contain. That evening we all went to eat at Rufinos, a little restaurant that was a favourite of ours in a beautiful little village called Benahavis. We spoke about the character Ronnie and what truth I could bring to him. Fuck me, I thought, I was Ronnie. We also talked about a couple of peripheral roles in the film that needed to be cast and, as I lived out there, could I help as the aggravation of bringing people over from the UK was not really that cost effective. I put up the name of my mate Michael Maxwell for the biscuit man at the beginning of the movie and another couple of friends, Joanne and Sylvia, for smaller parts. I drove Michael, Joanne and Sylvia up to Nerja two days later to meet Nick and the casting director Gary Davis and they all got the parts.

The character Ronnie didn't have many lines in the movie but a lot to do, so it was up to me to shape up a worthy skin. I called Nick up and suggested a few ideas, one of them being bringing Alfie and Barney in as Ronnie's kids. He loved the idea. It was nice to know that Nick was the kind of director who was open to suggestions.

Over the next eight weeks I think I drove him a bit mad with my script ideas. Another suggestion was in the scene where Geoff, who played the psychotic Sammy, asks Ronnie to shoot a lad who fucked the gang over. In the original script Ronnie shoots him. I suggested that Ronnie refuses as he was a man of principle and shooting young lads wasn't what he was about. Again he agreed.

The movie was ready to go – I arranged to pick Geoff and Danny Dyer up at Malaga airport and take them to Almunecar, in the province of Granada, where the movie was going to be shot. Danny was getting a name for himself after doing *Human Traffic* and two other Nick Love films, *Goodbye Charlie Bright* and *The Football Factory*. Tamer was already out there. I picked them up in my convertible ten-year-old 3 series BMW 318i. The sun was beating down and the roof was off. I drove the scenic route to enjoy the beautiful vistas that lined the way to Almunecar.

The film unit were staying in a hotel made up of self-contained apartments which was a bonus as you were not tied down to eating in restaurants all the time. There were a few good parties held in those rooms I can tell you. Like when I was up in Scotland with the Kray play, we all decided that we would stay in our characters the whole time. Adam Bolton, who played Ronnie's mucker Danny, was to arrive the next week with Linda Henry, who played my wife Shirley, and Camille Corduri, who played Nora, Dan's wife. Adam and I gelled immediately and became pals just like our characters in the movie.

So there we were, a motley group of little-known East, South and West London actors ready to start the journey of filming which would change our lives forever. After a little pep talk from Nick, we hit the town. We found a little authentic Spanish restaurant and spent the rest of the night bonding.

We all got on like a house on fire and immediately became Charlie's gang. The maddest thing was that we were not unlike the characters we were to portray on film, apart from drug smuggling and ironing out Dutch bods.

A week later the whole cast was out there. Georgina Chapman, who was playing Carly, and her partner Harvey Weinstein, whose company Miramax was producing the movie, hadn't shown their faces as they were living it up in a big villa situated in the hills.

I think Linda and Camille found the all-male environment a little overbearing and they didn't dwell too long around us. I used to go back home to Ali and the kids most weekends. One weekend, when I was away, Weinstein invited the cast up to his villa on the hill for a bit of dinner. When they were around the table, Geoff decided to light up a joint. Weinstein wasn't impressed and said as much whilst sucking on a big expensive cigar. He told Geoff to out the joint and Geoff told him to out the cigar. He stormed off in a huff. I think Weinstein thought he held a bit of sway around the unruly, South East London lads sitting around his table but this wasn't Hollywood, more like Cricklewood.

I personally found Weinstein to be alright. He was what he was: a money-making, high-end, successful, old-school movie producer. Who knew what he was up to. Karma will get you every time sooner or later.

My first scene in the film was me and my boy Alfie sitting in a bar when Tamer and Danny pull up in an old Merc and ask if I'm going out to Charlie's Bar in the evening. Before Nick shouted action I took stock. There I was with my little boy, acting in a movie being produced by Harvey Weinstein. I took a deep breath and smiled at Alfie…what a mind-bending journey we had been on. Nick shouted action and that was it, we were off. It's a funny scene with Tamer ending up being called a 'cardboard gangster cunt'. You couldn't write it.

One of my favourite scenes in the movie is when the gang assassinates a Dutch mob. We were shooting it in a port in Nerja as it was the same architect who designed Puerto Banus in Marbella, so it looked the same as Banus did in the eighties.

We were all given automatic weapons and blank ammunition and were positioned behind some parked cars. On action we jumped up and started emptying the guns; it was such a buzz. You can see how guns hold a fascination to some people. They give you such a power surge when firing them. I think it took about 150 rounds to get the scene but we could have gone on shooting all night. Mine and Geoff's characters, Sammy and Ronnie, started to form a rift with each other in the film and that started to spill out off set as well. I forget what it was about but we fell out big time. Sometimes when you are so into your characters it happens. It happened a day before we shot the Sunday roast scene and it comes across as well. Next time you watch the movie, look at Geoff's face when he looks at me in the scene.

When we finished filming, we'd usually sit at the hotel bar and chill out. The management and the bar staff must have wondered what planet we were from sometimes as we would all talk in London slang and usually come back at night covered in blood.

Another great touch in the movie was when we were going to

assassinate the mayor and we had to decide which of us would do the fowl deed. It was decided with the time-honoured tradition of spuds. One potato, two potato, three potato, four. A reminder of all our school days. Of course Ronnie got the short straw and we all know what happened to him. I still get people calling out to me on the street about how well I'm looking after ending up headless.

One weekend, when I was home, I ran into a friend of mine, Mac, who was running a bar called Linekers in Puerto Banus.

He asked if I'd bring the actors down for the night and he'd lay on a VIP thing for us. I put it to the lads – Danny, Roland and Tamer were up for it but the others weren't for some reason. So we called it on for the next Saturday. We arrived at Linekers to crowds of Danny and Tamer *Football Factory* fans. Danny was mobbed by girls as always. Mac had cleared a space for us. A lot of my pals from Bermondsey were there and it turned into a great night. I wasn't drinking but was riding the buzz from everyone else. Tamer and Danny were happy to spend their time having photos taken and socialising. Then someone, like always, had to spoil it and it all kicked off. Someone accused someone else of trying to muscle in on his girlfriend. An empty bottle of Dom Perignon was unduly smashed over the unfortunate's head, then his mates waded in and, before long, the fight spilled onto the brass-ridden back line of Puerto Banus.

Myself, Roland, Danny and Tamer slipped through the long grass before the Spanish scuffers arrived. But that's Spain for you – never a dull moment.

We drove back to the film unit the next day, back to the safety of guns, gangsters and *The Business* set. It was such a great movie to be involved in. When it wrapped, it felt like something special had been achieved. We had all been on a journey together but, most importantly, we had got the job done. I think the film stands out as a great British gangster movie and helped us all in our careers as everyone involved went on to work in some good stand-out films in the future. So I thank Nick Love for the trust and taking a chance on me for the part. It most definitely looms large in my little legend.

Life in Spain went back to normal but I got much more TV work in the UK. It meant going back and forth constantly. Alfie had a year to go before secondary school. We couldn't afford to send him to an international school and we weren't happy with the Spanish state education so we started to throw about the idea of selling our house and going back to the UK. We could move in with Ali's mum – she was in her fifth year of remission and Ali wanted to be close to her until we found something of our own. I got a call from Kate for an audition for a two-hour special on ITV's *The Bill*. I went back to the UK and got the part – my second stint on the show. I was to be the first character ever to shoot someone dead in the series. While I was back in the UK I stayed at Ali's mum's house in Surrey as she was going out to Canada to visit her sister who lived out there.

One night, after finishing work, I received a phone call from Ali to tell me her mum had died in an accident. Two steps forward and three steps back again. Our world came crashing down. I felt useless as I was in the UK and Ali was out in Spain. I wanted so much to comfort her, I would have jumped straight onto a plane but I was halfway through shooting *The Bill* special. I know it sounds callous but that is the nature of the beast in this area of work and Ali understood. It was a horrible and sudden departure from Spain. We had been there for five years. I had run a bar, created a blues band, made three films, commuted back and forth for TV work in the UK, Ali had created a successful Arts company, I had faced my demons and got some control over my drinking and drug use.

The kids had been to international school and Spanish school and our relationship had gone down many winding roads. It was time to set foot on terra firma again. After Jane's funeral, we moved into her house to sort all that needed to be sorted and went about starting again. It was a tough time, especially for Ali who had such a beautiful, loving relationship with her mum.

We put the Spanish house up for sale and hoped for the best. The kids started at a lovely little school up the road in Farnham. They were so relieved to be back in an English-speaking environment again. A new start and with it, new adventures.

The Business premiere was in Edinburgh and was to open that year's festival. All the actors, plus Harvey, were to be there. We all met up at the hotel, it was like we had never been apart.

As we got out of the cars to enter the cinema, we stepped onto the red carpet. The press were calling my name. I stood still and my whole life flashed before me like a timeless dream. 'Knock, knock, knock, i' the name of Beelzebub' but this time flashing cameras met my eyes and the shouts of my name were warm and welcoming. Eddie Webber had at last arrived so I will end this story here on the positive and take the opportunity to thank you for taking the time to indulge me and my little life.

I'm sure the future holds many more adventures for me and my tribe. The road, as always, I'm sure will carry on being long and winding with many more foxes coming out of the wood work dancing the way to the puppet master, but about that defining moment on the red carpet all that can be said in my mind is *Hi-Diddle-Dee-Dee...*

Stunned, shocked and elated. Our wedding day

Left: Ali's parents
Right: My mum and Charlie Potatoes

Charlie came up trumps with the best best man speech

My two beautiful boys
My oldest Alfie (left) and youngest Barney (right)

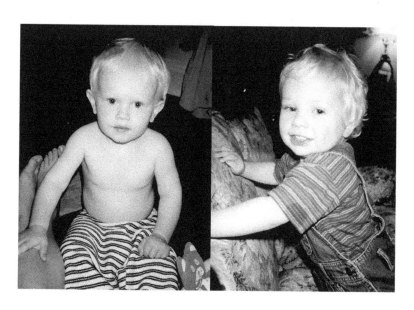

My first professional headshot

Inside The Firm at Edinburgh Fringe

Ronnie looking sharp in The Business

A signed copy of The Business *script*

The Business
(working title)

by
Nick Love

3rd Draft
9th August 2004

Vertigo Films
The Big Room Studios
77 Fortess Road
London NW5 1AG

Tel: +44(0)20 7428 7555
Fax: +44(0)20 7485 9713

(c) 2004 Vertigo Media

Ronnie and Sammie (The Business)
Myself with Tom Bell, Craig Kelly and Cathy Murphy of Oh Marbella!

My family on a rooftop in Spain

AFTERTHOUGHT

I've met some great people and some downright duplicitous bad people on my journey but they are all part of life's great mix of experiences – the cake has a little while longer in the oven but I'm sure, when it comes out, it will be perfectly cooked…I hope so anyway.

It's 2019 and life is still ever changing. Alfie and Barney have flown the nest and are going on their own adventures in life, both amazing men in their own right, and our hearts burst with pride for the two of them. Alfie graduated with a first-class degree from BIMM (British Modern Music Institute) in Brighton and is playing in a great band called 'Comforts', but most importantly, he is happy.

Barney is on the three-year BA course at East 15 Drama School and again what's most important, he is happy and is, if I may say, a fantastic actor. My sometimes long and winding pal Geoff Bell has a saying: 'If it's in the cat, it's in the kitten'. God knows where their happiness stems from having had me wrapped round them all their lives – probably their mum. In a strange twist of fate, my good friend Richard Graham who I starred alongside in the TV Lock Stock adaptation is now teaching Barney in drama school.

Ali and I have started to go our separate ways across the universe but I'm sure, in time, we will be part of each other's future lives…it's been emotional, Al. I'm still wrestling with my demons but I am sober and drug free thanks to the influence of friends involved in AA and friends who care for my welfare.

I've continued on my journey searching for peace of mind and a few years ago I was down in the dumps still looking for some spiritual path to tread, with a bottle of red wine hanging out the corner of my mouth. I drunkenly typed 'Guru' into YouTube and the smiling face of Sri Ramana Maharshi appeared. I started listening to his teaching and it sent a feeling of excitement through me. Investigating more, I found out about the Ashram that was founded in his name in Tiruvannamalai, Tamil Nadu, India. What else was there to do but buy a plane ticket and head out there? It was one of the most amazing and life-changing journeys I have had since Israel. I stayed for five weeks, a book in itself.

The Maharshi promotes the philosophy of self-enquiry through meditation – to find out who we really are in the nonphysical sense and seek The Self 'I', to try and find equilibrium of mind and heart. It's a difficult process but with practise one can achieve a great peace of mind and sense of being. I'm also a great fan of the teachings and the work of PD Ouspenski. Both philosophies marry well together.

I went on to work with Nick Love again in the movie *The Firm*. Check it out, it's a great film and I believe a great social comment. I find Nick a soulmate who I also commend for his journey from A to C. I look at him as a great human. I have sixty-three TV and film credits on IMDb, five successful stage plays under my belt, written five scripts and now, a book. Who would have thought, eh?

Mum lives a peaceful life in Bermondsey and is still running around for her brood, thanks Mum. For the ol' man, on the other hand, life is not so peaceful.

There were so many other people I would have liked to have mentioned in the book but I'm sure they all know who they are and know the love or hate I have for them.

I was sometimes shocked when writing my story, remembering some of the events from all those years ago; some happy and some sad, but it all means nothing unless we can take lessons from it. The lesson I have learnt in life is to be mindful of my actions as they usually only hurt or make happy the people I truly love.

"Anything that is not permanent is not worth striving for."

- Sri Ramana Maharshi.

Photo Acknowledgements

Photos used are from the author's personal collection, with the exception of those credited below:

Page 233: photo by Geoff Bell
Page 234: photo by Johnny Gates
Page 232: photo by Peter Attard